MICHIGAN BUSINESS PAPERS
Number 67

Dedicated to
KEN, BOB, and KAY
who contributed so much to their
mother's professional advancement.

Michigan Business Papers #67

Preparing Professional Women for the Future:
Resources for Teachers and Trainers

Edited by
V. Jean Ramsey

The Division of Research
Graduate School of Business Administration
The University of Michigan
Gilbert R. Whitaker, Jr., Dean
Alfred L. Edwards, Director, Division of Research

The University of Michigan, as an Equal Opportunity/Affirmative Action employer, complies with applicable federal and state laws prohibiting discrimination, including Title IX of the Education Amendments of 1972 and Section 504 of the Rehabilitation Act of 1973. It is the policy of The University of Michigan that no person, on the basis of race, sex, color, religion, national origin or ancestry, age, marital status, handicap, or Vietnam-era veteran status, shall be discriminated against in employment, educational programs and activities, or admissions. Inquiries or complaints may be addressed to the University's Director of Affirmative Action, 5080 Administration Building, Ann Arbor, Michigan 48109, (313) 763-0235.

Library of Congress Cataloging in Publication Data

Preparing professional women for the future.
 (Michigan Business Papers, ISSN 0076-7972; #67)

 Consists of original and rev. versions of papers presented at the Conference on Women and Organizations in 1982 and 1983 and held at Western Michigan University in Kalamazoo.

 Bibliography: p. 231
 Filmography: p. 247

 1. Women in the professions—Addresses, essays, lectures. I. Ramsey, V. Jean. II. University of Michigan. Graduate School of Business Administration. Division of Research. III. Conference on Women and Organizations (1982: Western Michigan University) IV. Conference on Women and Organizations (1983: Western Michigan University) V. Series.

HF5006.M46   n. 67   [HD6054]   330 s   85-827

ISBN 0-87712-239-3   [658.3′1245]

Contents

Preface

Let me begin by relating my experience in developing and offering courses and training programs for women in management at Western Michigan University—a tale I suspect is not uncommon. About five years ago, I began to feel that young women in our undergraduate business program were leading somewhat "protected" lives in academia and were unprepared for the realities of organizational life awaiting them. So, I set out to develop a course, and from that sprung training programs for professional women in the university and local community. But what sets this experience apart from courses and program development in my discipline (organizational behavior and theory) is the fact that all was done in relative isolation from others with similar interests and expertise—I had never taken a course in women in management, I knew no one who had developed such a course, there was little in the literature describing such things.

Contrast this feeling of isolation (and deprivation) with those of the last three years as I have looked out on roomfuls of individuals from across the nation, from numerous organizations and institutions, who are involved in teaching courses, conducting training programs, and developing programs for professional women. These participants in the Conferences on Women and Organizations have gathered together for the last three years, in 1982 and 1983 at Western Michigan University in Kalamazoo, and in 1984 at Simmons College in Boston.

While the Conference programs of papers, panel discussions, and workshop sessions were jam-packed with interesting and useful information, the real value of the Conferences has been in the informal sharing which has occurred in the hallways, at the receptions over wine, at the breaks over coffee, around the table at meals, wherever two or more people came together and held a conversation. All of us come away each year with new ideas, techniques, materials, contacts, as well as a renewed sense of the worth and importance of what we're doing in, and through, our own organizations and institutions.

In an effort to expand that "sharing," the best papers and sessions from the 1982 and 1983 Conferences on Women and Organizations were selected to include in this book. Most were written or rewritten especially for this purpose. It is hoped that this "sampling" of the work that teachers and trainers are doing for and with the professional women will be another vehicle for the networking which has begun as a result of these Conferences.

The book was conceived as a set of resource materials for individuals designing and teaching courses, conducting training workshops, or developing programs for professional women. As such, it highlights current issues facing professional women, shares some of the latest findings of research on professional women, and describes effective training programs.

Margaret Fenn, Professor Emerita of the University of Washington, Fulbright Lecturer and well-known author, was the keynote speaker for the first Conference on Women and Organizations in 1982. Just as she set the tone for the first conference, she establishes the theme for this book in Chapter 1: Women must not only be competent, but must develop confidence in their own competence and that of other women; only then will they obtain the much-needed credibility. In her words, "to stay on top and enhance her potential, a woman must recognize the need for these competencies [administrative, technical, interpersonal], devise and find continual ways to improve them, and have the confidence to use her competencies."

Of central importance to those of us teaching and training professional women in Fenn's notion that "knowledge about" the necessary competencies, gained through reading, observation, and reflection, is insufficient. It must be supplemented with "acquaintance with," through experimentation and practice.

This concern is echoed in Chapter 2, Current Issues in Teaching and Training Professional Women. Krystal Paulsen, in her article "Professional Women: What Do Organizations Want?" found that women seem adequately prepared for "what to do" in a limited range of positions, but have little sense of "how to do it" as they make the transition from the university to the work world. One of the reasons for this, Paulsen suggests, is that "So often as we develop programs, classes, or workshops, we do so in a void—without the intimate, firsthand knowledge of what professional women will face, what skills they will need, and what organizations are expecting of them." In order to provide a "reality reference" for educators and trainers, she reports what representatives from several industries and organizations identify as the needs of their professional women and their advice on how organizational needs and academic preparation and training can be more effectively aligned.

The next paper, "Working Parents: Issues and Strategies for Family Management," explores the many issues faced by working parents and suggests strategies for coping with these problems and opportunities. Sandra Morgan, through an extensive literature review, has presented what is known about this complex subject in an eminently understandable and practical way. Anecdotal material from two panel discussions of working parents adds a sense of humanness which will be of great use to us as we share this information with our students. She, too, cautions that "lecturing about the situation will do little to prepare women for the somewhat distant and obscure challenge of balancing work and family." We must find more innovative ways to increase students' awareness of the issues and their skill in finding and using coping strategies.

The final paper in Chapter 2, "Teaching Undergraduate Women in Management Courses: Issues and Ideas," by Diane McKinney Kellogg of Bentley College and Lynda L. Moore of Simmons College, is "must" reading for anyone designing or teaching a Women in Management course for undergraduates. The instructor's challenge, in their view, is to "address both the academic curiosity students have about how things are different in organizations (with more women wanting to join the higher ranks), and to help them answer more practical questions about how they will plan their own lives and careers." And they've given us practical suggestions for meeting this challenge, e.g., early exercises, interviews with women managers, student projects, personal journals, sample course outlines.

Chapter 3, "Critical Skills for Professional Women," contains descriptions of training programs detailed enough for others to use or adapt the materials to conduct their own workshop or training module. In the first manuscript in this Chapter, "Professional Negotiations: How to Get What You Both Want," Theresa Clow has designed a workshop based on the belief that developing effective negotiations skills increases a professional woman's ability to influence circumstances in a positive way, rather than always having to react to situations initiated by others. The workshop material she has included can be adapted to programs which vary in length from a few hours to an entire semester. Like many of the manuscripts in this book, Clow's is chock full of sample activities, exercises, and simulations. In her own words, "concepts presented during the introduction to the seminar gain depth and meaning for the participants as a result of their participation in various activities and simulations."

Janine Moon shares with us a workshop on conflict, which is "directed toward women who are uncomfortable in conflict situations and tentative about their personal ability to handle conflict effectively." Lecture notes complete with visual aids, as well as individual and group activities, are included.

Shirley Van Hoeven's workshop on male-female communications has, as its major purpose, increasing awareness of male-female roles and perceptions and resultant communication behaviors. Combining lecture notes and exercises, the materials are adaptable, in whole or in part, to workshop or classroom settings.

In "Career Design: How to Find a Good Fit," Brenda Beckman shares a process for helping professional women make good career choices—good for them and good for the organizations that employ them. The workshop takes participants through a process of recognizing their own values, personality traits and styles, relating those appropriately to career choices, assembling a plan for developing the necessary knowledge, skills, and experiences to enter and advance in a career, and developing a professional networking plan.

Krystal Paulsen believes that experiential training can "effectively increase women's awareness of how organizations—because they are grounded in the male culture and experience—require a success standard with which most women are unfamiliar, but to which they can become sensitized." Her workshop, "Criteria for Promotability: When Doing a Good Job Isn't Enough," is designed to help professional women identify the success criteria in their own work environments (covert as well as overt) and to provide them an opportunity to actually practice and modify their behaviors in a risk-free simulated environment.

Reality Shock. What is it? Who is affected? How important is it? When does it occur? Is it fatal? What can be done a about it? These are the issues addressed in the workshop designed by Marie Hodge to help women entering the world of work understand the realities of their first job. The material included is useful to us as counselors and advisers to young women, as teachers and trainers of reentry women, as members of educational institutions making programmatic decisions, and as members of and consultants to organizations struggling to deal with a high first-year attrition rate.

Chapter 4 contains the results of research and writing on topics which should be useful in keeping those of us teaching and training professional women up-to-date. Each manuscript has a section on implications for teachers and trainers which contains specific suggestions for integrating the findings into our classes and training programs.

The first paper, by Claire Scott Miller, reports the results of a recent survey of 167 organizations and 400 dual career couples in northeastern Ohio, conducted by RESOURCE: Careers. The most significant finding was that attitudes toward work and family are changing: the couples, well-educated and fast-tracked, reported that their number one priority is family. Organizations are aware of these changes and seem to favor a variety of new approaches, such as cafeteria benefit packages, flexible hours and work places, and child care assistance.

"Motherhood and the Career-Minded Woman" by Dorothea Nuechterlein contains evidence to suggest that male and female college students share many expectations concerning possible equalization in marriage roles, but only the males realize this. This suggests an important task for us as teachers and trainers—opening the channels of communication between young men and women so they can exchange and clarify their expectations of marriage roles. Included as an appendix to the paper is an instrument which can be used to begin this process.

Nuechterlein also suggests that full participation in careers by women is often limited by the male model inherent in the opportunity structure. As she states so eloquently, "Instead of using men as the center of the universe and determining how nearly women can duplicate their strengths, I think we could do much more than we are at present to reevaluate positions and the qualities needed to fulfill their requirements."

A portion of that male model—that "stopping out" is damaging to one's career—is addressed in the next paper, "The Impact of Perceived Career Interruptions on Individuals and Organizations," by Linda Ellison Sugarman. Sugarman found that while many young women plan to postpone motherhood until at least their late 20's, most expect to interrupt their careers for pregnancy and/or child rearing. She raises the question of whether these young women are realistic in their assessment of the impact this career interruption will have on their careers. Organizations have been slow, at best, in responding to these new career patterns.

Carol Michael and David Hunt present a comprehensive model of mentorship and share results of an exploratory study of mentorship in male-dominated professions. The Michael and Hunt research is particularly important given the scarcity of research on female mentors and mixed-sex mentor protégé relationships. Did you know, for example, that a different spelling of protégé is suggested when referring to a woman—protégée? And you'll find, in their section on implications for teachers and trainers, some excellent suggestions for incorporating the topic of mentorship into the career training and development of professional women.

Two different looks at Equal Employment Opportunity are taken in the next two papers. Barclay and Fields explore employee attitudes toward it, while Gleason examines the costs to individuals in insisting on its enforcement.

Lizabeth Barclay and Mitchell Fields found that women are not homogeneous in their attitudes toward Equal Employment Opportunity. Attitudes vary according to their views on the appropriate roles of women and according to the type of position they hold (male- or female-dominated). Their findings suggest that training programs designed to deal with Equal Employment Opportunity should take these varying attitudes and job levels of women into account.

Sandra Gleason, in her paper, "The Costs of Seeking Redress from Discrimination," describes the experiences reported by women who filed sex discrimination complaints against the federal government. She argues that teaching and training to prepare professional women to deal with discriminatory treatment in the work place should be refocused from a narrow emphasis on the identification of legally protected rights to a broader focus on training women to make well-informed decisions about how to assert their rights with the lowest personal and professional costs.

Kathleen Brannen and Randolph Feezel present an intriguing paper on the role of sports in developing female managers. In it, they take a philosophical look at women and sports participation, share student opinions on the relationship between sports participation and career development, and suggest ways in which we can help women without sports training learn to play "catch-up." Incorporating some of their suggestions into our courses and training programs may result in a whole new "ball game" for men and women in organizations.

Finally, in the spirit of sharing, so essential to the Women and Organizations Conference, Chapter 5 contains an annotated bibliography of books and an annotated bibliography of films and video tapes.

In closing, let me share with you some impressions I have formed as a result of my three years' involvement in the Conferences on Women and Organizations:

— Women still have a long way to go—not only must they continue to struggle with the old problems of acceptance, but they also must deal with new problems of role conflict, dual careers, and others. The need for developing courses and training programs for professional women is far from over.

—   We know more about the "what is" for professional women than we do about the "what to do." We must continue to develop, articulate, and share strategies for success in today 's and tomorrow's organizations.

—   There is a great deal of talent and competence among those who have taken responsibility for training and teaching the professional women of the future.

There will come a day, perhaps, when whether one is a male or a female in an organization or profession is inconsequential. But until that day arrives, there is still much to be learned and much work to be done. I invite you to be a part of that effort.

Competence, Confidence, and Credibility: Keys to Progress

Margaret Fenn, University of Washington

As working women change their expectations, more are becoming alert to the possibility of progress up the ladder in their own or other organizations. As more and more women aspire to managerial positions, educators, advisors, and women themselves come to recognize that there are certain keys to successful progress and performance. Two of those keys, Competence and Confidence can be acquired. The third, Credibility, must be ascribed. Thus, the willingness to earn one's competence through study, experimentation, and experience requires understanding what is needed, and investing one's self in order to acquire competence. As competence levels grow, self-confidence frees a woman to continue to experiment and experience, increasing both her competence and her self-confidence. As women become aware that other women can and do perform well, the knowledge frees them to recognize and accept the fact that other women also have skill, ability, and the willingness to perform. Thus, confidence in women allows the endorsement of women as credible participants. Continued and spreading endorsement results in the ascription of credibility to others. It is only as a woman's credibility becomes portable that she can move freely throughout organizations and invest her energies in performance, rather than investing them in reestablishing her credibility as a performer.

Competence

Women who aspire to managerial positions need to understand that competence extends through a multitude of levels. In general, we can classify those competencies in three broad areas: technical, administrative, and human competencies. Each of the levels will impact her performance and credibility, yet she seldom understands that they are different, even though related. Attention to each of the levels must be constant and continuous.

1

Technical competence

Competence in the technical area deals with the specific knowledge and skill required to get the job done. The area of technical competence is the saleable skill of successful performance. A file clerk must have technical competence in knowledge of the filing system in use, and the physical ability to complete the filing process. A surgeon must have the knowledge of anatomy and physiology, and the skill to use that knowledge in cutting, sewing, and adjusting human bodies. A seamstress needs skill in cutting, sewing, and adjusting, but the technical knowledge is related to material, drape, and form for covering the human body, rather than invading it.

Technical competence for a first-level supervisor is related to the kind of skill and knowledge needed by her workers. She must have enough knowledge of the work to understand, appreciate, and anticipate the skill needed for successful performance, although she may not be skilled in the work herself. A supervisor's technical competence is limited by the ability of others to perform, and by her special competence in organizing and directing the work flow through her own unit.

Technical competence is acquired through the investment of time and effort on the part of the woman herself. She needs intellectual understanding of the parts and processes involved, whatever the job. She can acquire much of this intellectual competence by reading, studying, observing, and asking questions. However, her intellectual understanding must be supplemented by skill development which comes through experimentation and practice. Skiers can learn the fundamentals of skiing by reading, watching, and analyzing the movement of others, but they do not become technically competent until they have experimented on skis and mastered the slopes.

The ability to perform is what is meant by technical competence. A successful woman is constantly broadening her ability to perform in a wide variety of areas. An indication of willingness to grow is her continual attempt to expand her technical competencies. Women aspiring to managerial positions in the modern organization can move from the technical skills of physical performance to broaden their technical competencies in using the tools of management. Computer technology is a must in today's world. A future manager does not necessarily have to be able to program a computer, but she must have basic skill in using programs to accomplish specific objectives. Since managers are responsible for managing all resources, women must become technically competent in extracting information whether it be statistical data about production or sales, or financial information from accounting data. Women can't afford to ignore opportunities to constantly increase their technical competence in all areas that relate to their current and future positions.

Although technical competence, meaning the ability to perform, is very important for the first-level supervisor, as she rises through the organization the demands on her technical ability "to do" lessen, and the demands needed for administrative competence rise.

Administrative competence

Administrative competence deals with the ability to marshal, organize, and use resources efficiently and effectively. Administrative literature uses the terms plan, organize, and control to introduce managerial responsibilities. Women aspiring to progress in their organizations need to acquire the skills and abilities to perform in those areas.

Normal progress in organizations usually moves a woman toward administrative responsibility from technical performance through supervision of the performance of others. Progress for a woman who was a highly successful performer into supervision of other performers is a difficult step. It is not unusual for the most proficient performer to be elevated into the role of supervisor. Both she and the organization err in believing that the skills for performance are the same skills necessary for supervision. This is not the case. The supervisor who recognizes that she was elevated because of her output record has a double disadvantage. She knows that none of the other producers do as well as she, and they, too, know it. She also recognizes that her new measure of success will be dependent on her ability to get others to perform satisfactorily. These conflicting demands often result in less than satisfactory behavior for the new supervisor. Errors may be supervising too closely, setting standards too high, or continually performing the work to speed it up. Her new supervisory responsibilities dictate that she should ensure adequate training for each performer, and create a climate of support while they experiment and master their skill.

The woman who takes that first step into management must recognize that managerial competencies are different than performance. She must recognize and be concerned with money, material, machinery, and people. She must learn how and where to acquire the resources which she will need. This entails planning on a long-range basis as well as on a short-term one. Part of that planning must be concerned with organizing those resources to maximize their usage. Thus, both planning and organizing must be concerned with using time and space as adjuncts to the other resources at her disposal.

A nursing supervisor must be concerned with the quality of patient care, the efficient use of supplies, and work flow patterns which mesh with other unit needs such as therapy, diagnosis, dietary, and housekeeping. A manager in a retail store has similar administrative responsibilities. Meeting and satisfying customer needs is primary. This must be accomplished by having the desired merchandise in sufficient quantities, styles, colors, and sizes readily available for display and delivery. Her floor space must be well designed for maximum utility. Her sales staff must be trained and motivated to respond and satisfy the customer. She is financially responsible for buying, pricing, display, markdown, and security.

The manager in an insurance company, a manufacturing organization, a financial institution, or a radio station each needs understanding, training, experimentation, and proficiency in planning what resources are needed; acquiring those resources; organizing the resources and whatever supporting units are necessary; administering usage of the resources; supervising others who also use the resources; and controlling the expenditure of energy as well as the physical consumption of the resources themselves. The setting varies, the style of managing varies to reflect the person and climate, but the competency for administration remains separate and distinct from the competency of actual performance which we have called technical competence.

Administrative competence is reflected in appropriate behavioral patterns. Women often overlook the fact that behavior can be adapted to meet the requirements of the situation. The role of worker for a technically proficient person is quite different from the role assumed by an administrator. The range of contacts and the attendant role requirements vary greatly from worker to administrator. The first-level supervisor is mostly concerned with internal relations within her unit. As a consequence, she tends to focus her attention within her unit. She adapts her behavior to that of teacher, trainer, monitor, disciplinarian, communicator, and rewarder. As she adapts to her role, she begins to discover that her attention to supervisory acts must be expanded so that she can respond to the needs of her workers, and represent their best interests elsewhere in the organization. Her behavior changes to allow her new awareness of the additional demands of supervision to be reflected. She listens more effectively, she exposes herself to ideas and information from her workers, she begins to seek access to communication links upward and outward from her own unit.

Beyond immediate supervision, the manager discovers that, out of necessity, she must expand her range of contacts within the organization. She must deliberately establish contact with supervisors and managers who precede and follow her unit tasks in a work flow. She begins to notice that there is much give and take in an exchange within the organization which is not formally designed. To be an effective representative of her unit's needs, she must find ways to become a member of the nonformal relationships which exist within the formal organizational context. As she acquires skill in the administrative process, she realizes that much of her attention to planning, acquiring resources, organizing, and utilizing those resources requires time and attention outside her own unit.

Externally directed relationships are as important as those which are internal to her own unit. It is difficult for a woman to get tapped into the organization's nonformal network. She must extend her contacts through her own initiative. She can initiate interaction by developing a deliberate strategy. She must know and be known by the manager whose work precedes her units. She also must make contact with those whose work follows her unit's. She must know those who can and do provide service for her unit, as well as those who monitor it. Purchasing agents, personnel, public relations, marketing, advertising representatives may be sources of information and service her unit needs. Industrial engineers, accountants, schedulers, and planners may audit her unit. To function effectively in her managerial role, she must know and be known. She must attend meetings, read communications, contribute, and socialize.

Administrative competence is built on understanding and appreciating technical competence but is separate and distinct from it. Neither technical nor administrative competence is acquired through reading and listening. Both require experimentation, reflection, and practice. As a woman moves forward in an organization, she can be helped by others who serve as confidants, role models, and tutors. A supportive climate which allows and encourages experimentation frees the budding manager to learn and grow. Growth entails mistake and failure as well as constant success. Learning can occur when mistakes are recognized, acknowledged, and worked through so that knowledge and understanding result. As in acquiring technical competence, administrative competence building is constant and continuous. Technical and administrative competencies are dependent on the third level of competence . . . that of interpersonal relations.

Human competence

The ability to relate effectively to others is what is meant by human competence. Accepting the difference in others, appreciating those differences, and understanding the needs of others is reflected in inter-personal relations. An effective manager exhibits competence in dealing with others in a wide variety of roles.

The ability to accept others is the basis for developing effective inter-personal relationships. Acceptance recognizes that differences exist. All persons are prejudiced, meaning that each carries a model that we prejudge others' actions against. Prejudgment can lead to stereotyping and discrimination. The effective manager accepts the fact that she has prejudice, but she guards against stereotyping. She accepts and deals with humans as individuals, rather than as members of a class. A manager who recognizes that differences are useful can draw on those differences as a means of expanding the human resources available. Listening carefully, providing opportunity for growth and development of others' talents, creating a climate that fosters contribution from others, treating others fairly and consistently contribute to successful relationships. These traits apply to all persons, those within her area and those who are external to it.

Women in organizations have discovered that the structure of the organization and the technical aspects of the job influence the behavior of people. Appropriate role behavior must be studied and practiced if a woman wishes to increase her competence in interpersonal relations. For example, the woman who manages a centralized service department will change behaviors in dealing with others who use that service. Centralized services, whether they be diagnostic units in a hospital, maintenance units in a factory, or secretarial services in a law firm, become scarce resources to their users. The manager of a scarce resource requires an ability to satisfy the demands of the users of that service in her external relationships. At the same time, she must buffer her workers from external pressure, and support their efforts. One can predict in advance that such demands are conflict prone; thus, the successful manager in such situations must adapt her behavior to manage conflict. She must be well acquainted with the users of the service and be willing to bargain, trade favors, and slip schedules occasionally. At the same time, she must know her workers well enough to be able to encourage, cajole, reward and motivate each of them in terms that are meaningful to them. Such behavioral requirements are given in the job.

Behavior for the manager of an auditing unit has different requirements. The auditor must recognize that her unit will be viewed with suspicion by those whose work will be audited. Thus, her behavior toward external contacts will, of necessity, be formal and distant. She will have to probe harder for information. Her unit will be suspect and her internal contacts must be protective. If a member of her unit has been rebuffed or accused of snooping by other workers, the auditor must understand her worker's sense of rejection.

Regardless of the focus of activity for her unit, the manager develops a style of dealing with her unit members (internal direction) and with important others outside her direct linkage (external direction). To be effective, she must maintain her contacts throughout the organization. Her access to nonformal communications, and her sphere of influence are reflections of her skill in interpersonal relations. Human competence is acquired in much the same manner as technical and administrative competence. "Knowledge about," gained through reading, observation, and reflection is implemented by "acquaintance with" through skill building exposure and learning. Continual attention is required in refining technical, administrative, and human competence. Skills get rusty through lack of use. Knowledge gets superseded. To stay on top and enhance her potential, a woman must recognize the need for these competencies, devise and find continual ways to improve them, and have the confidence to use her competencies.

Confidence

Self-confidence grows through experimentation and success. As a woman acquires technical skill and puts that skill into practice, she expands her confidence. As she masters and practices administrative competence, she becomes more sure of her ability. When she reflects on her skill in dealing with others, she acknowledges that she has competence in human affairs.

An example of the acquisition and use of a technical skill which contributes to administrative skill is the ability to use a computer. Since computers are essential in today's world, the ability to use computers is a technical skill a woman must acquire. Computer use has been simplified so that one does not have to be a mathematician, a statistical expert, or a philosopher to use a computer. Machine jargon has been simplified so that humans can use human language, not "computereze," to give commands. Software programs designed to fit most requirements are readily available. The hardware and the auxiliary parts have been reduced in size and complexity. Gaining technical skill in using a computer to manipulate data for personal use, as well as for use at work, is a must for a manager in today's world. Technical skill for the average user does not mean being a pro-grammer, nor an installer, nor a maintenance specialist. It does mean under-standing what is needed from the computer and the way to acquire the needed information. For a person who is timid about using machinery, acquiring skill in computer use gives a wonderful sense of accomplishment and a new boost to confidence.

A sense of confidence encourages display and use of that skill. Display is recognized and acknowledged by others, reinforcing a sense of confidence in abili-ty to perform. Computer use contributes to administrative efficiency. Data can be accumulated and used on forecasting, planning, organizing, and controlling.

Administrative skill results in similar contributions to confidence. A first line supervisor who plans, organizes, implements, and controls even one aspect of successful change in her unit will experience a flush of confidence in herself. Sup-pose a supervisor recognizes the need for an additional person in her unit. She must justify budgeting for the additional slot by presenting her request with full documentation of the work to be performed, the cost of each addition, and the pay off expected. She must define the qualities an employee needs to succeed at that work. She marshalls her facts and arguments and presents them to her superior. She may have to sell her idea. If she is successful, she must then select the new employee, orient the person and the department, establish the work routine, train that person, and supervise her performance.

Opportunities for confidence building are numerous. First, she has planned suc-cessfully. Secondly, she has been successful in selling her plan. Her selection of the proper employee should continue to build her skill and confidence. The ability to define the job, train an employee, to perform it, resolve human and technical difficulties in implementing the plan are all ways to build confidence through suc-cessful performance. The manager of that supervisor becomes more confident of her supervisor's ability to supervise. She recognizes that if she trusts her employees, they live up to that trust by acting in ways that are trustworthy.

As a woman gains confidence in herself and her ability, it frees her to become more confident of other women's ability and willingness to perform. One of the real obstacles to women's success is that organization members continue to lack confidence in other women's ability and willingness to perform. Surprising as it seems in today's world, most women employees still prefer male bosses. Whether this preference stems from cultural bias, experience with less than skillful bosses, or reflects power differentials in organizations is uncertain. The fact remains, however, that women do not have confidence in other women. It is difficult to succeed as leaders if you don't have followers. It is difficult to place your work-life fate in someone in whom you lack confidence. On the other hand, it is difficult to manage women when you do not have confidence in their ability to perform—this uncertainty in the credence of others results in behaviors that convey doubt. If either a woman manager or an employee works under a state of suspicion the results are limited.

On the other hand, as she experiences success in her own performance, either the worker or the manager are freed to become more confident of both the ability and the willingness of other women to work. As the manager becomes more competent in her administrative role, she gains in self-confidence. As her self-confidence grows, she is freed to recognize that other women also have competence in a technical sense. As that competence is demonstrated, the sense of trust grows. When the manager knows a woman can perform, she is more apt to create a work environment that encourages skill use. As the worker experiences the satisfaction of doing a good job and having it recognized, she becomes more open and willing to invest the energy to do a good job. As both her ability and her willingness are demonstrated and recognized, the greater her trust and confidence in her manager. A constantly expanding sense of confidence in one's self frees one up to become confident in others. Hence, the second "C," confidence, and the first "C,"competence, can be acquired. Each is related to the other, but both are necessary to insure success.

Credibility

As women acquire competence and confidence, they are accorded credibility by others. A strange difference in the awarding of credibility to males and females exists. Men are expected to succeed as organization members. As they are recognized as able, they earn a credibility which becomes portable. It goes with them as they move in the organization. On the other hand, women may acquire credibility based on performance in particular settings. This credibility must be earned whenever a stranger enters that setting, or whenever they move into another unit. Their credibility is not portable. It applies in a limited sense to a particular job in one setting.

This difference in portable credibility is very costly for women. They must invest countless ergs of energy, and countless hours in reproving their ability and willingness to perform. Each time they are faced with the necessity to prove their capability, their self-confidence is eroded. Every time a woman's confidence in self is tested, she must rethink her confidence in other women. Trust is tenuous at best. Confidence is eroded by doubt. Doubt of self opens the floodgates of doubt of others.

It is only as women free themselves from self-doubt, and doubt about others that they can build a support base for one another. Only as they recognize that competence and confidence are acquired and can be permanent are they freed to support one another. It is vital that women make acquired credibility a portable commodity for women. It is only after acceptance and support of one another is assured that a framework of acceptance allows a credible woman to move with her confidence intact. The third "C," credibility, necessary for success of women, is grounded in her competence, and demonstrated through confidence. It requires the trust, confidence, and support of all organization members. The support of women for women is required for success in organizations.

Conclusion

Modern work structures are moving away from the day of rugged individualism toward an era of teamwork in support for one another. If women are to climb the ladder of success in these organizations, they must constantly attend to investment in personal competence. Technical, administrative, and human competence contribute to self confidence. Confidence in self frees a woman to be confident in the willingness and ability of other women. Trust and confidence build a support here for the portability of credibility. All three "C's" are necessary for women to continue to succeed as organization members. We must all lend a hand. In solidarity there is hope.

Professional Women: What Do Organizations Want?[1]

Krystal G. Paulsen, Upjohn HealthCare Services

"More and more . . . women are creating community, sharing work, and discovering that in the sharing of work our relationships with each other become larger and more serious. In organizing a women's self-help clinic or law collective or a writing workshop, in editing a magazine or creating a center for women's work like the Women's Building in Los Angeles, in running a press that publishes "lost" books by women or contemporary work that may be threatening or incomprehensible to male editors, in participating in a women's prison project or a crisis center, we come to understand, at first hand, not only our unmet needs but the resources we can draw on for meeting them. . . . "[2]

And more and more, as instructors and trainers, we need to do exactly this, create community so we can understand our unmet needs and the resources we have to draw on to meet these needs. So often as we develop programs, classes, or workshops, we do so in a void—without the intimate, firsthand knowledge of what professional women will face, what skills they will need, and what organizations are expecting of them. Creating community—opportunities to directly interface with organizations— provides us with the necessary knowledge. What's more, organizations are demanding it of us.

This paper represents a summary of one such community effort. Panel representatives from several diverse industries and the federal government addressed a series of questions to help trainers and university faculty understand what organizations identify as the needs of their professional women and what organizations are providing to meet the needs. The group then advised how organizations' needs and academic preparations and training can be more effectively aligned so that women can be better prepared to join and progress within their own and other organizations.

Each panel member was asked to consider the following questions:

- What is your organization doing to prepare women?
- Are preparations within your organization increasing?

- Are there any areas of skill development your organization emphasizes more than others?
- Are universities doing a good job preparing women for entry into organizations?
- How should universities and trainers be preparing women for organizations?
- What can we do to better align our preparations with what your organizations need?

Their responses, summarized as follows, offer a reality reference for educators and trainers as to what organizations most value in regard to the behavior, skill, knowledge, and attitudes of their women employees.

What Is Your Organization Doing to Prepare Women?

Before investing in preparing their women employees, the organizations are recognizing they first must provide for hiring women, and some of the represented organizations are actively committing themselves to this goal to assure equitable opportunity.

After that, all the organizations are making available a variety of management development seminars and in-service training. Although not all have designated these programs "for women only," an effort has been made to provide for extensive "cross-training" providing women the opportunity to participate in familiarization programs to learn the nontraditional, semiskilled, and technical jobs. One organization is actively recruiting and training to get more women managers in engineering, financial, and data processing departments. As one individual said, "We are looking at the raw data to insure we get women not only in higher levels of management but in the mainstream or meat of the business." In addition, flexible and part time schedules, as well as scholarships, are being made available to women to encourage on-going education.

One organization's investment is unique and comprehensively directed toward better preparing women and minority employees. They have developed advisory panels to create an officer-to-women managers' network. Financial support is provided to the panels to assure contact and communication between upper management and the lower level management. A Women in Management group was formed as an off-shoot: it exists to create programs and seminars especially for women, and their meetings provide opportunities to share experiences, successes, and network opportunities. Another program was begun to identify "women promotables" and to involve them in succession planning and special training. These efforts provide highly visible mainstream job opportunities and allow the women to attend senior management assessment programs. Additionally, this organization's commitment to encouraging opportunities for women is reflected in their long-range strategic planning and monitoring efforts. They have modified the way they look at ratios and percentages of women in management, attempting to move women into nontraditional management areas and analyzing their progress job group by job group.

Are Preparations Within Your Organization Increasing?

The responses were mixed. In some, the opportunities are being enhanced and efforts specifically directed to the women employees. In others, women are provided the same opportunity as their male counterparts to enter upper positions, but no programs exist which are designed specifically to promote female upward mobility; no unique opportunities or specialized preparations are being provided for women.

Are There Any Areas of Skill Development Your Organization Emphasizes More Than Others?

The organizations represented are looking for women to increase their management skills in general, preferably in conjunction with actual experience as opposed to education alone. Skills specifically identified as essentials were interpersonal, listening, risk-taking, and assertiveness. One emphasized the need for developing behavior that produced future managers who would be results- and profit-oriented and have a "win-over" effect as exhibited by Lee Iaccoca. These managers need to demonstrate the ability to respond to and even enjoy ambiguity, all the while demonstrating flexibility.

Emphasis was heavy on women's need to acquire technical and scientific skills relative to research and development, as well as line production and management skills in areas such as manufacturing, product control, quality control, and manufacturing engineering. Computer and financial backgrounds were encouraged.

Although these are the skills and behaviors the represented organizations value, few of the organizations are actively assuming responsibility for providing the training internally. They are looking for educators and trainers to meet these needs and develop the skills the organizations seem prepared to reward.

Are Universities Doing A Good Job Preparing Women For Entry Into Organizations?

The most generous and minority response to this question indicated that from the standpoint of selection and on-the-job performance, women coming from university settings seem to be adequately prepared. The more vehement and majority opinion, however, was that preparations are inadequate especially for women; universities are not doing a good job because they remain out of touch with practical organizational application and don't prepare women to adapt to a political environment or to acquire organizational savvy. In summary, women seem adequately prepared for "what to do" in a limited range of positions, but have little sense of "how to do it" as they make the transition from the university to the work world.

How Should Universities And Trainers Be Preparing Women For Organizations?

Women need at least the same types of technical, professional, and managerial competencies as their male counterparts to be competitive in organizations. Their knowledge base must be equivalent if women are to have the opportunities available to men. Yet, universities must respond to organizations' needs to have women skilled in the areas of interpersonal, assertiveness, risk-taking, and career planning abilities. Women will be better prepared when they realize, too, that they must take personal responsibility for preparing themselves by taking advantage of training opportunities available in corporations and local institutions.

Women need to be made aware of the power structures and political environment of organizations and of the need to develop political savvy in response to the organization. They need to be encouraged for their ambition and assertiveness and learn not to feel ashamed of these traits. They must be reminded of the need for maintaining a sense of humor and be made cognizant of the high price they will personally pay for success. Women will pay the same price men do: long hours, wearisome travel, and pulls on personal and family life. These costs shouldn't be gilded.

A special emphasis was placed on the need to prepare women to develop their unique skills as women, encouraging them not just to emulate men but to work on using feminine qualities to enhance their management capabilities.

What Can We Do To Better Align Our Preparations With What Your Organizations Need?

The overwhelming recommendation was that the university should first establish lines with the business community to learn what organizations need and then listen to what the business community says instead of telling it what it needs. Several practical suggestions were offered.

- Use women from industry as guest speakers, faculty members, course developers, case history studies, and as research and survey references.

For instance, A Women In Management course for senior students can be designed to utilize local professional women as speakers who realistically address professional demands and the skills and attitudes necessary to respond successfully to those demands. Community business people can be invited to act as advisory faculty for curriculum development and course design.

- Identify through industry the kinds of jobs anticipated within the next 15-20 years and counsel women of these needs. The panel representatives specifically identified the areas of engineering, finance, and data processing; generally they cited most semiskilled and technical jobs as ripe opportunities for women. National and local labor market surveys as reported respectively by *Working Woman* (January 1984) and the Management Center at the University of Toledo, Ohio (1983) provide specific direction for career and skill development needs.

- Educate the men who head up the corporate power structure; they are tomorrow's officers who can influence the change necessary to provide new and on-going opportunities for professional women. Provide them with reports of the opportunities for women in their own firms and bring to their attention the accomplishments and aspirations of those women who perform successfully.

- Stress to those women who aspire to a career the need for awareness training so they can develop sensitivity to the needs of their particular organizational environment. Help women build confidence so they learn to assert their ideas and participate in decision making and team efforts. Encourage development of organizational savvy through use of co-op programs so women can acquire knowledge of the workings and impact of organizational politics on career development.

- Teach practical application of knowledge through co-op programs. Solicit intern placement of women business students in organizations so they can tackle specific, practical problems and learn by doing much as medical students learn by practicing under a trained doctor.

- Subscribe to trade journals and keep them in university libraries to reinforce the need for technical knowledge. More importantly, use the trade journals as required course readings. Trainers and educators need to assume responsibility for integrating relevant, up-to-date, state-of-the-art information.

- Create networking opportunities, either formal or informal, for students with career women. These opportunities can take the form of a student's spending a day or a week with a professional woman in her workplace. Groups like The Professional Women's Dialogue at Western Michigan University provide, through scheduled luncheon meetings, opportunity for professionals to interact with students, respond to student questions, and provide experienced feedback on case studies used as dialogue promptings.

- Encourage women to participate in their communities through their Chambers of Commerce or other such community business associations and professional organizations where they can get acquainted with local business needs and professional standards.

- Develop more flexibility in accepting combinations of subject areas for university degrees such as dual majors in marketing and manufacturing engineering or a dual major in marketing and natural resources.

- Solicit ideas from local industries for implementing technology-based training in the university using faculty, machinery, equipment, and ideas from corporations.

All these efforts will help minimize adjustment from the university to the organization without which tomorrow's professional woman's success will be hampered and her opportunities for promotion slowed.

Implications For Teachers And Trainers

The implications of the comments shared by the panel members are important. First, the feedback from these organizational representatives help us gauge whether our areas of interest are indeed "reality based" and practical in their application. A significant point, too, is that organizations are looking to universities and trainers to prepare women. Our jobs are secure, but our performance evaluation is mixed at best. The outcry is for establishing a stronger bond between organizations and educators for increased opportunities to communicate; for an increased receptiveness to the organization's need for practical skills; and for a sensitivity to their political environment and the skills necessary to survive in it.

If we are to align, we must be involved with one another, we must establish community. We must continually acquaint ourselves with the unmet needs, remembering that organizations consider universities and trainers as the most significant resources for meeting those needs. Alignment of the two is assured to be possible, hoped for, and indeed, necessary if women in organizations are to have better opportunities and increased success.

NOTES

1. Based on the opening panel discussion at the Second Midwest Conference on Women and Organization, May 17-18, 1983, with the following participants:

- *Dr. Laura Heinrich,* Corporate Director of Training for Pneumo Corporation. She has also worked for General Electric Company, owns her own consulting firm of Heinrich Association, and has been a faculty member of Kansas State University, University of Alabama, and University of Cincinnati.

- *Carrie Rosener* is Federal Women's Program Manager and R.N. for the Battle Creek Veteran's Administration Hospital. She works with top management in any area regarding the hiring and promotion of all women at the V.A. Hospital to assure that V.A. women at all levels don't get dead ended but get the proper cross-training to qualify them for promotions.

- *Diane Storey* is Management Training Specialist for the Corporate Management Development Department of the Kellogg Company. With a background in Counseling and Personnel, Diane's efforts concentrate in programs such as Listening Skills, Assertiveness Training, Interaction Management, and Targeted Selection Training.

- *Sheryl Walker* is a Staff Supervisor for Michigan Bell Telephone Company. She has been with the company for fifteen years where she worked her way up from an entry level non-management position. Sheryl has held line, field, staff, and training and development positions and is actively involved in women's organizations and issues in the company.

2. Rich, Adrienne, "Conditions for Work: The Common World of Women." In Sara Ruddick and Pamela Daniels (Ed.). *Working It Out,* New York: Pantheon Books, 1977, p. xviii.

REFERENCES

Management Center, University of Toledo, Ohio, Toledo Area CETA Consortium and Private Industry Council, Principal Sponsors, "Lucas and Wood County Labor Market Survey," 1983.

Rubin, D.K. "Who Makes What, Where?" *Working Woman,* Fifth annual salary survey. January, 1984, 59-63.

Working Parents:
Issues and Strategies for Family Management[1]

Sandra Morgan, Illinois Institute of Technology

"We only talk to each other 15 minutes a day."

"We have no problem coordinating the family—everyone shares tasks and we're all home for dinner."

Guess which statement was made by a parent of a preschooler and which was made by a parent with highschoolers. Both observations reflect some problems addressed by working parents—those of time management, division of household tasks, and finding time to share as a family.

In this paper, written primarily as an aid to those who teach preprofessional women, I introduce the situation of working parents and present a variety of parental issues through literature review and case examples. Suggested strategies for coping with these problems and opportunities are shared, and finally implications for the teaching and training of professional women are discussed. The anecdotal materials come primarily from two panels composed of working parents, one at the 1983 Women and Organizations Conference and the other at the Careers Interest Group Workshop during the 1983 National Academy of Management Meeting[2]. Since the panels included both single and married parents of preschool through grown children, their comments serve to illustrate the wide range of issues dealt with by most working parents.

Of course, some issues primarily affect working couples while others are unique to the single parent. This paper focuses on parental issues, while noting some specific differences attributable to marital status.

The Current and Projected Status of Working Parents

Male parents have always worked in large numbers, but now female parents also are working more, especially those who are heads of households. Not only

19

are there more women in today's work force than at any time in the past (almost 47 million in 1981 according to the Bureau of Census, 1982), but more of these women are parents. The trend for mothers, even those with preschool age children, to work has been increasing steadily since the 1950s and is expected to grow. In 1950, only 12 percent of married women with children under 6 were in the labor force. This figure climbed to 19 percent in 1960, 30 percent in 1970, and 45 percent by 1980. Of single working women, 55 percent had preschool children in 1980 (Bureau of the Census, 1982) and 62 percent of married mothers with school age children were in the work force in 1980 (Bianchi and Spain, 1983).

The past decade's increase in separation and divorce has resulted in a doubling of families with children under 18 headed by single parents since 1970, to 7.8 percent of all households in 1982 (Bureau of the Census, 1982) and, of course, the great majority are headed by women. Only 10 percent of these 6,547,000 single-parent households are headed by men.

If past trends continue as expected, most of today's young women will marry and have children; in 1980, 92% of ever-married women were mothers by age 40 (Bianchi and Spain, 1983). It is also expected that the trend for mothers, both single and married, to enter the work force will continue, both because of economic necessity and because of a desire to contribute their talents to a work world that is increasingly open to women.

Issues of Working Parents

Parental issues seem to fall into four categories: career, interspousal, child care, and household management. Themes such as time, stress management, personal time, and overload tend to run across all categories. Table 1 shows the major issues and subissues covered in the following pages.

Of course, parents' views of the issues discussed below are influenced by their profession, job requirements, type and flexibility of organization, age, number and spacing of children, marital status, reference groups, support systems, and income level. For instance, one can imagine that an MD doing her residency in emergency medicine would have different child care requirements for her preschool child than would a purchasing manager in a Fortune 500 company.

Career issues

Individuals, couples, and organizations all are becoming increasingly concerned about the effects of balancing work and family life. In some early studies (Rapoport and Rapoport, 1971), the dual-career family was viewed as a new pattern; pioneer couples reported experiencing negative sanctions from relatives, friends, colleagues, and neighbors. We might hope that the sanctions have diminished and even been reversed, so that the working parent now would have social support systems aiding

TABLE 1

Issues of Working Parents

Career-related
- Career interruption or reduction for children
- Changes in view of career/family balance
- Which is primary career; affects on decision making
- Timing of reentry

Child care
- Selection of caregivers
- Amount of time parent(s) spend with child(ren)
- Distribution of labor between parents

Household tasks
- Division of labor (family, hired help)
- Basic housework (meals, cleaning, shopping, laundry)
- Other housework (e.g., gardening, repairs, auto maintenance, errands, financial, medical care, durable shopping)

Interspousal
- Money
- Communication
- Competition
- Lack of time for each other

Overarching themes
- Overload
- Time management
- Stress
- Lack of personal time

---

him or her. However, panel members and authors present examples of lack of support for dual-career families, especially for the woman. One panel member reports that she feels pressure "not to allow home life to interfere with work" from her colleagues.

In a 1981 study of the Fortune 1300, Catalyst found that 76 percent of the 376 companies responding agreed that "companies were concerned about two-career family problems because such issues could affect recruiting, employee morale, productivity, and ultimately corporate profits" (*Career and Family Bulletin*, 1981, p. 4). In the Catalyst survey of 85 two-career couples, a majority of wives and husbands felt that family was more important than career. Among panel members, most also felt that family would come ahead of work in a crisis situation, but that a workable balance was possible. The strategies parents use for balance will be discussed later.

Several specific career issues emerged in panel discussions: what happens when a career is interrupted for children, changes in aspiration level and job after children, and whose career takes precedence during moves or changes.

It is clear that employed women have fewer children on average than women of the same age not in the work force. In 1980, employed women aged 18 to 34 averaged .8 children while those of the same age at home had an average of 1.7 children. While there are numerous studies on the relationship between labor force participation and fertility (Bianchi and Spain, 1983), it is difficult to find specific data on who dropped out to have and rear children and the length of their absence from the paid work force. A 1983 study of dual-career couples in Northeastern Ohio found that 71 percent of the women took pregnancy leaves of six months or less and that those reporting longer absences from work were generally in the 45-64 age bracket (Resource, 1983). A 1980 Catalyst survey of two-career families reported that 36 percent of women were back at their jobs within 1-8 weeks, 32 percent took 9-18 weeks, 19 percent took 19-33 weeks, and 10 percent took longer. The median time off for childbirth was twelve weeks (*Career and Family*, 1983). Among panel members, most spent some time at home with their first child. The senior panelist (children now ages 14-24) worked part time for nine years before returning to full-time work. One other panelist worked half-time until her child was two and recommends "enjoying a period of time with your baby" before work and social commitments take over. According to Catalyst (*Career and Family Bulletin*, May 1981), 93 percent of women between 15 and 44 (over 80 percent of all employed women are in this age group) are expected to have at least one child and are "increasingly likely to return to the work force within a year following the birth of their child due to either the pull of an emotionally satisfying career or the need for the income the job provides, or both" (p.1).

The decision about length of leave for child-rearing is affected particularly by potential loss of pay (even the most generous disability payments tend to cover only eight weeks' leave), lack of alternatives for infant care (Kamerman and Kahn 1981), and fear of losing ground in one's career.

With the exception of a couple holding industrial positions, all panelists made major changes in their career direction and aspirations after childbirth. The chief adjustment was the change to a position or organization with a more flexible schedule or fewer hours. Panelists felt they redefined career priorities to "buy time and flexibility." Three panelists, both male and female, also mentioned that they preferred their new situations (research and academic environments) because they were allowed to discuss children and family issues with their colleagues. In a literature search, no articles were found that discussed change in job, organization, or aspiration level after children were born, although there are many references to work-family conflict and interference (Pleck, 1982). A different perspective (Gallese, 1981) claims family concerns do not prevent women from getting ahead. However, the Gallese data are about women MBA's, a highly selective, and presumably highly motivated group.

The third major career-related concern of married panelists was that of whose career takes precedence when a move is considered. The Catalyst study (*Career and Family Bulletin*, 1981) found that although most husbands and wives claimed their careers were equally important, in practice they tended to reflect traditional patterns. The most frequent pattern was for couples to move because of the husband's job opportunities. Blumstein and Schwartz[3], in their nationwide study reported in *American Couples* (1983) present data that support this. One of their major findings is that the member of the couple with the greater earnings has a generally more powerful role in family decision-making, and in most situations, the husband is the chief wage earner.

Among panelists, one couple reported that their greatest source of stress had been "a geographic career move" (for the husband's career). Another dual-career male felt that "neither partner can maximize career," while one female parent says her husband's career has always come first. Her support for this was "you can be replaced in your career. If you dropped dead tomorrow, they'll find someone. But you can't be replaced at home." (This was the oldest panelist and the same one who reported staying home the longest with children.) In general, the panelists felt the career person earning the most had the primary career, whether this was the man or woman, and in all cases but one it was the husband. As the primary breadwinner, the higher earner therefore earns the right to have greater influence in career-related decisions, such as job change and location.

Child care

The major child care concerns for panelists were the amount of time spent with children (there seemed to be an implicit assumption that this time was quality time), selection of care givers and distribution of child care responsibility between parents in the two-parent families. A first priority for full-time working parents was "quality child care" and three of the families had live-in or full-day housekeepers.

It is clear that, as Sheila Kamerman (Kamerman and Kahn, 1981) says in her comprehensive study of national child care policy in six industrialized countries (France, Federal Republic of Germany, German Democratic Republic, Hungary, Sweden and the United States)

> If women are to bear and rear children at the same time as they participate in the labor force, traditional assumptions regarding women bearing sole or primary responsibility for child care and child rearing become increasingly untenable (p. 2).

However, in *American Couples* (Blumstein and Schwartz, 1983), data showed that "Fathers would help out with the children, but the primacy of the husband's work was almost inviolable" (p. 136). Catalyst (*Career and Family*, 1983) reports that to the extent that a husband shares in daily child care and household management and has responsibility for planning and responding to the logistical arrangements for child care, the stress of balancing work and family roles becomes easier to manage. However, according to Pleck's review (1982) of earlier research and of two large mid-1970s national surveys of time use, husbands do not participate more in child care when their wives are employed. Of course, there are differences in measures: for example, one study (Robinson, 1977) showed that husbands of employed wives spend an average of 19 minutes more per day in child "contact" (time in all activities in which a child is present, which includes considerable leisure time, as well as time in which the wife is present) but not in child "care." And one must also keep in mind the noncomparability between studies based on self-report and those on time diaries, as well as those that survey only wives versus those that receive reports from both spouses.

Literature covering options in child care shows that the United States offers a sparse and limited menu compared with other nations (Kamerman and Kahn, 1981). In fact, in fifteen countries, the law requires employers to set up a day nursery when they employ a certain number of working women (Séguret, 1981). A concrete example comes from the 1981 Catalyst study: only one percent of corporations surveyed provided on-site day care although 20 percent favored the practice. Choices of child care options (e.g., centers, family day care, siblings, mother at home) are discussed in Michelson (1980), but he notes that day care centers, while offering excellent care of children, are logistically difficult and women using them experience greater time pressures.[4]

Some personal experiences from panelists include a "babysitter who drives the kids to the doctor," having guilt about not being the perfect mother (from lack of time with a preschooler), getting one partner (not both) involved in social and family events, and making sure one partner has a "flexible schedule to accommodate problems as they happen."

Household tasks

While the literature abounds with discussions of household division of labor from sociological, psychological, mental health, and economic perspectives (Ericksen, Yancey, and Ericksen, 1979; Farkas, 1976; Gross and Arvey, 1977; Morgan, 1978; Robinson, 1977; Robinson, 1980; Walker and Gauger, 1973), panelists barely mentioned it. The industrially employed couple felt "pressure to keep the house up" and a woman with two preschoolers says she is "not meticulous" anymore. One suggestion from an academic couple was, "Don't divide household tasks on the basis of sex roles, give them to the one who dislikes the job the least." A different panel family reports that total household management tends to be handled by the wife. Hall (1972) reports a major coping technique for reducing role conflict is to let the level of household maintenance slip. In Blood and Wolfe's 1960 study it seemed that husbands of employed wives took over "an appreciably larger share of the housework" (p. 63); however, this apparent contradiction disappears when one realizes that time use studies demonstrate that husbands of employed wives do a higher proportion of family work only because wives' absolute level goes down, not because husband's goes up (Pleck, 1982). This lack of attention to the topic by the panelists may indicate a successful resolution of the issue for their families, but I suspect there is an on-going need for negotiation and renegotiation in order to achieve continuous satisfaction.

According to the literature, it seems that both employed parents are doing less household work now than 10 years ago. While this may accurately reflect shopping and cooking trends (much more prepared food is eaten; more families eat out more often), it fails to include other types of household work such as taking the car for repairs, filling out insurance forms, supervising the plumber, finding someone to mow the lawn and shovel snow, doing taxes. Since many two-job couples choose to hire household help, finding, training, and supervising such assistance must be counted as part of household management as well.

Interspousal concerns

The concerns a couple may have about money (Is there enough? How do we share expenses? How do we decide what to buy for the baby?), communication (How do I really know what he/she is thinking and wants?), competition (Her career seems to be off to a flying start, what about mine?), and lack of time together both before and after a child comes are frequently discussed in both academic and popular literature. A main theme seems to be that of identity (Bebbington, 1973; Rapoport and Rapoport, 1969). If the partners have succeeded in clarifying their own identities as career-oriented and family-oriented rather than "masculine" or "feminine," then working out interspousal concerns will be a management task rather than a philosophical or ideological (and therefore more difficult) one. Blumstein and Schwartz (1983) present a large quantity of anecdotal material dealing with these interspousal concerns. Also, their resolution relates significantly to stress, time, and overload which are discussed in the next section.

Overarching Themes

The four themes that flow throughout the literature on working parents and the panelists' experiences are stress, overload, time management and time for self. The Rapoports (1969) identified the sources of strain for dual-career couples as dilemmas of work overload, identity, role-cycling (i.e., family and career stages in conflict), discrepancies between personal and social norms, and social network dilemmas. Their categories encompass the divisions currently identified by panelists and researchers.

Stress

Recent writers have indicated that conflicts between professional and parental roles create special stress for the woman partner (Holahan and Gilbert, 1979), but earlier work often looked at the mental health of husbands with employed versus nonemployed female spouses (Burke and Weir, 1976). The results of the studies have been contradictory. Sometimes employed women seem healthier (Gove and Geerken, 1977; Kessler and McRae, 1982) and sometimes not (Aneshensel, Frerichs, and Clark, 1981; Radloff, 1975); sometimes husbands of employed wives show more psychological distress (Burke and Weir, 1976; Kessler and McRae, 1982), yet other researchers find the opposite (Locksley, 1980). A critical variable that is often overlooked in the work on mental health and distress has been the partners' occupational status. There are some indications that the effect of wives' working only has a negative effect on the mental health of husbands in white collar, managerial, and professional occupations.

Overload

Of course, whatever one says about stress and distress, there is no denying that working parents are victims of overload. Pleck (1982) reports that working parents of preschoolers have the longest work week (including family work) of all (84 hours for fathers, 109 hours for mothers) and that employed parents of preschoolers sleep less than any other group. In another study, once children have grown and left the home, working women's work week drops from 86.2 hours to 68.9 (Greenglass, 1983) with the major change being the drop in hours in home work, i.e., housework, child care, maintenance, finance. Women in this study appeared to have very high standards about combining career and family and did not admit they were overworked. They "took for granted that they ought to be able to accept their dual role without complaint."

Lack of personal time

With this attitude, it comes as no surprise that personal time and time for spouse suffer. Essentially, what has to get done (professional work, household tasks, and child care) gets done, but there may not be time left for self and/or spouse. Panelists shared their experiences of putting friendships on hold, giving up sports, and omitting personal reading time (except for work-related reading). In the 1980 Catalyst study of dual-career couples, a primary complaint was lack of time for spouse. One danger is that working parents, especially women, will fail to make the time to recharge their batteries (keeping in mind that "recreation" is derived from "re" and "creation") and that their health (Greenglass, 1983), their work, and their families will suffer.

Time management

In order to cope with the internal and external demands on them, employed parents must become proficient time managers. In the Catalyst couples' survey

(1981), wives and husbands agreed that the most difficult problems in combining career and family were "allocation of time" and "financial issues." There are many strategies suggested for the individuals and couples who want to improve their time management skills (Embers, 1981; Gabriel and Baldwin, 1980; Hall and Hall, 1979; Lakein, 1974; Silcox, 1980). These fall into five primary categories: simplifying, delegating, eliminating, saying "no," and negotiating. However, in order to implement one or more of these strategies, a working parent must be clear about his or her priorities (Bailyn, 1978; Embers, 1981). Embers suggests that couples make

> . . . individual and joint resolutions which define the relative importance of work to family life and result in each partner having a clear hierarchy of commitments which may change over time (p. 27).

Strategies Parents Use to Cope With Multiple Demands

Although this paper focuses on coping, a panel member claimed a major goal was to "reach the level above coping." What does this mean and how can a parent reach it? Panel members shared a wide variety of strategies they used successfully for managing, improving, and enjoying their situation. The range of suggestions was broad, from "hire help" to "make sure you take mini-vacations as a couple." However, there was basic agreement on the critical approaches (Table 2). This list is somewhat reminiscent of Greiff and Munter's (1980) guidelines for managing pressure, which advises executives to not abuse their bodies, to delegate, to be aware of emotional vulnerability and to pace themselves. Hall and Hall's (1979) book also focuses on strategies for the two-career couple. On the topic of tradeoffs, panelists (especially women) found they gave up personal time, friends and social life in order to attain a comfortable work/home balance. Other things that slipped were the level of upkeep in the house (parallels Hall's finding, 1972), giving up personal reading (novels, newspapers, magazines), cutting back on time for spouse, omitting nonessential care items such as facials, and canceling out "alone time."

Single parents' coping strategies

Several recent studies suggest that the length of time as a single parent may be associated with the salience of certain coping strategies. Kazak and Linney's study (1983) suggests that social support systems are most important for recently divorced mothers, but that three years later, success in being self-supporting is a powerful predictor of life satisfaction.

McLanahan, Wedemeyer, and Adelberg find that a single mother's support needs depend "not only on the availability of friends and/or relatives, but also on the fit between the role orientation of the woman and the way her network is organized

(1981, p. 610)." Some "stabilizers" want to maintain their predivorce role as wife and mother; others, labeled "changers," attempted to establish a new identity as a career person and relied successfully on loose-knit networks.

TABLE 2

Coping Strategies

- Apply management techniques (decision-making, clear communications, time management, goal-setting, teamwork) at home.
- Rely on support systems, both paid and unpaid.
- Make priorities clear and review them periodically.
- Realize there are tradeoffs—you can't have it all.
- Play and relax together (e.g., ski, run, do yoga, mountain climb).
- Have plans ready for emergencies.
- Take care of your body and your relationship with your spouse.
- Decide whose career is primary for times when push comes to shove.
- Make sure one parent has a flexible schedule.

Panelists' suggested strategies

Two excellent, but hard to implement, pieces of advice came from panelists who suggested picking the right spouse (i.e., secure, energetic, cooperative, sense of humor) and having reference groups that support your decision to be a working parent. A poignant example came from a parent of a preschool daughter: "My mother praises me for spending so much time with her (the daughter), but my wife's mother criticizes her for letting me take over so much child care." It is almost a no-win situation, particularly for the woman who may feel held back or discriminated against at work because of her children (Rosen, Jerdee, and Prestwich, 1975) and also criticized by (usually older) family members who feel she is a poor mother, wife, and housekeeper because she has a career. Although panelists did not mention it, my informal survey of working parents shows that most socialize primarily with other working parents with similar age children and try to avoid situations with opportunity for criticism from their relatives (e.g., big family gatherings, prolonged in-law or parental visits).

From observing the apparent health of the panelists' marriages and/or families, I would conclude that it may not be necessary to do what Meredith, a Boston television personality who had gone through a recent divorce tells her friend who complains of "...husband problems, baby problems, job worries, baby-sitter blues, and wave after wave of tension" (Gresh, 1983, p. 131 ff):

> Well, you can't do it all. Once you reach our level you've got to choose, and you can only have two out of three selections. You're not going to give up your child, so it's either your career or your husband. (She stirred her Bloody Mary and took a sip). So your husband goes.

Meredith's example is one extreme. At the other extreme is the naive view of a 25-year old financial consultant who feels she can have it all. Her comments are:

> You know something? I'm glad I'm not 33 today. There's a big difference between older women and those of us on the way up. Most women in their thirties have dead-end careers and can't make up their minds whether they want to be mamas or stay at their jobs. Me? I want it all—career, marriage, and a family when I'm ready for it and when I find the right man for it. But it will have to be later, when I'm established and in my thirties. That's why I'm working hard now. Whem I'm 30, I expect to be making $100,000 a year, and when I marry I want someone who is a working father—committed to helping at home—someone who likes kids but is not threatened by my career (Gresh, 1983).

Teachers and trainers must be aware that most of the solutions to working parent dilemmas lie somewhere between these two extremes. In the next section, some guidelines for these trainers are offered.

Implications For Teachers and Trainers

From the preceding review of literature on working parents and anecdotal material from working parent panelists, we can draw several implications for preparing young women to join the professional work force. It is assumed that two trends will continue. The first is the positive trend for younger men and women to shun traditional sex role behaviors and stereotypes. Organizations also are beginning to help their employees get located together with spouses (Lublin, 1984), pay for child care (Catalyst, *Career and Family,* 1980), allow employees time off for childbirth and child rearing without penalty (*Career and Family Bulletin,* May 1981) and provide slower career tracks for men and women who choose not to neglect family in order to display a meteoric rise through the ranks (Bailyn, 1978).

For the educator/trainer of preprofessional women, the major foci might be on both the process and content of learning the coping strategies of working parents. Obviously, lecturing about the situation will do little to prepare women for the somewhat distant and obscure challenge of balancing work and family. Therefore an experiential and case discussion approach would be pedagogically sounder. Assuming one's objectives in a course or workshop were to increase the students' awareness of the problems and teach them coping strategies, a reasonable curriculum would include empirical studies, popular literature, and case histories dealing with the aforementioned issues. Of course, the content would be adapted to the specific group of participants—engineering students might be interested in different career variables than would nurses, for example.

A major thrust in training professional women should be imparting managerial skills such as effective communication, time management, decision making, goal setting, planning, and change strategies and guiding the students in applying these to home and family management. Of course, since the family realm is never textbook simple, one should not be led to believe these techniques will always work. Probably educating these women to take care of their bodies, thus building energy for family management, and to manage stress well will be equally as important as the so-called "managerial skills."

The new professional woman will still have to fight the old battles of sex-role stereotyping and family work overload; however, with both managerial and personal skills to rely on, she will most likely manage difficult situations with more aplomb and equanimity than her unprepared sister.

In summary, let me just share some of the comments I heard when I asked my friends, mostly working parents of preschoolers, how they coped:

"You are on the edge all the time."
(married female, teacher, child 26 months)

"I don't sleep anymore."
(married female, professor, children 4, 2)

"I get up in the morning; I put my clothes on; I go through the motions. That's how I survive."
(married female, publisher's representative, child 3)

"It's taken me a long time to learn to take care of myself."
(married female, graduate student/swimmer, children 21, 18, 15)

"It got a lot easier when my daughter reached 3 years and I discovered I needed only 4½ hours sleep per night . . . and sometimes less."
(married male, professor/author/consultant, child 50 months)

NOTES

1. Thanks are owed to Richard Cohn, Marrey Embers, and Jim Stoner who read and provided valuable comments on drafts of this paper. I also want to thank all the panel members who willingly shared their personal experiences.

2. Panel Composition

Panelist(s)	Estimated Age(s)	Occupation(s)	Children
Married F	35	Assistant professor	2 preschool
Married F	30-35	Researcher/administrator	1 infant
Married M	30-40	Law professor	1 preschool
Married M & F	35-40	Industrial managers	2 school age
Single F	38-40	Human resource manager	1 high school
Married M & F	35-45	Professor; librarian	1 school age
Married M	45-50	Professor; author	1 preschool
Married M & F	45-60	Manager; professor	4 high school, college

3. These sociologists studied the private lives of 6,000 couples, beginning in 1975. The volunteer subjects included married and cohabiting couples both heterosexual and homosexual. Each partner completed a 38-page questionnaire and more than 300 couples were subsequently interviewed face-to-face. *American Couples,* the first report on the study's findings, focuses on money, work, and sex.

4. It is interesting to note the phrasing of this report: "Women using them . . . " rather than "families . . . " or "parents . . . " The probable reason for this is that in the majority of cases, the employed mother is the parent responsible for delivering and picking up the child in an out-of-home care situation. Michelson's report on the time use in 800 Toronto families states, "Tension in women's travel is not a function of total distance covered in the day, but the *extra* distance the child-care drop-off adds to the home-to-work trip."

REFERENCES AND SUGGESTED READINGS

Andrews, F. and Withey S. *Social Indicators of Well-Being.* NY: Plenum Press, 1976.

Aneshensel, C. S., Frerichs, R. R., and Clark, V. A. Family Roles and Sex Differences in Depression. *Journal of Health and Social Behavior,* 22 (1981): 379-93.

Bailyn, L. The "Slow Burn" Way to the Top: Implications of Changes in the Relation Between Work and Family for Models of Organizational Careers. MIT, Sloan School of Management, 1978.

Bane, M. J., Lein, L., O'Donnell, L., Stueve, C. A., and Wells, B. "Child Care Arrangements of Working Parents." *Monthly Labor Review,* October 1979, 50-56.

Bebbington, A. C. "The Function of Stress in the Establishment of the Dual-Career Family." *Journal of Marriage and the Family,* 1973, 530-37.

Bianchi, S. M. and Spain, D. *American Women: Three Decades of Change.* U.S. Department of Commerce, Bureau of the Census, August 1983.

Blood, R. O., Jr. and Wolfe, D. M. *Husbands and Wives.* Glencoe, IL: Free Press, 1960.

Blumstein, P. and Schwartz, P. *American Couples.* NY: Morrow, 1983.

Burke, R. J. and Bradshaw, P. "Occupational and Life Stress and the Family." *Small Group Behavior,* 12 (1981): 329-75.

Burke, R. J. and Weir, T. "Relationship of Wives' Employment Status to Husband, Wife, and Pair Satisfaction and Performance," *Journal of Marriage and the Family,* 38 (1976): 279-87.

_____. "The Type-A Experience: Occupational and Life Demands, Satisfaction, and Well-Being." *Journal of Human Stress,* 6 (1980): 28-38.

Career and Family: Maternity and Parental Leaves of Absence. NY: Catalyst, March 1983.

Career and Family Bulletin. NY: Catalyst, May 1981 and Winter 1981.

Corporations and Two-Career Families: Directions for the Future. NY: Catalyst Career and Family Center, 1981.

Cunningham, A. M. "The Time-Pressured Life." *Savvy,* December 1980, 38-52.

Embers, M. Time and Balance in the Lives of Dual-Career Women: An Exploration of the Time Management Literature. Qualifying paper, 1981, Harvard Graduate School of Education, Cambridge, MA.

Ericksen, J., Yancey, W., and Ericksen, E. "The Division of Family Roles." *Journal of Marriage and the Family,* 41 (1979): 301-12.

Evans, P. and Bartoleme, F. *Must Success Cost So Much?* NY: Basic Books, 1980.

Farkas, G. "Education, Wage Rates, and the Division of Labor Between Husband and Wife." *Journal of Marriage and the Family,* 38 (1976): 473-84.

Feinstein, K. W. (Ed.). *Working Women and Families.* Beverly Hills, CA: Sage Yearbooks in Women's Policy Studies, Vol. 4, 1979.

Fogerty, M. P., Rapoport, R., and Rapoport, R. N. *Sex, Career, and Family.* London: Allen and Unwin for P.E.P., 1971.

Gabriel, J. and Baldwin, B. *Having It All,* NY: Warren Books, 1980.

Gallese, L. R. Family Doesn't Keep Woman from Getting Ahead. *The Wall Street Journal* (May 4, 1981).

Glick, P. "Children of Divorced Parents in Demographic Perspective." *Journal of Social Issues* 35 (1979): 170-82.

Gove, W. R. and Geerken, M. R. "The Effect of Children and Employment on the Mental Health of Married Men and Women." *Social Forces,* 56 (1977): 66-76.

Greenglass, E. R. Type-A Behavior and Role Conflict in Employed Women. Unpublished paper, 1983, York University. Toronto.

Greiff, B. S., and Munter, P. K. *Tradeoffs: Executive, Family, and Organizational Life.* NY: NAL, 1980.

Gresh, S. "Three Lives." *Boston Magazine,* June 1983, 100 ff.

Gross, R. H. and Arvey, R. D. "Marital Satisfaction, Job Satisfaction, and Task Distribution in the Homemaker Job." *Journal of Vocational Behavior,* 11 (1977): 1-13.

Haggman, K. W. "Family Reorganization of Divorced Mothers and Their Children." Qualifying paper, 1976, Harvard Graduate School of Education. Cambridge, MA.

Hall, D. T. "A Model of Coping with Role Conflict: The Role Behavior of College Educated Women." *Administrative Science Quarterly,* 17 (1972): 471-86.

_____. *Careers in Organizations.* Santa Monica, CA: Goodyear, 1976.

Hall, F. S. and Hall, D. T. *The Two-Career Couple.* Reading MA: Addison-Wesley, 1979.

Holahan, C. K. and Gilbert, L. A. "Conflict Between Major Life Roles: Women and Men in Dual-Career Couples." *Human Relations,* 32 (1979): 451-67.

Household and Family Characteristics. U.S. Department of Commerce, Bureau of the Census, Current Population Reports. Washington, D.C.: March 1982.

Kamerman, S. B. and Kahn, A. J. *Child-Care, Family Benefits, and Working Parents—A Study in Comparative Policy.* NY: Columbia University Press, 1981.

Kazak, A. E. and Linney, J. A. "Stress, Coping, and Life Change in the Single-Parent Family." *American Journal of Community Psychology,* 11 (1983): 207-20.

Kessler, R. C. and McRae, J. A., Jr. "The Effect of Wives' Employment on the Mental Health of Married Men and Women." *American Sociological Review,* 47 (1982): 216-27.

Kleiman, C. "MBA Isn't Always Ticket to the Top for Women." *Chicago Tribune* (Dec. 28, 1981).

Kopelman, R. E., Rosensweig, L., and Lally, L. H. "Dual-Career Couples: The Organizational Response." *Personnel Administrator,* 27 (1982): 73-78.

Lakein, A. *How to Get Control of Your Time and Your Life.* NY: NAL, 1974.

LaRossa, R. and LaRossa, M. M. *Transition to Parenthood.* Beverly Hills, CA: Sage Library of Social Research. 119, 1981.

Lipman-Blumen, J. "The Implications for Family Structure of Changing Sex Roles."*Social Casework,* 57 (February 1976): 67-79.

_____, and Tickameyer, R. "Sex Roles in Transition: A Ten-Year Perspective," *Annual Review of Sociology,* 1975, 297-337.

Little, L. *Work/Family Policies: An Innovation Theory Approach.* Suffolk University, Boston, MA, 1983.

Locksley, A. "On the Effects of Wives' Employment on Marital Adjustment and Companionship." *Journal of Marriage and the Family,* 42 (1980): 337-46.

Lublin, J. S. More Spouses Receive Help in Job Searches When Executives Take Positions Overseas.*Wall Street Journal,* (Jan. 26, 1984): 31.

Marks, S. "Multiple Roles and Role Strain: Some Notes on Human Energy, Time and Commitment." *American Sociological Review,* 42 (1977): 921-36.

McLanahan, S. S., Wedemeyer, N. V., Adelberg, T. "Network Structure, Social Support, and Psychological Well-Being in the Single-Parent Family." *Journal of Marriage and the Family,* 43 (August 1981): 601-12.

Michelson, W. *Child Care Under Constraint Project.* Executive summary, mimeo, undated.

_____. "Spatial and Temporal Dimensions of Child Care." *Signs: Journal of Women in Culture and Society* 5 (1980): S242-47.

Miller, J. and Garrison, H. H. "Sex Roles: The Division of Labor at Home and in the Workplace." *Annual Review of Sociology* 8 (1982): 237-62.

Morgan, J. "A Potpourri of New Data Gathered from Interviews with Husbands and Wives." In G. Duncan and J. Morgan (Eds.), *Five Thousand American Families—Patterns of Economic Progress,* 6. Ann Arbor, MI: Institute for Social Research, 1978.

Nadelson, T. and Eisenberg, L. "The Successful Professional Women: On Being Married to One." *American Journal of Psychiatry* 134 (1977): 1071-76.

News, Bureau of Labor Statistics, Washington D.C., (Dec. 9, 1980): 1-2.

Nuechterlein, D. *Motherhood vs. Seniority: The Dilemma of the Career-Minded Woman.* Paper presented at Women in Organizations Conference, Kalamazoo, MI, May 1983.

Nye, F. I. (Ed.). *Family Relationships.* Beverly Hills, CA: Sage Focus Editions, 46 (1982).

Olson, D. H. and McCubbin, H. T. and associates. *Families: What Makes Them Work.* Beverly Hills, CA: Sage, 1983.

Pepitone-Rockwell, F., ed. *Dual-Career Couples.* Beverly Hills, CA: Sage Focus Editions, 24, 1980.

Pleck, J. "Husbands' and Wives' Family Work, Paid Work and Adjustment." Wellesley College Center for Research on Women, Wellesley, MA, Working Paper No. 95, 1982.

Radloff, L. S. "Sex Differences in Depression: The Effects of Occupation and Marital Status." *Sex Roles* 1 (1975): 249-65.

Rapoport, R. and Rapoport, R. N. *Dual-Career Families,* London: Penguin Books, 1971

_____. "The Dual-Career Family: A Variant Pattern and Social Change." *Human Relations* 22 (1969): 3-30.

_____. *Dual-Career Families Reexamined: New Integrations of Work and Family.* NY: Harper and Row, 1976.

RESOURCE: Careers, Report of Dual Career Project, Cleveland, 1983.

Robinson, J. *How Americans Use Time: A Social Psychological Analysis.* NY: Praeger, 1977.

_____. Household Technology and Household Work. In S.F. Berk (Ed.), *Women and Household Labor.* Beverly Hills, CA: Sage, 1980.

Rosen, B. and Jerdee, T. H. "Sex Stereotyping in the Executive Suite." *Harvard Business Review,* March-April, 52 (1974): 45-58.

Rosen, B. Jerdee, T. H., and Prestwich, T. L. "Dual-Career Marital Adjustment. Potential Effects of Discriminatory Managerial Attitudes." *Journal of Marriage and the Family,* 37 (August 1975): 565-72.

Séguret, M.C. "Child-Care Services for Working Parents." *International Labor Review,* 120 (1981): 711-25.

Shenon, P. "What's New with Dual-Career Couples." *New York Times* (March 6, 1983): F29.

Silcox, D. with Moore, M. E. *Woman Time.* NY: Harper and Row (Wyden Books), 1980.

Skinner, D. A. "Dual-Career Family Stress and Coping—A Literature Review." *Family Relations,* 29 (1980): 473-81.

Staines, G. L., and Pleck, J. H. *The Impact of Work Schedules on the Family.* Ann Arbor, MI: Institute for Social Research, University of Michigan, 1983.

Voydanoff, P. "Work Roles as Stressors in Corporate Families." *Family Relations* (Oct. 1980): 489-94.

Walker, K., and Gauger, W. "Time and Its Dollar Value in Household Work." *Family Economics Review* (Fall 1973): 8-13

Weiss, R. S. "Growing Up a Little Faster: The Experience of Growing Up in a Single-Parent Household. *Journal of Social Issues.* 35 (1979): 97-111.

Teaching Undergraduate Women in Management Courses:
Issues and Ideas[1]

Diane McKinney Kellogg, Bentley College
Lynda L. Moore, Simmons College

"What am I going to face out there, as a woman in the business world?" This seems to be the question on the minds of undergraduate women anticipating a career in business. Young women are growing up in a world where some women are making it, but it appears to be difficult. They wonder what they can expect to face, and if it's worth it to them personally, to try. Similarly, young men wonder how all these changes in women's roles are going to affect them personally and professionally. "Will it be harder for me to get promoted? Is my wife going to want to work instead of taking care of our children?" These concerns as well as others underlie the interest in "Women in Management" courses being taught in a large number of business schools.

The instructor's challenge in teaching these courses seems to be to address both the academic curiosity students have about how things are different in organizations (with more women wanting to join the higher ranks), and to help them answer more practical questions about how they will plan their own lives and careers. While the course typically focuses on the effects of having women and men acting as colleagues in the workplace, students are thinking about and raising questions about how to make women and men colleagues on the homefront as well. Academic instruction can influence the choices students will make about the nature of their male-female relationships in general: with their bosses, colleagues, and subordinates as well as with their spouses, friends, boyfriends, and girlfriends. Thus, experience shows that instructors can expect the course to have an impact on students both academically and personally.

1. The authors would like to acknowledge the contributions of V. Jean Ramsey who joined the authors in a panel discussion of these issues at the 1983 Conference on Women and Organizations.

35

In planning coursework for the training of undergraduate women, a number of issues need to be addressed:
What are the characteristics of the registrants?
What are the goals of the course?
What content areas should be covered?
What pedagogy will result in the most learning?
What resources have others found useful?

What Are The Characteristics Of The Registrants?

Most students take the course as an elective. Students may have a friend who recommended the course, or they may themselves be curious and hopeful that taking the course can help them succeed in business. Men often take the course for the same reasons, but sometimes are persuaded by a girlfriend or a fiancee who want them to take the course! Whatever the reason for registering, the elective nature of the course helps assure that most students will be interested in learning and will have an open attitude toward course material.

Even though one does find a more open attitude in an elective than in a required course, many instructors also find that "traditional" undergraduates (aged 18-22 with little or no full-time work experience) have a difficult time acknowledging that women still face problems as they enter and move through organizations. Students seem to assume that since equal opportunity laws were passed some twenty years ago, both organizations and the people in them must have changed their ways. They don't expect to face the same problems.

This is an understandable perspective for today's undergraduates. They were born in the late '60s, and reared by parents who were aware of sex role socialization and may have attempted to raise their daughters in nonsexist ways. Also supporting their optimism was the rhetoric of the equal opportunity legislation. Schools were asked to spend as much money on girls' sports as they did on boys' sports, and they knew it was illegal to pay women less or refuse to promote someone just because she was a woman. Today's undergraduates grew up in times which encouraged optimism for women.

However, the new attitudes did not result in immediate changes. Their parents' espoused values may have been consistent with the values which encouraged women to join the professional workforce, but in practice women cared for the children and the home while men were the breadwinners. The role models to back up the newly-espoused values simply were not (and still are not) easily seen in the lives of young children growing up. Neither in homes nor in those work environments with which they were familiar did they see women in numbers equal to men in all settings and roles.

Their own educational experiences reinforced their optimism. Students often point to the fact that there are as many males as females majoring in business now, and that every year the professional schools get closer to a 50-50 ratio in male and female students entering programs. In their earlier educational experiences, girls' sports were strongly emphasized, and boys could take home economics. In fact, Betty Friedan points out that " . . . American girls grow up feeling free and equal to boys. . . . All this gave girls the feeling they could be and do whatever they wanted to, with the same freedom as boys" (1963, p. 75). The educational system does come close to giving males and females equal opportunities, which may lead young women to assume that the same pattern will persist in the work world. Not so, says Epstein (1971, p. 62): at college graduation, suddenly the expectation of "marriage" takes over for young women, and "career" for young men. Nonetheless, students taking Women in Management courses may still cite their educational experiences as evidence that "things are different now."

This optimism is not necessarily "bad," it is simply something which needs to be taken into consideration when planning course content and the sequence of learning experiences. Students may need more factual information early in the course . . . current data on the percentage of women in the professions as opposed to hourly-wage jobs or statistics and research on the incidence of male vs. female promotion in certain industries. It may be important to present some bad news early in the course to help students recognize that "problems" do exist . . . that the rhetoric still doesn't match the reality.

In summary, undergraduates who take a Women in Management course as an elective do want to know more: they're curious. But they're not convinced the problems women once had in the business world still exist today.

Male registrants

Both males and females register for Women in Management courses. Instructors informally polled report that usually two or three men register, and some instructors report ⅓ to ½ of the class is male, depending on the reputation of the course. Some titles encourage men to register: Women and Men in Management; Women and Men as Colleagues in Management; Women in Management: Male, Female, and Organizational Perspectives; Gender Issues in the Workplace.

Dorothy Hai (1982) presents both sides of the question of whether courses "should be" only women, or open to men as well. The argument favoring women only points to research which suggests that women participate more in female-only groups and therefore will develop leadership and communication skills more effectively in that setting. Also, "women feel more comfortable in female groups discussing such issues as sexism, personal experiences with discrimination, etc." (1982, p. 39). Alternatively, since the work world and the world in general is made up of both sexes it is more realistic to have students discuss these issues in a mixed group, and practice skills in a mixed-sex setting. Also, it is just as important for males to understand the problems and think about the solutions as it is for females.

Many find the second argument favoring a mix of sexes more persuasive. It is easy to split the class into one-sex discussion groups when those advantages are wanted for particular topics, and still have the benefit of both male and female perspectives in relation to most of the issues.

Also, the rationale behind the "support groups" which sprang up early in the feminist movement was that women needed other women—they were discouraged and needed to be encouraged, they were alone in their personal dilemmas because of the isolation of the housewife role, they were alone in their work because they were pioneers in jobs new to women. However, traditional undergraduates have not yet had the difficult experiences that made all-female support groups so vital. These women have experienced only educational organizations where they feel both sexes have had equal opportunity and equal access.

Though the "need" for a support group may arise for these women in the future, they may not yet feel that need and may, at first, find an all-female group more problematic than useful. However, there is much to be said for placing women in all female groups to learn to identify, support, and work with one another. In addition, some women tend to feel more comfortable talking about sensitive personal issues and female identity issues in an all-female group.

Alternately, assuming men are encouraged to register, the Women in Management class has the potential both for "educating" the male peers of undergraduate women and for generating lively discussions between the sexes. Giving both sexes a legitimate environment for openly discussing gender issues seems to be a rare opportunity—one which could affect, for the good, attitudes of the males and females who will populate the business organizations of the future.

Course Goals

Goals for courses instructing undergraduate women may fall into three general categories: cognitive, affective, and skill development. The cognitive area involves acquiring new information and knowledge concerning academic topics as well as developing conceptual and analytical skills. The affective area is concerned with attitude development and personal feelings related to the subject matter. The skill development area includes those goals which focus on increasing students' abilities to perform more effectively on the job, e.g., communication, assertiveness, and delegation skills. This area also includes career planning skills such as writing résumés, developing interviewing skills, and managing the entry process.

One professor described her initial goal as a combination of cognitive and affective: "to introduce students to and make them think about issues they are likely to face as they enter organizations." After some experience with the course, she found students did want to develop skills such as assertiveness and leadership, she added a personal growth and development component.

One might have very specific skill development goals related to career planning, where the course helps students choose a major, write a résumé, interview well during the job search process, learn how to read the organization's norms, understand office politics, develop specific on-the-job skills, and make well-informed career moves in the future.

One professor focused both on personal career management and on managing others' careers. The rationale for this approach notes that every graduate will have at least one career to manage, her own. However, those who move into management positions will also face increasing responsibilities in managing the careers of others: developing subordinates to take over so that one can move on; meeting corporate human resource development goals; and creating a skilled support staff. One can point to EEO (equal employment opportunity) policies, increasing demands for more managerial talent, the scarcity of good managers, and the ethics of one's organizational responsibility to subordinates as evidence of the growing importance of managing careers. This dual focus, on students' careers and on the careers of others, served as the organizing theme for course material in the cognitive, affective, and skill development areas. (See Appendix II for readings used in this course.)

Experience suggests that a number of approaches to teaching the course can be effective, and receive the support of students, faculty and administrators alike. However, the course seldom stays in the area of cognitive learning alone because the topics seem to create considerable "affect." Even if one were to have only cognitive goals (for giving students new information about the experience of women in organizations today), female students hoping to join those organizations in the near future will be thinking about the significance of the information for their own lives. Thus, the course inevitably touches on the affective domain as well. Therefore, since it is necessary to plan on "managing the affect," instructors should shape the goals, instruction, and evaluation to include both the cognitive and affective domain.

For example, a course may commonly begin with some discussion of the differences in male and female socialization which have led males to have a stronger career orientation than females have. Student reactions vary, but because those personal reactions are inevitable and sometimes emotionally laden, it is important that the instructor plan for dealing with the reactions, rather than leaving them unattended and up to the student to deal with.

"Attending to the affect" can be as simple as leaving time for class discussion around specific lectures, either during or after, putting students in discussion groups to meet weekly, or asking students to write an entry in a personal journal after each class session. Whatever the approach, attitudes and emotions seem to be stirred by many of the topics covered. This presents a rich opportunity for the instructor to help students develop their personal understanding of the issues, and to develop healthy attitudes toward themselves, and toward the problems they may encounter as they begin their careers.

While cognitive and affective areas are an inevitable part of women in management courses, the area of skill development needs careful thought. Instructors should assess their own professional preparation and competence, particularly for dealing with sensitive skill areas (self-awareness and in-depth interpretation of childhood experiences) before incorporating skill training into the course.

*Avoiding overlap of course goals with other courses in the curriculum.*The decision of whether or not to include skills training should also consider whether or not those skills are being taught in other courses in the curriculum. Courses in Leadership, Interpersonal Relations, and Career Planning (or workshops offered by a student service office) may be sources of overlap in instruction. Certain management courses take a competency-based approach in the first place, and intend to teach students skills in delegation, communication, planning, motivating, and leading.

Some educators feel that some of the topics which might be covered in a Women in Management course are appropriate for Introduction to Organization Behavior courses. Since 50 percent of the students are women and 50 percent of the population of organizations are also female, some feel these topics should not be treated as "special," but should be part of the regularly required curriculum.

Katham and Weathersby discuss ten topics which they feel belong in Introductory OB courses. That list is titled "Dilemmas faced by women in organizations" (1983, p. 4) and includes devaluing women's work roles, socialization pressures, expectations vs. reality, sex structuring and numbers, social conformity and informal influence, power, economic reality, gender differences in self-definition, intimacy and sexuality, and balancing work and private life.

Should a full faculty have such a strong commitment to these issues as to have these topics covered routinely, an elective on women in management may not be necessary. However, it is difficult to foresee that this will generally be the case. Introductory courses traditionally have a difficult time covering all the required topics in the first place, without going into detail at very many places along the way.

The purpose of electives in leadership, organizational change, interpersonal relations, and small business management is to give students depth in topics which merely are touched on in the introductory courses. One might more commonly expect a Women in Management course to be seen in a similar light: the subject is important to introduce, but since one cannot do it justice in an overview course, an additional elective is called for.

If getting the course incorporated into the curriculum in the first place is an issue, one may appeal to the American Assembly of Collegiate Schools of Business (AACSB) accreditation guidelines which call for affective skill development in the business school curriculum.

Topics To Be Covered

Topics one might consider covering in a Women in Management course include:

1. Differences in male and female socialization

2. Impact of socialization
3. Career decision-making for women
4. Stages of career development for women
5. Women's adult and moral development
6. Identity development for women
7. Differences in male & female management and leadership styles
8. Differences in male & female communication
9. Fear of success and women
10. Women and competition
11. Women and power: personal and structural
12. Women and authority
13. Women and stress
14. Women and conflict resolution
15. Androgyny
16. The minority female manager
17. Mentors and sponsors for women
18. Networking
19. Sexual harassment
20. Organizational politics and women
21. Dual career couples/families
22. Working mothers and childcare alternatives
23. Organizational career planning for women
24. Government legislation affecting women
25. Sexuality and intimacy
26. Business travel
27. Multiple role management
28. Maternity and paternity benefits
29. Nonconformity—dilemmas for women in predominantly male work groups
30. Structural discrimination/tokenism

Pedagogy

The sequencing of topics to be covered, and the way in which each topic is introduced to students may be more important to the success of the course, in terms of real student learning, than the actual topic areas one selects to include or exclude.

Given the age and life experience of the traditional students, the foundation-laying sessions of the course seem to be particularly important. Students need first to understand there is a problem, before they can be expected to analyze causes of those problems and think through solutions.

Laying the groundwork

Initial course experiences need to create a receptive, discussion-oriented feeling about the classroom. Students need to be open to the course material, to each other and to the instructor.

Given some expected skepticism from students, the instructor may need to be the first to set the tone of open exploration, rather than didactic prescriptive approaches to the course content. This can be done by introducing oneself in perhaps a more open fashion than may otherwise be called for on the first day of class. Hearing the instructor trace her own process of changing attitudes, with life and career experiences, can help the students see a model of the kind of process they are beginning, and can expect to continue as the course progresses.

One instructor describes her course as "highly experiential and exploratory in nature." She begins the class with an "icebreaker" intended to get the students talking to each other, hopefully about personal issues, and setting a tone of personal sharing for the course. One idea is to ask students to introduce themselves by telling a story about how they as a child first came to discover that girls and boys were different. Or about what their parents thought girls and boys "should" and "should not" do. Humorous stories and predictable tales about task differentiation in the home serve to get students laughing with each other and admitting to backgrounds which were "All-American" though not usually what they hope to replicate in their own homes.

"Joshua In a Box," a four-minute cartoon designed to illustrate the "boxes" that women individually and collectively may face in career and life planning, can also be used as an ice-breaker. (See Chapter 5 for a list of this and other films.)

Yet another idea involves having students draw pictures, using crayons or colored magic markers, which illustrate their current and predicted future career and life situations. This activity effectively tends to stimulate other ways of thinking and feeling about one's own career and life decision making.

A case study of a young woman's early socialization experiences, "Melissa's First Twenty-Two Years" (Keys, 1980) may help lay a foundation by acting as a bridge between students' own experiences and some of the issues to be dealt with in the course. Students usually recognize that Melissa's socialization hasn't led to firm career preparation and since they relate to her so closely they also come to question whether their own early experiences encouraged or discouraged a career orientation.

Guest speakers

Once the early groundwork has been laid, guest speakers may be an important source of learning. Meeting women in the professional working world helps students "connect" to that world. Simply asking speakers to trace their career history and respond to questions seems to be adequate structure. Not only can guest speakers tell students "what it's really like out there," but they can also serve as role models. Young students are looking for a clearer picture of what they will be like as professionals, and role models help them better visualize themselves as professional women.

It seems important to have at least two or three guest speakers, if they are to be used at all, in order to avoid creating a single model of professional women. We all seem to have the stereotypic picture of the woman on the cover of *Savvy* magazine, who is highly extroverted, wears a feminine blouse with the Malloy-dictated navy-blue skirted suit, and has a live-in housekeeper. Having a variety of guests, with a variety of personal ties and lifestyles (married, single, with and without children) can help to break down this stereotype and teach students that professional women come in all shapes, sizes, colors, and personality types. They also have a wide variety of career paths.

Case studies

The Simmons College case book (1976), contains descriptive studies of women's lives and career experiences. These can also serve to put students in touch with real people in real work situations. The cases need to be carefully selected to demonstrate a wide variety of issues, but students who are accustomed to the case approach to learning find case discussions instructive.

Interviews with women managers

Still another way of getting students connected to the working world is to send them out into organizations to interview with women managers, and write a short case study. Students may be asked to focus on women's experiences with specific course topics or stages in women's careers . . . but the real purpose is to have them meet someone in a one-to-one situation.

Interviewees are flattered to be interviewed, and students universally have positive experiences with this assignment. A class session devoted to exchanging stories about their interviewees proves to be particularly lively.

If the course has a career development component, the interview can be expanded to become an "informational interview," which will encourage students to ask questions about the interviewee's career area and company. (See Appendix II.)

Research on women: developing a critical perspective

A portion of the course can be used to help students distinguish between sound and unsound research, and to prepare better to analyze people's behavior in organizations. Many of the early conclusions about differences between males and females have since been refuted, and it is helpful for students to be familiar with both the earlier conclusions and the more recent studies. Nina Colwill, in *The New Partnership* (1982) does a particularly nice job of summarizing a great deal of research and drawing useful conclusions applicable to the workplace. For example, she points out (p. 114) that what we once saw as communication differences between males and females we are now seeing as differences accounted for by power: it simply happens that the women originally studied were in lower power positions while males were in high power positions. Our conclusions were sex-conscious rather than power-conscious.

Kanter, in *Men and Women of the Corporation* (1977) reaches a similar conclusion. She points out that when employees express a preference for a male boss over a female boss, they are really expressing a "preference for power" (p. 197). It is easier to work for a boss who has power than one who does not. In fact, "powerless" bosses, both male and female, exhibit controlling behavior, supervise closely, are rules-minded, and overly protective of their "turf." These characteristics were once thought to be female-specific. Again, the research was sex-conscious but not role-conscious or power-conscious.

A third example: sexual harassment is better understood not as something that "men do to women," but as a phenomena also explained by power differences . . . people in lower positions of power can suffer greater career damage and so are more vulnerable as victims, where people in positions of higher authority can take more risks as initiators.

This theme of decreasing students' sex-consciousness and increasing their consciousness of role as the dependent variable explaining research conclusions is a welcome one for men in the course, too, who don't want to be accused or blamed for "the problem." Finding examples of men in low-power positions who feel vulnerable, who are not career-oriented, and who have higher loyalties to their families than their companies, who are nonassertive, and leave the office at exactly 5 o'clock helps students to understand the significance of role in explaining behaviors previously thought to be sex-specific. Helping students make these intellectual recognitions predisposes them to better understand both the women and the men they will encounter in the workplace.

Student projects

Putting students into work groups of two to five for a project not only gives students a chance to get to know a few people well (where one hopes more personal discussions can take place) but it gives students a chance to explore topics of their own choice. Giving students 30-60 minutes of class time can generate interesting results. Some creative projects reported have included:

1) Interviewing successful women and writing up a series of case vignettes for class discussion;

2) Arranging a panel of dual-career couples to come to class;

3) Role-playing role-reversal incidents with male as home manager and female as breadwinner then conducting a class discussion;

4) Exploring the psychology of the "superwoman syndrome";

5) Replicating Rosen and Jerdee's study of managers' attitudes using their peers, the managers of tomorrow, as respondents;

6) Attending a training workshop on assertiveness and reporting on the experience to the class.

The options are limitless.

Current periodicals

Students may be required to find articles and readings which illustrate the topics covered in the course. Having them search for articles from newspapers, current periodicals, or from academic journals from the recent three or four years structures an opportunity for students to read for themselves and share with classmates up-to-date information being generated about women professionals. One professor asks students to submit a xeroxed copy of the article with a full reference citation, attaching a cover sheet to each article with a 100-word description which summarizes how the article relates to the topic as it was discussed in class.

Personal journals

Students usually have personal reactions to the class which don't get expressed in the class setting, even when discussion is encouraged. Asking students to react in a personal way to each class session, reading, or to their own experiences concurrent with the course can facilitate the depth of learning for students. The journal encourages students to consider more personally, and to think beyond the academic bounds of the information.

At first, students may not know how to use a personal journal toward their own learning, and so it may be useful to read some sample entries, and to clearly differentiate between class notes and journal entries. Suggesting questions at the end of class sessions can help students find a specific direction for writing a journal entry. How did you feel after the guest speaker? Did you agree with the author? In full, in part? How would you have dealt with the dilemma Caroline faced in the Caroline Miller case? Have you ever felt sexually harassed, but didn't know what term to attach to it? Describe the incident. One hopes that students will be able to shape their own questions as the course continues.

While journals are well-liked by students, and thought to have a great deal of learning value, instructors report spending considerable time reading and responding to them. Thus, an alternative might be to ask students to write two or three "learning papers," where at various points in the course students summarize their personal learnings to date. (See Appendix II.)

Resources Available

We have included as Appendices excerpts from two course outlines, one taught to a mixed-sex class and the other to an all-female group. Each lists complete references for materials students are asked to read, as well as other supplementary materials which may be useful to instructors. Other resource material can be found in Chapter 5.

Conclusions

Preparing undergraduate women for careers in business organizations is a challenging task. Instructors face the challenge of keeping up with the rapidly growing body of information and research related to women and organizations. At the same time, different organizations are changing at different rates such that women face a growing range of situations. While new companies in the fast-growing high-technology field seem to be more welcoming to women, America's older, more traditional companies are slow to change: women may still feel quite unwelcome there. Thus, instructors must regularly assess course goals and instructional material to see that the preparation undergraduate women are getting does indeed use information addressed to the realities of business organizations today.

Regardless of the challenge, more and more professors are teaching Women in Management courses, and increasing numbers of undergraduate women are preparing to begin careers in business. Graduates who have taken Women in Management report that they have often reflected on the course, reporting that they felt much better prepared for their work experiences as a result.

APPENDIX I
Excerpts from a Sample Course Outline
Women and Men as Colleagues in Organizations
Dr. Diane McKinney Kellogg
Bentley College
(male and female registrants)

Session #   I. Male and Female Socialization

1. Introducing Ourselves and the Issues
2. Male Socialization (Film: "Men's Lives")
3. Female Socialization (Film: "She's Nobody's Baby")
4. Understanding Your Own Life Script

    (Submit personal journals for ungraded review)

II. Research on Women: Fact and Fallacy

5. Stages of Moral Development + Fear of Success Myths
6. Characteristics of Managerial Women: past, present, future
7. "My Career History" (Guest Speaker #1)
8. Communication and Power: Male/Female Differences
9. Wives & Breadwinners: Sources of Well-Being

    (Submit case study of woman manager you interviewed)

III. Women and Organizational Realities

10. Secretaries and Managers
11. Structural Barriers: Opportunity, Power, and Powerlessness
12. Impact of Stereotyping on Managerial Decision-Making
13. Women Managing Men
14. "My Career History" (Guest Speaker #2)

IV. Men and Women Working Together

15. Women and Newcomers to the Professional Workforce (Film: "A Tale of O")
16. Men as Newcomers to the Homefront (Film: "Men Under Siege")
17. Reading the System's Norms + Understanding the Politics
18. Sexual Attraction, Intimacy, and Working Relationships

19. "Working with Professional Women, and Marrying One" (Guest Speaker #3)

    (Submit Take-Home Essay Exam)

V. Current Issues

(Group presentations will be based on these, or alternative approved topics.)

20. Mentors and Networking
21. Dual Career Couples/Families
22. Maternity and Paternity Benefits + Childcare Alternatives
23. Sexual Harrassment
24. Strategies for Moving Up
25. Dressing the Part + Image Management
26. Androgyny and Role Reversal
27. Stress Management + Time Management

    (Submit Personal Journals)

Required Readings

(Numbered to correspond to session #'s above.)

All books used in the course are available in paperback at low cost, and would be excellent additions to your library: they will be even more useful in the future as you begin your career. Articles are on reserve in the library: each student may make one xeroxed copy. *Harvard Business Review* reprints can be purchased at the bookstore, as can *Savvy* Magazine. Please read *Savvy* regularly as we will discuss articles from time to time.

2. Pleck, J. H. "Men's Power with Women, Other Men, and Society." In *The American Man*, Elizabeth and Joseph Pleck (Eds.). New Jersey: Prentice-Hall, 1980.

3. Colwill, N. *The New Partnership*. Palo Alto, CA: Mayfield Publishing, 1982, Chapters 1 and 2.
   Bem, S. and Bem, D. "Case Study of a Nonconscious Ideology: Training the Woman to Know Her Place." In D. J. Bem, *Beliefs, Attitudes, and Human Affairs*. Brooks/Cole, 1970.

4. Keys, D.E. & "Melissa." *Melissa's First Twenty-Two Years*. Northern Illinois University, 1980.

5. Colwill: Chapters 4 and 5.
   Gilligan, C. "Why Should a Woman Be More Like a Man?" *Psychology Today*, June 1982.

6. Hennig, M. and Jardim, A. *The Managerial Woman.* New York: Pocket Books, 1976.
   Keown, C. F. and Keown, A. L. "Success Factors for Corporate Women Executives." *Group and Organization Studies,* December 1982, 445-56.

8. Colwill: Chapter 7.

9. Baruch, G. Barnett, R. and Rivers, C. *Lifeprints.* New York: McGraw-Hill, 1983. Scarf, M. "The More Sorrowful Sex." *Psychology Today.* April 1967.

10. Kanter, R. M. *Men and Women of the Corporation.* New York: Basic Books, 1977, Chapters 3 and 4.

11. Kanter: Chapters 6 and 7.

12. Josefowitz, N. *Paths to Power: A Woman's Guide from First Job to Top Executive.* New York: Addison-Wesley, 1980.
    Rosen, B. and Jerdee, T. H. "Sex Stereotyping in the Executive Suite." *Harvard Business Review,* March-April 1974.

13. Schrank, R. "Two Women, Three Men on a Raft." *Harvard Business Review,* May-June 1977.

15. Colwill: Chapter 9
    Kanter: Chapter 8

16. Prescott, E. "Real Men Do Wear Aprons." *American Demographics,* 1983.

17. Kennedy, M. M. *Office Politics.* Chicago: Follett, 1980.

18. Spelman, D. and Crary, M. "The Barbara Dibella Case." Unpublished manuscript. Waltham, MA: Bentley College, 1984.

20. Missirian, A. K. *The Corporate Connection.* Englewood Cliffs, New Jersey: Prentice-Hall, 1982.

22. Wheatley, M. and Hirsch, M. S. *Managing Your Maternity Leave.* Boston: Houghton-Mifflin, 1983.

24. Lee, N. *Targeting the Top.* New York: Ballantine, 1980.

Sample Essay Questions

1. After reading the "Foreword" to Roszak & Roszak's book *Masculine/Feminine* respond to the final question they pose: "How can we call off the game?"

2. Discuss an experience you have had recently, or an incident you have observed, which demonstrated the existence of stereotyped assumptions about females and/or males. How would you "explain" the attitudes you saw? How did *you* feel about the incident?

3. Discuss the concept of "powerlessness," as defined by Kanter. How do her conclusions relate to the characteristics stereotypically assigned to women in general? "Women bosses" in specific?

4. After rereading Schrank's conclusions (1977), discuss how women can be more effective leaders. Assume that Schrank's conclusions are accurate—that men do tend to unconsciously or consciously fail to support women as their leaders.

5. Defend the statement: "Sexual harassment is more an issue of misuse of power than misuse of sexuality."

6. What *can* a mentor do for you, and what can a mentor *not* do for you, in helping you get ahead in your career?

7. If you want to make sure that you don't take a position which has little power built into the role, what questions would you want to ask an interviewer, and why would you want that information? (Discuss at least four questions.)

APPENDIX II
Excerpts from a Sample Course Outline
Behavioral Implications of Women in Management

Dr. Lynda L. Moore
Simmons College
(female registrants only)

Required Texts

Bolles, R. N. *The Quick Job Hunting Map* (advanced version). Berkeley, California: Ten Speed Press, 1979.

_____. *What Color is Your Parachute?* Berkeley, California: Ten Speed Press, revised edition, 1984.

Forisha, B. and Goldman, B. *Outsiders on the Inside: Women and Organizations.* Englewood Cliffs, N.J.: Prentice-Hall, 1981.

Harragan, B. *Games Mother Never Taught You: Corporate Gamesmanship for Women.* New York: Warner Books, 1978.

Hennig, M. and Jardim, A. *The Managerial Woman.* New York: Pocket Books, 1980.

Josefowitz, N. *Paths to Power: A Woman's Guide from First Job to Top Executive.* Reading, MA: Addison-Wesley Publishing Co., 1982.

Miller, J. B. *Toward a New Psychology of Women.* Boston: Beacon Press, 1976.

Required Readings

Dalton, G. W., Thompson, P. H., & Price, R. L. "The Four Stages of Professional Careers—a New Look at Performance by Professionals." *Organizational Dynamics,* 1977, 43-60.

Dolotin, S. "Voices from the Post-Feminist Generation." *The New York Times Magazine,* November 21, 1982.

Dowling, C. "The Cinderella Syndrome." *The New York Times Magazine,* March 22, 1981.

Friedan, B. "Twenty Years After the Feminist Mystique." *The New York Times Magazine,* February 27, 1983, 34-36, ff.

Gilligan, C. "Woman's Place in Man's Life Cycle." In Carol Gilligan, *In a Different Voice.* Cambridge: Harvard University Press, 1982.

Sassen, G. "Success Anxiety in Women: a Constructivist Interpretation of Its Source and Its Significance." *Harvard Educational Review,* 1980, *50*(1), 13-24.

Shreve, A. "Careers and the Lure of Motherhood." *The New York Times Magazine,* November 21, 1982.

Stiver, I. P. *Work Inhibitions in Women.* Stone Center for Developmental Services and Studies, 1983, Wellesley College, Wellesley, MA.

Tavris, C. "Women's Wants: The Cinderella Complex." *The New York Times Review of Books,* July 12, 1981.

Informational Interview Analysis

Instructions to Students:

You are required to interview a woman who is currently working in your preferred career. She must be someone you do not currently know. You should use any and all existing resources to network in order to find the appropriate person to interview (relatives, friends, peers, professors, friends of friends, alumnae network, etc.). Your interview should not last more than one hour. Questions for the interview are listed below.

Suggested questions for your informational interview

Purpose:

1. To find out as much as you can about the career that is special to you.
2. To experience that the working world is only inhabited by *people.*
3. To gain experience in making contacts within a particular occupational network.
4. To develop some knowledge of the interviewing process.
5. To gain some insight into the problems and opportunities that professional women face in organizations.

Richard Bolles suggests using the following questions to guide your interview:

1. What do you especially like about your career?
2. What are your dislikes about this career?
3. How did you obtain your present position?
4. What advice would you offer someone who would like to enter this occupation?
5. Who do you know in your field that might be willing to talk to me? May I use your name as a referral?

Additional Questions:

1. How did you decide to go into this career?
2. What specific skills are needed for this type of work?
3. How promising is the future of this work?
4. Can you recommend academic courses or experiences that might enhance my chances of breaking into this field?
5. How does working in this field affect one's personal life?
6. What are the opportunities for advancement in this career field?
7. Have you found any barriers to your career success because you are a woman? If so, what are they and what strategies did you use to overcome them (if any?)
8. Do you feel there are any special considerations that women need to be aware of in planning to write their careers?

Remember to Write a Thank-You Note

Requirements for the paper

You are required to write an analysis of the informational interview from two perspectives. The first perspective is the content. From the questions provided as well as your own, what did you learn about the career, and this individual woman's career and life decision-making process? About being a woman in that career? The second perspective is the interview process itself. What did you learn about interviewing someone? Did you feel that you were effective or ineffective? Why? Be specific and identify particular behaviors and attitudes which contributed to a successful or unsuccessful interview.

The paper should be maximum of five pages, typed, proofread, and stapled together. No extensions will be given on due dates.

Learning Paper Assignments

First paper

The purpose of the first learning paper is to help you assess where you are right now in terms of personal career development, and to consider where you'd like to be in the future. Assessment of your present state should be based on what has happened in the past; goals for the future should include some sort of plan for reaching them.

How would you describe yourself as a person and as a woman right now? What values are especially important to you? What concerns do you have? What do you *like* to do? What personal characteristics help you, which hinder you, in terms of getting along with other people—which is what a career in management is all about? What is your likely future, given where you are now?

In responding to these questions, think about what has occurred in the past to make you the kind of woman you are, to orient you toward the career you have in mind. These may be events from school, family, job, social, or other situations. Why are you here now? What do you hope to get out of it?

Think about the future. How do you hope to be different in a year? Two? Five? Twenty? How might this course help you get there? That is, how can you use this course to meet your own goals and needs?

Be as specific as you can in writing this paper. If you find it difficult, don't be surprised. Most people seldom encounter themselves in such concrete introspection as I'm asking of you. Some even find it painful. Remember, unless you contract specifically otherwise, the paper will not be seen by anyone other than the instructor. So put down what you want to. If you draw a blank on some of this, just say so; don't bother generating useless verbiage. Papers are due at the end of the second week of class.

Second paper

The second learning paper is to help you assess what you think you've learned from the course, if anything. A good place to start is with the goals of your first paper. How have you done in relation to what you set out to do? What helped or hindered your progress toward your goals? What particular things in the course made an impact? Have your goals changed? If you had it to do over, what changes would you make? (For example: drop the course, set different goals, behave differently, etc.)

As with the first paper, the second should be your honest engagement of the issues, with nothing forced. Be specific in expressing yourself.

Be sure to hand in your first learning paper along with the second. Put both papers in a sealed envelope with your name on the outside.

REFERENCES

Cases on Women in Management. Boston: Simmons College, 1976.

Colwill, N. *The New Partnership.* Palo Alto, CA: Mayfield Publishing Company, 1982.

Epstein, C. F. *Woman's Place: Options and Limits in Professional Careers.* Berkeley, CA: University of California Press, 1971.

Friedan, B. *The Feminine Mystique.* New York: W. W. Norton, 1963; Dell, 1974.

Hai, D. "Teaching 'Women in Management' Courses: Current Issues." *Exchange,* Vol. VII, 1982, 4, 38-40.

Kanter, R. M. *Men and Women of the Corporation.* New York: Basic Books, 1977.

Katham, J. and Weathersby, R. P. *Dilemmas of Gender: How do We Socialize Men and Women for Organizational Roles?* Unpublished manuscript. Durham, NH: University of New Hampshire, 1983.

Keys, D. E. and "Melissa." *Melissa's First Twenty-Two Years.* Northern Illinois University, 1980.

Professional Negotiations:
How to Get What You Both Want

Theresa L. Clow, Stephens College

Negotiation is an inevitable reality in human interactions and relationships. Individuals often rely on unexamined habits in their personal and professional transactions. It is necessary to analyze one's communicating behaviors consciously in order to enhance one's professional effectiveness and personal satisfaction. Perhaps one negotiation seminar participant best described this when she said: "I thought I was just communicating, but now I realize I should have been negotiating."

Negotiating expertise provides an opportunity for women to influence circumstances rather than react to situations. Appropriate fact-finding, preparation, and application of negotiation techniques encourage women to develop and pursue their own strategies and goals. Thus, negotiating becomes a way of life to increase each participant's success. This seminar focuses on negotiation as a means for collaborative outcomes in conflicts or situations where the needs of the individuals differ. The collaborative approach often demands more creativity, time, and energy. However, in professional relationships such extra effort is preferable so that both parties can "win" and the relationship can be maintained. Competitive strategies often fuel, rather than resolve, conflict.

This seminar emphasizes the development of insight into negotiation as a process and as a professional skill. This allows participants to begin to consciously initiate effective negotiation strategies to improve professional success on many levels. Negotiation skills can be applied to salary and benefit issues during interviews, as well as to facilitate better understanding and cooperation with superiors, subordinates, peers, and clients. A repertoire of alternative behaviors and means for analyzing such transactions allows women to influence agreements collaboratively and obtain positive outcomes.

55

Objectives

This seminar is designed to introduce women to the application of negotiation skills in a variety of business and professional situations. One objective of the seminar is to increase the participant's awareness of negotiation as an effective approach for improving professional relationships and to help her achieve desired results in dealing with others.

A second objective of the seminar is to develop each participant's negotiating abilities. The seminar emphasizes learning through personal involvement, experience, and analysis of experience in terms of negotiation concepts. Particular emphasis is placed upon the application of techniques in simulations. Thus, participants leave the seminar aware of the wide range of possible negotiation situations, having tested their own abilities through applying a variety of negotiating strategies during simulations.

Specific characteristics for successful negotiation are emphasized. These include developing a practical understanding of the negotiation process and the behaviors which are appropriate to specific issues involved in a situation. The seminar provides opportunities for developing appropriate communication behaviors to facilitate negotiations and arrive at satisfactory agreements that can be successfully implemented. The importance of managing negotiation by process and content is adressed. Participants improve their capacity to prepare resourcefully for negotiations, to implement strategies effectively, and to adjust their expectations and assumptions in the light of actual experience.

Finally, the seminar facilitates the development of the ability to recognize tactics employed by the other party and to use counter-tactics which will promote productive cooperation, reduce conflicts, and protect individual interests. Proper analysis of situations contributes to mutual understanding. Many apparent conflicts are misunderstandings caused by ineffective communication, and negotiation is a form of communication at its highest level. Participants are assisted in developing listening skills and the abilities necessary to clarify and convey a point of view.

A workshop or seminar on professional negotiations may be presented in several different formats depending upon the time available and the specific goals to be achieved. One's negotiating skills are continually tested beyond any seminar. The topic can consume a full semester of traditionally scheduled class periods; it fits easily into a two-weekend concentrated format, and may be presented effectively as an abbreviated module within other programs. The following outline is intended to present a full range of concepts pertinent to professional negotiations. Several activities and resources are suggested for each segment in order to allow a variety of applications.

Ideally, the workshop should include the introduction of information from a variety of sources, discussions which allow the participants to relate the information to their own experiences, and opportunities to engage actively in exercises and simulations in order to apply the information and obtain feedback from the instructor or the trainer. If time is limited it seems most appropriate to abbreviate all three aspects of the seminar rather than to eliminate any one of the approaches described above. The real learning often takes place during the processing phase of the simulations and exercises as participants examine and reflect upon their behaviors and the consequences of those behaviors. Thus, concepts presented during the introduction to the seminar gain depth and meaning for the participants as a result of their participation in various activities and simulations. The seminar environment provides a supportive and low-risk opportunity for participants to experiment with and practice their professional negotiating skills.

Workshop Outline

Content	*Design*
I. Introduction to Professional Negotiations (1 to 4 hours)	I. Lecture, discussion, and self-tests to provide over-view.
II. Body Language/Nonverbal Communication (30 minutes to 3 hours)	II. Mini-lecture, individual and group activities, slides, and photographs.
III. Verbal Communication and Listening (35 minutes to 2 hours)	III. Mini-lecture, group activity, and film.
IV. Assumptions and Expectations (15 minutes to 1 hour)	IV. Mini-lecture, logic, and dice games.
V. Preparation and Creativity (10 minutes to several hours)	V. Mini-lecture, creativity quiz, and simulations.
VI. Needs, Trust, Openness, and Collaborative Strategy (30 minutes to several hours)	VI. Mini-lecture and simulations.

Introduction to Professional Negotiations

Procedure

Step 1: 30-60 minutes

Introduce participants to the variety of books, articles, and resources available which address the topic of negotiation. Solicit individual definitions of negotiation and individual experiences involving negotiation. Share definitions of negotiation provided by various authors and present the variety of applications suggested by the authors. Describe the relevance and importance of negotiation in personal and professional interactions. Explain the objectives and the format of the workshop. Briefly introduce the various issues and concepts relevant to negotiations. Any of the following steps work well alone or in combination for introducing participants to the process and importance of negotiation.

Step 2: 45-55 minutes

Hand out and discuss information which capsulizes the negotiation process and which describes some of the characteristics of skilled negotiators (Supplement I).

Step 3: 60 minutes

Several authors have included self-tests in their books which allow participants to begin to describe their own behaviors and styles of negotiation (Cohen, 1980; Warschaw, 1980).

I A: Introduction to professional negotiations

Negotiation may be viewed as a spectrum or continuum which places bargaining, win-lose situations, and conflict at one end and joint problem-solving, win-win situations, and cooperation at the other end (Rohrer, Hibler, and Replogle Inc., 1981, p. 93).

Characteristics of skilled negotiators

Characteristics of skilled negotiators may be summarized as follows:

1. Practical understanding of the negotiating process and behaviors which are appropriate to the issues involved.
2. Characteristic use of certain communication behaviors to facilitate the flow of negotiation and arrive at satisfactory agreements that can be successfully implemented.
3. Ability to manage negotiations by process and content control.
4. Capacity to prepare resourcefully for negotiations, to implement strategies effectively, and to adjust expectations and assumptions in the light of actual experience.
5. Ability to recognize tactics employed by the other party and to use counter-tactics which will promote productive cooperation, reduce conflicts, and protect individual interests (Rohrer et al., 1981, p. 92).

II: Body Language/Nonverbal Communication

Procedure

Step 1: 15-20 minutes

Many messages are conveyed through eye-contact, stance, tone of voice, gestures, and other elements of body language. Negotiators must be aware of the messages they send and receive through these nonverbal channels. Knowledge of nonverbal behaviors allows the negotiator to use these behaviors strategically for intended results. This also improves the negotiator's ability to analyze such behaviors in others. Participants should be introduced to these skills by sharing information from a variety of sources. A variety of activities may also be used to stimulate discussion, self-awareness, and consideration of these aspects of communication. The importance of context, gesture clusters, and patterns of nonverbal communication should be emphasized. Nonverbal communication is structured much as sentences are structured in verbal language. Isolated movements may be misleading.

Step 2: 10-15 minutes

Ask participants to "freeze" and consciously consider their current body position and possible message they are sending. Is their body accurately reflecting their current feelings? To what extent is their posture habitual and to what extent is it unique to the current context?

Step 3: 10-15 minutes

Ask participants to shake hands with several others and try to be conscious of their own and the other's stance, eye-contact, and hand shake. Discuss reactions and differences. Ask if they were ever taught to shake hands and how they learned their own style? Explore different messages which can be conveyed.

Step 4: 45 minutes

The exercise entitled "Cooperative and Competitive Communication" (Ruben and Budd, 1975, pp. 74-75) involves nonverbal communication and related issues pertinent to collaborative negotiations. The exercise involves subgroups of five members each of whom must nonverbally communicate and cooperate in order to construct individual three-inch squares from variously shaped and sized pieces of cardboard.

Step 5: 20-30 minutes

The game "Red Handed" (Fluegelman, 1976, p. 71) involves participants who attempt to conceal the location of an object within a group while "it" tries to determine who is holding the object. Participants discover how easy it is to mislead and be misled using only body language and nonverbal communication.

Step 6: 20 minutes

Slides or photographs depicting people in various settings can be used to engage participants in an analysis of various postures and gestures. This often exposes differences in perception among individuals, an important point to raise in discussion of body language and nonverbal messages.

III: Verbal Communication and Listening

Procedure

Step 1: 5 minutes

Introduce the need for negotiators to refine their verbal communication skills in order to facilitate clear and effective transfer of information and needs. Listening is equally critical for the accurate understanding of the other party during negotiations.

Step 2: 30 minutes

The exercise entitled "Self-Disclosure and Listening" (Ruben and Budd, 1975, pp. 21-23) allows participants to examine their individual styles of communication. Triads are asked to share with each other how and why they communicate as they do. The triad members rotate in the roles of Speaker, Listener, and Judge which allows them to each practice their speaking and listening skills, in addition to helping participants to recognize differences in communicaiton styles.

Step 3: 30 minutes

The film, "The Power of Listening," McGraw-Hill, Catalog Number, 12-1637, is very good for this topic.

IV: Assumptions and Expectations

Procedure

Step 1: 10-15 minutes

Recognizing each individual's assumptions facilitates the development of appropriate strategies and alternatives before and during negotiations. It is important to distinguish between assumptions and facts in order to arrive at mutual understanding and agreement. Assumptions are often the source of conflict and disagreement and must be exposed in order to resolve conflict and reach agreement. Assumptions are inherent in our behavior and functioning in the world. We assume others will stop at a red light. Unexamined assumptions often interfere with communication. A thorough exploration of each side's assumptions is a critical first step in the negotiation process. Assumptions about one's self, the other party, and the issues involved contribute to certain expectations. Negotiators should examine their own expectations and anticipate the expectations of the other party. If assumptions are clarified, then realistic expectations can be formed.

Step 2: 30 minutes to 1 hour

The difficulty in trying to determine another's assumptions can be experienced with the dice games presented in Supplement II.

IV A: Assumptions and Expectations

Two dice games

These games, "Petals Around the Rose" and "Bulls in the Pasture" create confusion for participants. Participants commonly approach the task with certain assumptions regarding the rules of dice games which are based upon previous experience. The traditional rules for dice games do not apply in these games. Indirect clues to the logic of the games are reflected in each of the names of the games. The instructor should roll the dice and encourage participants to test a variety of assumptions until they discover the appropriate rules. Six or seven die should be used. Each game may take from 15 minutes up to an hour.

> *Petals Around the Rose:* Only threes and fives are relevant to this game. One counts the dots surrounding the center dot on the threes and fives in a throw of die. The total dots represent the petals around the roses. Example: A throw consisting of a two, a five, a three, a six, a one, and a four would contain six petals.

> *Bulls in the Pasture:* One is attempting to classify the number of healthy and the number of disabled bulls in a particular throw of the die. Die pairs of one, three and five represent healthy bulls while single one, three and five die represent disabled bulls. Example: A throw of a six, two fives, a four, a three and a one would contain one healthy and one disabled bull (from ADAPT Workshop, University of Nebraska-Lincoln).

V: Preparation and Creativity

Procedure

Step 1: 5-10 minutes

Successful negotiations require extensive fact-finding and preparation. Such preparation should include research about the other party as well as about the issues so that realistic positions and viable alternatives can be developed. The level of one's confidence in a negotiation often is directly correlated with the amount of preparation one has done. Strategies, alternatives, and agreements that are mutually beneficial often require considerable creativity. Participants should be encouraged to avoid either/or attitudes toward the development of alternatives and agreements.

Step 2: 30-45 minutes

Exercises in creativity can include asking participants to think about familiar items in different ways (Supplement III).

Step 3: 30-45 minutes

Two-Person Bargaining: The Ugli Orange Case (Hall, Bowen, Lewicki, and Hall, 1975, pp. 82-83) explores the dynamics of two-person bargaining, but can be adapted for teams. Creative problem-solving, initial fact-finding, and preparation can be emphasized by this case.

V A: Preparation and Creativity

Creativity quiz

1. Design a clock that has no moving parts on its face or any feature that changes visibly during normal use.
2. What needs more protection, a turtle or a rock?
3. Which weighs more, a boulder or a heavy heart?
4. Which grows more, a tree or self-confidence?
5. Provide an example of "repulsion-attraction."
6. Provide an example of "delicate-armor."
7. Provide an example of "frozen haste."
8. Provide an example of "disciplined-freedom."

There are no right or wrong answers for these questions. A sun dial or auditory clock are examples of typical answers to the first question. Democracy is often given as an example for the last question. Adapted from a discussion of Synectics exercises presented by Marilyn Ferguson, *The Aquarian Conspiracy*, Houghton-Mifflin, 1980, pp. 302-5.

VI: Needs, Trust, Openness and Collaborative Strategy

Procedure

Step 1: 5-10 minutes

The core of Nierenberg's approach to negotiation is identifying and satisfying needs; other authors also consider this aspect important to successful negotiations. The collaborative approach seeks to satisfy both parties' needs. Identifying needs promotes agreements which can be mutually beneficial. Trust and openness are essential in order to inspire reciprocal trust and openness in others. Such behavior speeds agreements and sustains lasting professional relationships. These elements create a positive environment based upon mutual respect and sincere desire for agreement. Collaborative techniques are based upon the belief in the potential for mutual satisfaction of needs combined with trust. Both parties can participate in creating collaborative agreements in which both parties' needs may be satisfied. Competitive strategies result in winners and losers. Collaborative strategies result in winners on both sides. Realistic agreements, which are collaboratively developed, sustain lasting professional respect and cooperation.

Step 2: 30 minutes to several hours

A variety of simulations may be used. Often the choice of simulations will be based upon the professional concerns and interests of the participants. The following simulations may be appropriate in length or topic for certain participants; however, instructors may want to develop their own. The book *Experiences in Management and Organizational Behavior* (Hall, et al., 1975) contains several applicable simulations:

> *The Disarmament Exercise,* pp. 85-93, demonstrates the potential for conflict with another group, how groups tend to emphasize only their own needs, and how problems are created by mistrust and differing expectations. It provides an opportunity to apply negotiation concepts and techniques. (One to three hours; pairs of groups with four to eight persons in each group.)
>
> *Coalition Bargaining,* pp. 130-34, explores the dynamics of trust between groups in a competitive situation, and emphasizes what happens when there are winners and losers in a negotiation. (One to two hours; three teams with four to eight members.)
>
> *Transactional Analysis,* pp. 143-46, presents the terminology of Parent, Adult, and Child and provides the opportunity for participants to reflect upon inter-personal relationships. (One to three hours; subgroups of three.)

Step 3: 3 to 12 hours

Two simulations developed by this author are briefly described below. Detailed descriptions of these simulations can be obtained by contacting the author. These are comprehensive simulations which provide participants with the opportunity to integrate the concepts and skills learned in all prior seminar activities.

> *Procurement Contract Problem* involves negotiating changes to an existing contract between the government and a construction contractor. The information provided to each side appears to be straight-forward and complete. It includes specifications and a small blueprint of the remodeling work. However, there are a number of ambiguities in this situation which require each negotiating party to make several assumptions. The situation seems deceptively simple and participants normally prepare their positions in a short period of time. Different prices and methods for pricing materials and labor can be provided to each side or parties may be asked to contact local firms and obtain their own pricing. If price data are provided, each side normally can prepare their position in one or two hours. The teams then begin negotiating and their differing assumptions often escalate competitiveness and conflict. The processing phase of this

simulation provides the opportunity for both sides to discuss their errors, behaviors, and agreement. The negotiation may take three to four hours. Video-taping of the process provides ample material for discussion of all the elements of negotiation.

Labor and Management Negotiation is a lengthy simulation which provides each side with the same information. The information is complete and no additional research is required for participants. Traditional issues of salary, benefits, and staffing are considered. This simulation is appropriate for large groups since six separate issues can be taken from the package for pairs of participants to negotiate. The over-all objective is to reach agreement on a total package which requires considerable collaboration within each group as well as between groups. This simulation requires three to four hours as a minimum for preparation and can take eight to twelve hours to negotiate a final agreement.

REFERENCES AND SUGGESTED READINGS

ADAPT Workshop, University of Nebraska-Lincoln, 1981.

Cohen, H. *You Can Negotiate Anything.* Secaucus, NJ: Lyle Stuart, Inc., 1980.

Ferguson, M. *The Aquarian Conspiracy.* Los Angeles: Houghton-Mifflin Co., 1980.

Fisher, R., and Ury, W. *Getting to Yes—Negotiating Agreement Without Giving In.* Los Angeles: Houghton-Mifflin Co., 1981.

Fluegelman, A., ed. *The New Games Book.* Garden City, NY: Doubleday and Co., Inc., 1976.

Hall, D. T., Bowen, D., Lewicki, R., and Hall, F. *Experiences in Management and Organizational Behavior.* Chicago: St. Clair Press, 1975.

Henley, N. *Body Politics.* Englewood Cliffs, NJ: Prentice-Hall, 1977.

Ilich, J., and Jones, B. *Successful Negotiating Skills for Women.* Reading, MA: Addison-Wesley, 1981.

Karrass, C. L. *The Negotiation Game.* New York: Thomas Crowell Publisher, 1970.

———*Give and Take.* New York: Thomas Crowell Publisher, 1974.

Knapp, M. .L. *Nonverbal Communication in Human Interaction.* New York: Holt, Rinehart, and Winston, 1978.

LaFrance, M., and Mayo, C. *Moving Bodies.* Monterrey, CA: Brooks and Cole Publishing, 1978.

Lewis, D. V. *Power Negotiating Tactics and Techniques.* Englewood Cliffs, NJ: Prentice-Hall, 1981.

Mayo, C., and Henley, N. M. *Gender and Nonverbal Behavior.* New York: Springer-Verlag, 1981.

Morrison, J. H., and O'Hearne, J. J. *Practical Transactional Analysis in Management.* Reading, MA: Addison-Wesley, 1977.

Nierenberg, G. I., and Calero, H. H. *How to Read a Person Like a Book.* New York: Simon and Schuster, 1971.

Nierenberg, G. I. *Fundamentals of Negotiation.* New York: Hawthorne Books, 1973.

———*The Art of Creative Thinking.* New York: Simon and Schuster, 1982.

Raiffa, H. *The Art and Science of Negotiation.* Cambridge: Harvard University Press, 1982.

Rohrer, Hibler, and Replogle, Inc. *The Managerial Challenge: A Psychological Approach to the Changing World of Management.* New York: New American Library, 1981.

Ruben, B. D., and Budd, R. W. *Human Communication Handbook, Simulations and Games, Vol. 1.* Rochelle, NY: Hayden Book Co., 1975.

Seltz, D., and Modica, A. *Negotiate Your Way to Success.* New York: New American Library, 1980.

Warschaw, T. *Winning by Negotiation.* New York: McGraw-Hill, 1980.

Zemke, R. "Negotiation Skills Training: Helping Others Get What They Want—Gracefully." *Training,* February 5, 1980, pp. 25-28.

Conflict:
If You Ignore It, It Won't Go Away

Janine A. Moon, United Telephone Company of Ohio

Conflict is, for most, both foreboding and fascinating. It's a very natural part of life that occurs everywhere: in interpersonal, organizational, national, and international relations. At least part of its fascination results in the diverse and seemingly "at odds" ideas and feelings most women have about conflict. On the one hand, women see conflict as negative, to be avoided at all costs. As girls, most women learn "only boys fight," "nice girls behave themselves," "be nice," and that boys learn "never hit a girl." So women shy away from conflict naturally: many have no productive experience with it, have never developed the skills to handle it, and so have no background with which to manage conflict constructively. On the other hand, many women are in organizations or work environments in which conflict is a normal, expected part of everyday operations. Conflicts come and go, some larger and more important than others, some handled more effectively than others, many with positive results, but most managed—not avoided.

The "at odds" idea, then, for women is this: to view conflict as bad/negative/destructive is in direct opposition to views fostered in environments in which women live. Often work environments seem to encourage constructive conflict—and this, for many women, is frightening since they see their own self image and ability to succeed in those environments as threatened. To change ideas and behaviors about conflict after 20, 30, or more years seems a big task, and to many women one that also invites failure. The situation appears to be a "Catch-22."

However, what women need to realize is that failure is *more* likely if women do not change or reorient beliefs and behaviors about conflict. Women's failure to learn to deal with and manage conflict creatively will lock them out of successful work and organization relationships and lessen their effectiveness in interpersonal ones.

So, *Conflict is O.K.* Comfort with and success in dealing with conflict increases in direct proportion to learning about and working with conflict, conflict resolution and reduction strategies, communication skills, and personal conflict handling styles. The information that follows is a basic workshop on conflict and covers many of these areas. The methodology is directed toward women who are uncomfortable in conflict situations and tentative about their personal ability to handle conflict effectively. This information can begin the learning process.

Objectives

This workshop is designed to help women recognize that "Conflict is O.K." and to encourage women to see conflict as another side of communication. One objective of the workshop is for participants to trace the cycle that conflict follows from beginning to resolution, thereby recognizing conflict as predictable, and having a natural pattern. Secondly, to examine conflict's nature further, participants consider personal conflict situations and list both constructive and destructive aspects of the conflict.

The predictability of conflict is further reinforced by the third workshop objective in which participants identify frequent areas of organizational conflict. Through guided discussion, participants share back-home examples of these areas and analyze the "why" behind their frequent recurrence.

A fourth workshop objective seeks to show conflict as communication while recollecting societal expectations of women as empathetic and naturally good communicators. Participants work to examine interpersonal relations through the communication dimensions of impact and ownership.

Finally, participants examine four conflict positions—the characteristics and appropriate applications of each. Then, participants consider each position and its relationship to the two communication dimensions. Participants then have a model to use in defining productive conflict and in determining a most appropriate position to adopt in interpersonal conflict situations.

Workshop Outline

Content	*Design*
Introductory Remarks (10 minutes)	"Warm up" discussion with a purpose of relaxing group; includes remarks on significance of conflict as a topic; participant objectives; direction of workshop; and definition of and examples of conflict situations.
I. The Conflict Cycle (15-20 minutes)	I. Short lecture with visual that details seven phases of a conflict cycle. Emphasis is on "Reflection" phase during which learning is most likely to occur.

II. Constructive and
Destructive Aspects of
Conflict
(15-20 minutes)

II. Part A: Individual exercise in which
participants describe (in writing) two
recent conflict situations, behaviors,
and positive and negative effects of the
conflicts.
Part B: Processing of this information (entire
group) with two desired outcomes: 1) emphasis
on the constructive or positive aspects of conflict; and 2) individual examination of written
lists for balance or imbalance of positive and
negative aspects.

III. Areas of Conflict or
Disagreement
(7-10 minutes)

III. Brief review or discussion (using
handout) of five areas around which
conflict frequently occurs: goals, policy,
priorities, methods, information.

IV. Self-Assessment:
Conflict Style
(5 minutes)

IV. Brief individual activity in which
participants indicate their conflict
style(s): first, their perceived style of reacting to
conflict; and second, their preferred style.
Discussion centers around reasons for *two*
styles.

V. Communication and
Conflict
(40-45 minutes)

A. Communication
Dimensions

B. Conflict Positions

C. Productive Conflict

V. Primarily lecture with some discussion shows how conflict falls, in
reality, on the communication continuum.

A. Description of dimensions and
their importance as factors in communication.

B. Description of conflict model: four positions,
characteristics, and appropriateness of each. Emphasis on each position being productive and
appropriate in certain situations.

C. Overlay of communication dimensions onto
conflict model demonstrates high-impact and
high-ownership conflict positions, and shows
"face" position as the most productive one.

VI. Personal Assessment
Tools
(5 minutes)

VI. Tools are not used in workshop.
Several are distributed and their purpose and
use explained. Other tools are referenced.

VII. Pulling It All Together
(5 minutes)

VII. Using easel, major workshop ideas
are reviewed and listed.

VIII. Closure
(3 minutes)

VIII. Participants complete (write) several
statements that best describe their learning for
the workshop.

I: The Conflict Cycle*

Purpose: to show conflict as cyclical, predictable, and falling into a pattern of recognizable phases; recognition of these phases can encourage learners to see conflict as natural and manageable.

Visual: The Conflict Cycle (I A)

Lecture notes

I. Anticipation Phase
   A. May be unconscious or planned.
   B. May get clues that conflict is coming—words, gestures, other nonverbal clues.
   C. Like *turtles*, we move slowly and observe carefully.

II. Wait and See Phase
   A. Become aware (consciously aware) of conflict brewing.
   B. Look for clues and gather information as we "wait and see" what happens next.
   C. Like *hawks*, we watch and wait.

III. Growing Phase
   A. Can grow slowly or quickly, but conflict *will* grow unless cause is removed.
   B. Will not "go away."
   C. Like *mushrooms*, the conflict will escalate.

IV. In the Open Phase
   A. Tension builds, battle lines are drawn, defenses are up.
   B. Options include:
      1. Appeasing, denying, suppressing the conflict—a retreat to Wait and See phase (temporary).
      2. Facing the conflict—move into next phase.
   C. Like *duelers*, we deal with the conflict in some manner.

V. Application Phase
   A. Work toward resolving conflict by applying method(s).
   B. May take several tries to find right approach.
   C. Like *alchemists*, we search for a formula that works.

VI. Settlement Phase
   A. Reached when all involved are satisfied.
   B. A truce is called.
   C. Like *doves*, parties involved may feel affection to each other.

VII. Reflection Phase
   A. Occurs when those involved reflect upon/analyze the conflict and learning from it.
   B. Often neglected or forgotton.

---

*From Lois Hart, *Learning from Conflict: A Handbook for Trainers and Group Leaders*

C. If omitted, little, if any, attitude or behavior change.
D. When completed, next conflict:
1. can be settled more easily.
2. with higher "win-win" potential.
E. Like *philosophers,* we ask ourselves such questions as:
1. what did I learn about myself/others/this organization?
2. what did I do that was effective in dealing with this conflict? what was in-effective or inappropriate?
3. what would I do differently if I could replay this?

I A: The conflict cycle

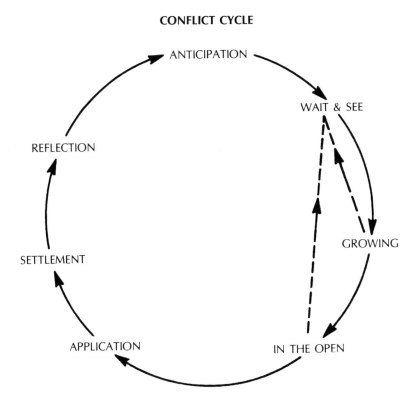

CONFLICT CYCLE

Reprinted by permission from Lois Hart, *Learning from Conflict: A Handbook for Trainers and Group.*

II: Constructive and Destructive Aspects of Conflict*

Purpose: to identify and briefly discuss both aspects of conflict, allowing participants to see the "positive" side of conflict.

Materials: 5 ×8 index cards
easel paper and marking pens

Procedure

Step 1: 5-7 minutes

Distribute a card to each participant. On one side of card, participant is to describe briefly the last two conflict situatioins in which s/he was involved (3-4 phrases or sentences each). Description should note those involved, what happened, and participant behaviors: active (yelling, screaming, gesturing, etc.) and/or passive (pouting, silence, etc.).

Then participants should list ways in which they and the others involved were positively and/or negatively affected by the conflict; and positive and negative results/outcomes of the conflict.

Step 2: 10-15 minutes

Using easel for listing, elicit destructive aspects and negative results of conflict from participants. To increase responses, facilitator might ask:

— what happens to individual/group morale?
— what is the impact on group relationships?
— what is the effect on work priorities/activities?
— what happens to feelings about people?

Post easel sheets on wall or board. Construct a similar list of the constructive aspects of conflict. Encourage respondents to explain and discuss the positive side of their examples—and to find a positive side where one does exist. Note that a cursory look often overlooks positive results. Facilitator might ask:

— what happens to emotions?
— what are the emotions that follow conflict?
— what happens to "the problem"?
— what positive outcomes do group members experience?

Step 3: 1-2 minutes

Summarize lists, emphasizing most important areas of each. Suggest that participants examine lists for a possible imbalance: heavy emphasis on negative aspects

---

*From Lois Hart, *Learning from Conflict: A Handbook for Trainers and Group.*

of conflict; little emphasis on positive aspects. Facilitator can, if necessary, supplement list(s) (II A).

II A: Constructive and destructive aspects of conflict
Sample List

Constructive

- Clarify issues
- Build cohesiveness
- Release emotion
- Solve problems
- Encourage creativity
- Surface problems
- Examine new approaches
- Grow individually

Destructive

- Create distance
- Develop resistance
- Divert energy
- Destroy morale
- Polarize groups
- Encourage distrust
- Show negative behaviors
- Increase value differences

III: Areas of Conflict/Disagreement*

Purpose: to examine briefly five areas around which conflict often occurs.

Visual: Areas of Disagreement/Conflict (III A)

Lecture notes

  I. Goals
    A. Areas we should be reaching toward.
    B. Usually judgments based on fact and opinion.
    C. Conflict results in differences in judging the information.

  II. Policy
    A. Sometimes viewed as "law," so is seen as bad, negative—and worthy of disagreement.
    B. Sometimes viewed as "guideline," so is seen as open to interpretation—and also worthy of disagreement.

  III. Priorities
    A. Since we value our jobs/tasks differently, our priorities will be different; conflict will result.
    B. Because we do have differing values, setting common priorities is cause for disagreement.

  IV. Methods
    A. The means to the end and usually open to debate.

*This material adapted from Bob Richards, *Managing Conflict Administrator's Guide.*

B. Determined by personal preference, comfort, use; trying to "set" methods can cause much disagreement.

V. Information
A. We infrequently have the same information.
B. Even if "same," it is colored by our perceptions and experience.
C. Different facts and opinions invite disagreement.

III A: Areas of conflict or disagreement

Areas of conflict or disagreement

1. GOALS

2. POLICY

3. PRIORITIES

4. METHODS

5. INFORMATION

IV: Self Assessment: Conflict Style*

Purpose: to have participants examine the disparity between their perceived conflict handling style and their preferred conflict handling style, if a difference exists.

Materials: 5 ×8 index card (used in previous exercise) "Conflict Continuum" (on easel paper) posted on wall (IV A)

Procedure

Step 1: 2-3 minutes

Participants should examine the Conflict Continuum and plot themselves on the continuum according to how they think they usually react to/deal with conflict. If the group is small (10-15), participants can physically line themselves up along the posted continuum. If the group is too large for this, participants can draw the continuum on the 5 ×8 cards and plot themselves at the appropriate place on the line.

For participants having difficulty plotting themselves, suggest that they consider their "gut" reaction to conflict: when a conflict is imminent, do they more often

---

*Adapted from Lois Hart, "Conflict Continuum" Exercise, *Learning from Conflict: A Handbook for Trainers and Group Leaders*

think "Ah, a challenge!" or "Oh no, not again!" (aggressive/tough or passive/meek)? This may help participants veer toward one end of the continuum or the other.

Step 2:

Now participants should consider the continuum again, and place themselves on the line where each would *prefer* to react to/deal with conflict. For some participants there may be little, if any, difference, for others the difference may be quite great.

Step 3: 3-5 minutes

Questions to consider:

— For how many is your *now* reaction and your *preferred* reaction the same? different?
— If you have a difference, why?
— What keeps you from reacting to conflict as you want to?
— How do you feel about the way you usually deal with conflict?

Step 4:

Summarize and key in on participant feelings about handling conflict. The more "OK" participants feel, the better they understand that all ways of dealing with conflict *are* acceptable at the appropriate time and place. "Toughness" and "meekness" are both appropriate, but the individual situation determines which approach will be more productive.

IV A: Self assessment: conflict style

CONFLICT CONTINUUM*

Passive   Aggressive

*From Lois Hart, *Learning from Conflict: A Handbook for Trainers and Group Leaders.*

V: Communication and Conflict

Purpose: to examine conflict and conflict positions (styles) as extensions of communication and, as such, to see how two communication dimensions—impact and ownership—influence conflict situations.

Visuals: Conflict Positions (V A)
           Communication Dimensions (V A)
           Productive Conflict (V A)

Lecture notes*

I. Communication and Conflict
   A. Communication: transfer of meaning with mutual understanding.
   B. Some ways of managing conflict improve communication; some ways close communication.
   C. If mutual understanding does not occur, conflict can result.
   D. So, conflict can be the *cause* or the *result* of poor communication.

II. Communication Dimensions
   A. Impact
      1. The force with which a message is received.
      2. The effect the message has on the receiver.
      3. A "high impact" message is believable, clear, and direct.
   B. Ownership
      1. The "buy in" of the receiver to the message.
      2. "High ownership" indicates receiver is willing to commit or agree to message.
   C. Implications
      1. Communication is highly influenced by these dimensions.
      2. Conflict is an extension of communication.
      3. Conflict handling positions or styles, as extensions of communication styles, are impacted by these dimensions; i.e., some conflict positions encourage high ownership but low impact, while others encourage low ownership but high impact.
      4. Awareness of impact and ownership in conflict positions will encourage the selection of the most productive position(s) for a particular conflict situation.

III. Four Conflict Positions
   A. Fight
      1. Definition: aggressively attacking problems and (often) views of others involved.
      2. Characteristics:
         a. imposition of views, solutions.
         b. noncreative approaches.
         c. nonlistening mode.
         d. defensiveness.

---

*From Bob Richards, *Managing Conflict Administrator's Guide.*

3. Appropriate uses:
   a. a need to control alternatives or solutions.
   b. possession of most of the facts of the problem.
   c. ownership not important.
   d. time or consequences constraints.

B. Flight
   1. Definition:
      a. "flight" from a problem.
      b. attempts to avoid unpleasantness by smoothing, soothing, or tossing to someone else (i.e., dropping the ball).
      c. compromise and voting are common solutions to problems handled from flight position.
   2. Characteristics:
      a. listening mode.
      b. encouragement of popular vote.
      c. pacification behaviors.
      d. little personal involvement.
   3. Appropriate uses:
      a. others have most facts to solve problem.
      b. personal, not job-relevant, conflicts.
      c. ownership is important.
      d. others are emotional, very upset.

C. Freeze
   1. Definition:
      a. attempt to avoid involvement.
      b. withdrawal from or ignoring of conflict.
   2. Characteristics:
      a. avoid personal contact.
      b. communication through paper, memos.
      c. routine-orientation.
      d. change-avoidance behaviors.
   3. Appropriate uses:
      a. confusion with issue, problem.
      b. lack of understanding about problem.
      c. legal, moral issues involved.

D. Face
   1. Definition:
      a. confrontation of conflict.
      b. a search for solutions.
      c. the most productive position.
   2. Characteristics:
      a. encouragement of creative solutions.
      b. listening mode.

       c. involvement of those affected.

       d. desire to *solve* problem.

   3. Appropriate uses:

       a. ownership is important.

       b. resistance needs to be overcome.

       c. facts are shared among those involved.

       d. creative solutions needed/desired.

IV. Communication Dimensions and Conflict Positions

  A. Dimension: Impact

    1. Low Impact: Flight and Freeze

       a. message not heard, vague.

       b. message has little credibility.

       c. receiver does not know speaker's stance.

    2. High Impact: Face and Fight

       a. message heard, understood.

       b. receiver knows speaker's position.

  B. Dimension: Ownership

    1. Low Ownership: Fight and Freeze

       a. others not heard.

       b. force used to make decisions.

       c. information not shared.

    2. High Ownership: Face and Flight

       a. others express feelings, opinions, ideas.

       b. creative problem solving encouraged.

       c. information shared.

  C. Productive Conflict

    1. High Impact, High Ownership.

    2. Face Position most productive.

From Bob Richards, *Managing Conflict Administrator's Guide.*

V A: Communication and conflict

Conflict Positions*

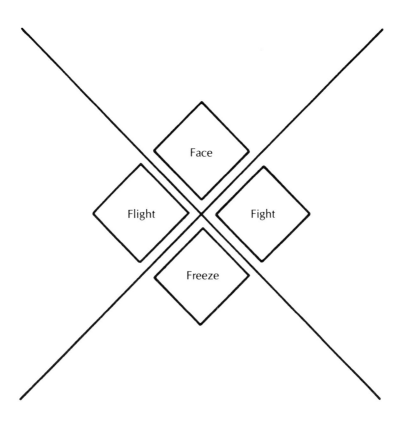

---

*From Bob Richards, *Managing Conflict Administrator's Guide.*

V A: Communication and conflict

Communication Dimensions*

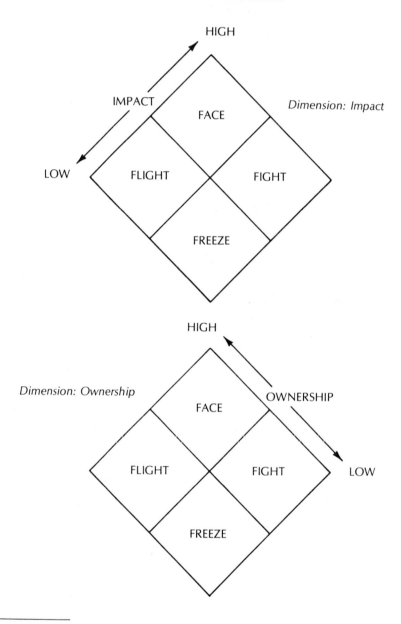

---
*From Bob Richards, *Managing Conflict Administrator's Guide.*

V A: Communication and conflict

Productive Conflict*

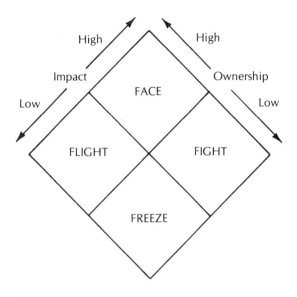

---

*From Bob Richards, *Managing Conflict Administrator's Guild.*

VI: Personal Assessment Tools

Purpose: to acquaint participants with instruments available for assessing conflict style.

Materials: *Managing Conflict Feedback Profile* (four booklet set)
References and Suggested Readings

Procedure

Step 1:

Distribute profile set to participants. Briefly explain purpose of each profile and use of scoring booklet. Encourage use of profiles with peers and others on- and off-the-job. (Materials may be ordered through Consulting Associates, Inc., 21333 Haggerty, Suite 311, Novi, MI 48050.)

Step 2:

Distribute "References and Suggested Readings" and note additional conflict instrument, Thomas-Kilmann.

VII: Pulling It All Together

Purpose: to review the workshop's major ideas.
Materials: easel

Procedure

Step 1:

Title easel page "Pulling It All Together."

Step 2: 3-5 minutes

Invite participants to name important ideas from workshop. List on easel, supplementing if necessary:

- Know personal view of conflict
- Know personal conflict handling style(s)
- Recognize four conflict positions
- Recognize importance of two dimensions
- Assess personal productivity and conflict handling
- Work on stronger communication
- Use Reflective Phase of Conflict Cycle
  - analyze conflict situations
  - identify alternative or more productive behaviors
  - be aware of or practice these behaviors

VIII: Closure *

Purpose: to have each participant note his/her workshop learnings.

Materials: 5 ×8 index card (used in earlier exercise)
            easel with learning statements listed

Procedure

---

*Adapted from Lois Hart, *Learning from Conflict: A Handbook for Trainers and Group Leaders.*

Step 1:

Post prepared easel page on which are listed 5-6 incomplete statements, e.g.

Closure
1. I learned that I . . .
2. I relearned that I . . .
3. I discovered that I . . .
4. I am disappointed that I . . .
5. I am surprised that I . . .
6. I plan . . .

Step 2:

On back of notecard, have participants complete responses to any 4-5 statements that best summarize their learning for the workshop.

REFERENCES AND SUGGESTED READINGS

Benne, K. D. "The Significance of Human Conflict." In L. Porter and B. Mohr (Eds.), *NTL Reading Book for Human Relations Training.* NTL Institute, 1982.

Blake, R. and Mouton, J. *The Managerial Grid.* Houston: Gulf Publishing, 1964.

Filley, A. C. *Interpersonal Conflict Resolution.* Chicago: Scott, Foresman & Co., 1975.

Hart, L. *Learning from Conflict: A Handbook for Trainers and Group Leaders.* Reading, MA: Addison-Wesley, 1981.

Richards, B. *Managing Conflict Feedback Profile and Administrator's Guide.* Consulting Associates, Inc., 21333 Haggerty, Suite 311, Novi, MI., 48050, 1978.

Schermerhorn, Jr., J. R., Hunt, J. G., and Osborn, R. N. *Managing Organizational Behavior.* New York: John Wiley & Sons, Inc., 1982.

Schmidt, W. "Conflict: A Powerful Process for (Good or Bad) Change." *Management Review,* December 1974, 4-10.

Thomas, K. "Conflict and Conflict Management." In M. Dunette (Ed.), *The Handbook of Industrial and Organizational Psychology.* Chicago: Rand McNally, 1975.

Thomas, K. W., and Kilmann, R. H. *Thomas-Kilmann Conflict Mode Instrument.* Tuxedo, NY: Xicom, Inc., 1974.

Turner, S., and Weed, F. *Conflict in Organizations.* Englewood Cliffs, NJ: Prentice-Hall, Inc., 1983.

VanNess, R. *I Win, You Win: Turning Conflict to Your Advantage.* Midland, MI: Pendell Publishing Co., 1981.

Male-Female Communication:
Who We Are Is What We Say

Shirley A. Van Hoeven, Western Michigan University

The 1980s bring with them a need and a necessity to integrate women's issues and communication problems into our more traditional courses on the campuses of colleges and universities throughout the country. The workshop materials in this chapter have been developed to meet this need. Three separate lectures entitled, Conflict: Games People Play and/or Game Theory; Conflict: Male/Female Roles Within the Organization; and, Conflict: Power in the Organizational Setting form the base of the workshop. These materials may be used separately or for a two-hour workshop.

Because of the changing roles of women in the organizational setting, as well as in the work force in general, academia should lead the way toward sensitizing males and females regarding conflictual communication issues and problems facing both sexes in today's world. The challenge facing educators is to bring this new awareness to the surface. A workshop setting is ideal because it provides "hands on" experience. Awareness is the first step toward any possible change. The steps between awareness and change include the following:

AWARENESS → CONFLICT → COMMUNICATION → CHANGE

It is important to increase the recognition of both males and females so that the conflict which arises because of awareness and/or knowledge can be managed in a productive and healthy process. The process is communication. Unless there is communication between males and females when there is conflict, there can be no change.

In the past, communication research has dealt with such categories as race, class, religion, political setting, and economic background but has given little attention to sex as a variable. In addition, most of the research on leadership and management is sexist, i.e., based on male samples only. This leads to the need for step one—awareness in communication between males and females in the organization.

Objectives

This workshop is designed for women who want to increase their awareness and knowledge of conflictual communication issues and problems facing males and females in today's organizational setting. One objective of the workshop is to demonstrate the impact of communication on male and female roles and behaviors within the organization. Particular emphasis is placed on the communication pattern of the individuals involved in the communication process.

A second objective of the workshop is to assess one's own communication behaviors in the communication transaction. It is necessary for individuals to be aware of their own communication behaviors before assessing others'. The workshop provides an opportunity for participants to assess their communication behaviors in interpersonal and group situations.

The concept of power is examined as it also impacts the communication process in male/female relationships. This concept of power is realized through the participants' personal involvement and experience as they take part in group work.

A fourth objective is to provide participants with a simulation that relates directly to the organizational setting. This simulation assesses males' and females' desire to work cooperatively and/or competitively with one another. An added variable in the simulation includes building the trust that must occur if individuals are to cooperate with one another.

A final objective of the workshop is to provide the participants with appropriate communication strategies and tactics applicable to the organizational setting. Use of these communication behaviors provides an opportunity for women to manage productively the conflict that occurs between males and females.

The outline which follows provides a variety of experiences for the participants. The workshop facilitator may wish to use one or all of these depending upon the length of the workshop. It is also possible to use some of the materials in a classroom setting, depending upon the direction of the course. The references and suggested readings provide added resources for those who desire to expand this topic beyond the workshop setting.

Workshop Outline

Content	*Design*
I. Impact of Power on the Communication Process (20-30 minutes)	I. Group exercises are good "openers" to help participants begin to think about the roles of males and females.
II. Male/Female Communication Within the Organization (30 minutes)	II. Lecture designed to give participants an awareness and understanding of the impact of

the communication process that occurs among males/females within the organizational setting.

III. A Role Wheel Approach: Assessing One's Communication Behaviors (20-30 minutes)

III. Group exercise designed to assess participants' communication behaviors in a variety of roles on a daily/weekly basis.

IV. Competition, Cooperation, and the Building of Trust (45-60 minutes)

IV. Dyad exercise that provides an opportunity for participants to assess their own styles of behavior in communicating with others using a game theory approach.

I: Impact of Power on the Communication Process

Purpose: to look at male/female roles that we as women are involved in on a daily/weekly basis; to assess our communication behaviors in these male/female roles.

Procedure

Step 1: 5 minutes

This exercise is a good "opener" for the workshop. It works best when there has been no discussion on the given topic. Ask the participants to list the names of 5 people who represent power to them. Do the same thing for the listing of 5 powerful positions in the United States (I A).

Step 2: 10 minutes

When participants have completed the above task ask them to place an M (male) or an F (female) behind each name and position they have listed. At this stage, discussion becomes very appropriate for leading directly to the listing of stereotypes that participants can think of that are attached to males and females.

Step 3: 15 minutes

The section on stereotyping should be facilitated in small groups. Divide the participants into groups of 4 to 6 and give groups 10 minutes to brainstorm as many stereotypes of males and females as they can think of. Discussion of the results of the brainstorming session provides an awareness of the impact of stereotypes on the communication process and also provides an opportunity for participants to talk and get to know one another.

I A: Impact of power on the communication process

List the names of 5 people who represent POWER to you:

1.

2.

3.

4.

5.

List 5 POWERFUL positions in the United States:

1.

2.

3.

4.

5.

Female Stereotypes	Male Stereotypes

II: Male-Female Communication Within the Organization

Lecture notes

Historically and traditionally, most of us have been taught by our leaders, parents, and teachers that conflict is bad and nonproductive. We have been taught to "stay in line," "don't rock the boat," and "keep quiet" when the "powers that be" speak and/or give assignments and directions. The child who questions is often tagged as a troublemaker when it comes to the classroom setting. This imprinting continues to follow most of us throughout our life experiences. Examples of these kinds of teachings are reinforced upon little girls when they are told "girls don't fight," "act like a lady," "girls don't talk like that," all of which imply that it is okay for boys to talk and behave in those manners. Therefore, to view conflict as necessary and productive when analyzing male-female communication is entirely new for many of us.

Communication is the first step to an awareness of the problems now facing women in the organization. The male-dominated organization puts up immediate barriers to the female seeking entry into a previously all-male setting. This awareness can only come through interpersonal communication, which is defined for this workshop as communication between people. It is based on a transactional model of communication where the receiver of the message is as important as the sender. Interpersonal communication can only take place when the intended receiver of the message receives the sender's message, and in turn sends feedback to the original message-sender. The sender and receiver then continually exchange roles.

The model below should help to explain this process.

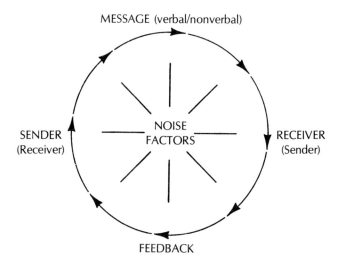

MESSAGE (verbal/nonverbal)

SENDER
(Receiver)

NOISE
FACTORS

RECEIVER
(Sender)

FEEDBACK

A breakdown in the communication process may occur when noise factors knowingly or unknowingly affect the communication process. These noise factors (or barriers), which may be physical, psychological, and/or environmental, will be addressed in this workshop.

Once both males and females become aware of the noise factors, interpersonal conflict can occur. Management of the conflict is the key to whether or not both individuals will change their communication style to achieve a healthy, productive working relationship. The diagram below indicates the process that must occur in order to bring about change.

AWARENESS → COMMUNICATION → CONFLICT → CHANGE

Before change can even begin to take place, it is necessary to understand how and why men and women conflict as they communicate. Females do communicate differently than do males, although few people today are aware of these differences. One very clear example of this difference occurs when men and women identify themselves. A man, in American society, usually identifies himself in relation to his job and/or position while a woman very often identifies herself in terms of a relationship with a man. For example, "I am Tom Brown, a professor at Western Michigan University" illustrates the male identification, while Tom's spouse identifies herself as Mrs. Tom Brown, whose husband teaches at Western Michigan University.

Women traditionally, when marrying, give up their independent identity. They lose their last name and in many situations also their first. For example, to most homes, mail is addressed to Mr. and Mrs. Ronald Jones, eliminating the woman's name completely. Many women today continue to have their checks and private stationery imprinted with their spouse's name only, again reinforcing their desire to be identified in a relationship with a male.

If women want to be as involved in the business world as men, they are going to have to work through this identity problem and become responsible to themselves for who they are. For many women this will bring conflict, both intrapersonal and interpersonal. Eakins and Eakins (1978) discuss this by giving examples from Bardwick's 1970 study of the way women who are skillful in arguing risk loss of social acceptance and approval. Their self-esteem and social acceptability depends very much on what they are, that is, on their personal acceptability in terms of how they look and sound.

Eakins and Eakins (1978) assess the women's sense of self as:

Being more dependent on the reflection she sees mirrored in others' eyes than a man is. Her selfhood may be defined more by the approval and acceptance she senses in others. Men have developed a sense of self-regard that does not depend as much on outside sources. (p. 52)

If this is so, is it not true that the woman, who in the organizational setting, uses certain behaviors inappropriate to her sex, may risk conflict, which if viewed negatively may prove to be a real threat to her self-esteem. If these behaviors cause noise factors to the communication process, which are psychological in nature, conflict will occur. Once women understand the cause of conflict, they can do something about it. Without this awareness on both the male's and the female's part, the behaviors will continue to take place. Women must develop sources of self-esteem that counteract the impact of rejection and criticism which occur from day to day in the organization.

Males have, for centuries, been rewarded for talking—for testing their ideas within a group. A man's success or self-esteem does not depend on whether the group accepts or rejects his ideas. Many women have not had the opportunity for, or the training in, articulating thought processes. According to the research cited, women have for years been the victims of conditioning. Eakins and Eakins (1978) cite Lakoff who discusses the use of the tag question, which they believe women use in conversational situations more than men and which they identify "as a device to avoid making a strong statement." (p. 39) A tag question is in between a statement and a question. An outright statement such as, "Bob left my office door open," becomes a tag question when stated, "Bob left my office door open, didn't he?"

There are situations in which it is legitimate or logical to use a tag question, but our concern is that women use this speech pattern more often than men. Since this is a less assertive style of communication than is using direct statements, women should consciously assess their own speech patterns and work at changing these less assertive behaviors. Some questions to ask one's self might be, "Am I requesting agreement?" "Am I avoiding conflict or confrontation?" or "Am I giving the impression that I am not sure of myself?" A person using the tag question gives the listener power and seems to look for the other person's approval and confirmation.

Eakins and Eakins (1978) discuss qualifiers as another communication technique used more often by women than men. Qualifiers are:

> Additions to our utterances that can soften or blunt the impact of what we say. They are used to avert or avoid negative or unwanted reactions to our words, and they seem to make our statements less absolute in tone. We use these devices in the beginnings, endings, and sprinkled throughout our utterances: Well, let's see, perhaps, possibly, I suppose, I think, it seems to me, you know, and so on. (p. 43)

The following examples of statements, plus statements that add qualifiers, demonstrate how qualifiers make the speech sound more tentative.

> You are incorrect.
> Perhaps, you are incorrect.
> We should go home.
> I guess we should go home.
> Yes.
> Well, yes.
> That's an average paper.
> It seems to me that's an average paper.

Another device discussed in smoothing personal interactions is what Hewitt and Stokes (1975) call a disclaimer. These mitigators are usually introductory expressions that excuse, explain, or request understanding or forbearance such as "I may be wrong, but . . . " or, "You may not like this, but. . . . "

Women have a tendency to use disclaimers more often than men. It may be useful and appropriate at times to use the disclaimer to soften negative reactions, but overuse can quickly weaken one's stand. If a woman is confident of her position, she must voice that confidence. Awareness and training again become the keys to change those speech patterns which automatically place women at a disadvantage in a male-dominated organizational system, where men make most of the final decisions.

As stated earlier, women cannot change something which they are not aware of; once men and women recognize these speech patterns, intrapersonal tension will often arise. This tension builds from within, forcing a person either to confront or to avoid the conflict that may occur when the issue is brought into the open. As soon as the conflict is verbally acknowledged by two or more people, a productive change can begin—a change which can only come through a collaboration among the people involved. Women must take advantage of the opportunity to collaborate, as a technique for managing conflict.

Thomas and Kilmann (1975) define collaborating as both assertive and cooperative—the opposite of avoiding. Collaborating involves time, patience, and concern for the other person or persons involved in the conflict. Attempts are made to work with the other person to find solutions which satisfy both parties. Participants explore their disagreements in order to learn from each other's insights and work toward a creative, manageable solution to an interpersonal conflict.

Women who manage conflict in this way may have difficulty working with men since research reminds us that men usually use a competitive style to manage conflicts. This, then, adds pressure on a woman who chooses to manage conflict productively and positively. Women should also be prepared to be competitive. For many women, this does not come easily, since women have traditionally been taught that competition is unfeminine. These teachings are imprinted at a very early age and usually are not dealt with until little girls become women who find themselves scholastically and professionally in a competitive world.

Developing communication skills to manage these conflicts comes through training and practice. And that is why we are involved in this workshop today. The following exercises willl provide an opportunity for all of us to work at the self-awareness level which should lead us forward to the process of communication, conflict, and change.

III: A Role Wheel Approach: Assessing One's Communication Behaviors

Purpose: to assess one's communication behaviors in male/female relationships; to examine perceptions of self in relationship to males.

Procedure

This exercise is designed to continue work on the awareness level of participants. This awareness should cause some conflict to surface if it has not already. The intent of this exercise is to work at assessing the "self" in relation to others (interpersonal communication) as a continuing process. Change may come at different stages for women; we as workshop leaders must be very sensitive to the fact that the women attending a workshop will be in a variety of stages. This exercise can be adapted to specific situations raised prior to the workshop setting. The time spent on this experience can also be adjusted to the needs of the participants (III A).

Step 1: 10 minutes

The role wheel should be filled in by participants first. Directions for completing the role wheel are as follows:

1. Think of all the female/male communication roles that you find yourself in on a daily/weekly basis.
2. In each section of the wheel put your own role first and the male role second—note example.

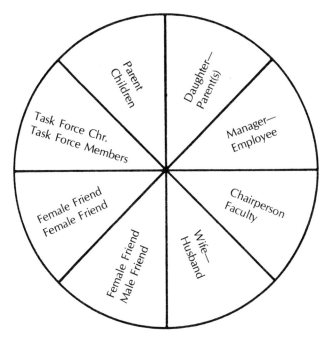

Step 2: 20 minutes

Discuss communication behaviors in the differing roles. Some questions to ask of participants:

1. Do you use the same communication style at home as you do in your professional setting? Why or why not?
2. What types of conflict arise in each of the roles in which you find yourself?
3. What are your communication patterns? Do you change these patterns because of the "other person" in the relationship?
4. Are you more comfortable in some of these roles than in others? Why?
5. Who controls the flow of communicaiton in each of the roles?

Step 3: 10 minutes

Finally, ask the participants to think of their daily or weekly communication behaviors and complete the "I AM" stems. For example: "I am an impatient listener," "I am concerned that my staff receives information necessary to feel a part of the organization," "I am an accommodator when it comes to conflict in the office."

III A: A role wheel approach: assessing one's communication behavior

ROLE WHEEL

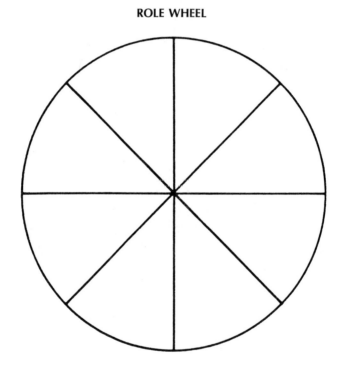

List Male/Female "Roles" that You Daily Find Yourself In

Perception Evaluation:

1. How do you see yourself?

2. How do others see you?

3. How does this affect the way you communicate with other males and females?

Think of Your Communication Behaviors (Interpersonal Relationships) Use these to complete the following I AM stems.

I AM

I AM

I AM

I AM

I AM

I AM

Role wheel prepared and constructed by Dr. Shirley A. Van Hoeven, Associate Professor, Communication Arts and Sciences, Western Michigan University.

IV: Competition, Cooperation and the Building of Trust

Purpose: to assess the competitive behavior of females; to examine whether males and females compete equally; to examine the impact of communication and the building of trust between males and females.

Procedure

Preparation information

The instrument used for this study is the Prisoner's Dilemma, a non-zero-sum mixed game, attributed to A. W. Tucker (1957). The game provides for a well-controlled interaction situation and provides the participants with the fact that the choices or decisions that they must make during the exercise are very similar to decisions that are made in real-life bargaining and conflict situations (Gallo and McClintock, 1965) (IV A).

Figure 1 shows the game used in the exercise. The cell entries shown in Figure 1 represent points gained or lost. The matrix in Figure 1 indicates that if Player A, B chooses A and Player 1, 2 chooses 1, both players lose 5 points. If Player A, B chooses B while Player 1, 2 chooses 1, Player 1, 2 gains 10 points and Player A, B loses 10 points. If Player A, B chooses A while Player 1, 2 chooses 2, Player

1, 2 loses 10 points and Player A, B gains 10 points. If Player A, B chooses B while Player 1, 2 chooses 2, both players gain 5 points.

The Game

The following squares list the scores each player will receive:

Player 1, 2

	1	2
A	Player 1,2 = −5 Player A,B = −5	Player 1,2 = −10 Player A,B = +10
B	Player 1,2 = +10 Player A,B = −10	Player 1,2 = +5 Player A,B = +5

Player A,B

Figure 1.   Prisoner's Dilemma Game

Figure 2 shows the playing cards used for playing the game. Three-by-five index cards work very well. Player A, B receives one A card and one B card while Player 1, 2 receives one 1 card and one 2 card. Players hold their playing cards out of their partner's sight while deciding their individual cell choice (a competitive or cooperative choice). When ready, players look up at their partner and flip their card choices simultaneously. Each player can take as much time as needed to make her or his competitive or cooperative cell choice.

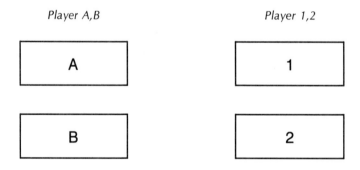

Player A,B   *Player 1,2*

Figure 2.   Playing Cards Used for Playing the Prisoner's Dilemma Game

Figure 3 shows the tables used for scoring Game #1 and Game #2, each of which consists of nine trials. Players record both their own and their partner's score following each trial. Scores are totalled at the conclusion of each game.

	Game #1			Game #2	
	(1,2)	(A,B)		(1,2)	(A,B)
1.			1.		
2.			2.		
3.			3.		
4.			4.		
5.			5.		
6.			6.		
7.			7.		
8.			8.		
9.			9.		
Total			Total		

Figure 3.   Tables Used for Scoring Game #1 and Game #2

Materials needed:

Rules for the game   Plain white 3×5 cards

Game sheet   Pencils

Playing cards   Armed desk chairs or tables and chairs

Step 1: 10-15 minutes

Instruct participants to sit facing one another with a desk or arm chair between. Pass out the game materials to the participants with the following verbal instructions:

> The object of the game is for each person to maximize your positive score. Read the rules for the game silently and thoroughly. Take your time. When you have understood and finished reading the game procedures look up at your partner and nod your head affirmatively. Play nine trials for Game #1, recording both your score and your partner's score. Total both scores and wait for further instructions. Do not talk to anyone during any time of the experiment.

Subjects then proceed to play Game #1 according to the rules and instructions given.

Step 2: 10-15 minutes

When all subjects have finished playing Game #1, pass a white 3 x 5 card out to the subjects with the following instructions:

You may write your partner a one-sentence message before playing Game #2. Write the message and when both you and your partner have finished, exchange the cards simultaneously. Read the message you received from your partner and go on to play Game #2. Play the nine trials recording both scores following each trial and at the conclusion of trial nine total both scores.

Step 3: 20 minutes

Discuss how the participants played in Game #1. Did they play to win, lose, or tie? Discuss the competitive and cooperative choices available to the participants. Remind people that a B-2 choice is considered a cooperative score and all other combination scores are competitive.

Van Hoeven (1976) predicts that females playing females in Game #1 will play competitively. Terhune (1968) concluded that when there is no opportunity for communication, there is more competition. Another reason may be that an initial reaction to any game situation is that someone must win or lose, although if participants read the game instructions thoroughly they will see this is not stated.

Before playing Game #2, participants have an opportunity to communicate with each other through a written message. Of interest to the participants should be the effect communication may have upon the increase or decrease of trust in playing Game #2. This writer agrees with Sereno and Bodaken (1975) when they state that "trust is an interpersonal communication factor consisting of feelings that the other person will not take advantage of you and has your concerns at heart; crucial to the development of meaningful intimate communication (p. 192)."

Step 4: 10-15 minutes

An important part of the after-game discussion should be talking about the type of message communicated between partners in the exercise. The opportunity to communicate with one another does not necessarily mean that trust will increase or even occur.

Results of Van Hoeven's (1976) research showed that when participants did not include trust in their communication message, their trust of each other decreased, while if one of the participants communicated a trust message, their trust of each other increased. When both participants communicated a trust message, trust increased significantly. These findings support the author's conclusions that the opportunity for communication among participants is necessary if their mutual trust is to be increased. The content of that communication then determines their increase or decrease of trust. Loomis (1959), Berlo (1960), Terhune (1968), and Doolittle (1976) found similar results in their studies of the effect of communication in increasing or decreasing trust between persons.

I V: Competition, cooperation, and the building of trust

THE GAME

Object: The object of the game is for each person to maximize her/his positive score.

RULES

1. Each will get two cards. One set of two cards will have a "1" and "2" on them; the second set will have an "A" and "B" on them.

2. With each trial, the players will simultaneously hold up one of his/her cards. That is, one player will hold up either "1" or "2" and the other player will hold up either "A" or "B".

3. Each player should independently determine which strategy will best maximize her/his positive score. Players should not indicate which card is going to be held up until the trial begins.

4. If Player 1, 2 holds up "1" and Player A, B holds up "A", then record the scores listed in box 1A. In this instance, both players lose 5 points.

   If player 1, 2 holds up "2" and Player A, B holds up "A", then record the scores listed in box 2A. In this instance, Player 1, 2 loses 10 points and Player A, B gains 10 points.

   If Player 1, 2 holds up "1" and Player A, B holds up "B", then record the scores listed in box 1B. In this instance, Player 1, 2 gains 10 points and Player A, B loses 10 points.

   If Player 1, 2 holds up "2" and Player A, B holds up "B", then record the scores listed in box 2B. In this instance, both players would gain 5 points.

5. After each trial, record the appropriate scores in the tables. There will be 9 trials within each game. You will play 2 games.

6. Please do not talk to your partner at any time during the game.

7. After you finish each game, wait for further instruction.

The Game

The following squares list the scores each player will receive:

Player 1, 2

		1	2
Player A,B	A	Player 1,2 = −5 Player A,B = −5	Player 1,2 = −10 Player A,B = +10
	B	Player 1,2 = +10 Player A,B = −10	Player 1,2 = +5 Player A,B = +5

	Game #1				Game #2		
	(1,2)	(A,B)			(1,2)	(A,B)	
1.				1.			
2.				2.			
3.				3.			
4.				4.			
5.				5.			
6.				6.			
7.				7.			
8.				8.			
9.				9.			
Total				Total			

REFERENCES AND SUGGESTED READINGS

Bardwick, J. "Psychological Conflict and the Reproductive System." In J. Bardwick, et al. (Eds.), *Feminine Personality and Conflict*. Belmont, CA: Brooks Cole, 1970, p. 4.

Berlo, D. K. *The Process of Communication*. New York: Holt, Rinehart and Winston, 1960.

Coser, L. *The Functions of Social Conflict*. New York: The Free Press, 1956.

Doolittle, R. J. *Orientation to Communication and Conflict*. Modcom, Science Research Associates, Inc., Chicago, 1976.

Eakins, B. W., and Eakins, R. G. *Sex Differences in Human Communication*. Boston: Houghton-Mifflin Co., 1978.

Frost, J. H., and Wilmot, W. W. *Interpersonal Conflict*. Dubuque, Iowa: Wm. C. Brown Co., 1978.

Gallo, P. S., and McClintock. C. G. "Cooperative and Competitive Behavior in Mixed Motive Games." *Journal of Conflict Resolution*, 1965, 9, 68-78.

Hewitt, J., and Stokes, R. "Disclaimers." *American Sociological Review*, 40, 1975, 1-11.

Loomis, J. L. "Communication, the Development of Trust and Cooperative Behavior." *Human Relations*, 1959, 12, 305-15.

Sereno, K. K., and Bodaken, E. M. *Trans-per Understanding Human Communication*. Boston: Houghton-Mifflin, 1975.

Terhune, K. W. "Motives, Situation, and Interpersonal Conflict Within the Prisoner's Dilemma." *Journal of Personality and Social Psychology*, Monograph Supplement, 1968, 8, 1-24.

Thomas, K. "Conflict and Conflict Management." In M. Dunnette (Ed.), *The Handbook of Industrial and Organizational Psychology*. Chicago: Rand McNally, 1975, 889-935.

Van Hoeven, S. A. "A Study of Competitiveness Between Sexes and the Effect of Communication Messages upon the Building of Trust." Unpublished doctoral dissertation, Western Michigan University, 1976.

Career Design:
How to Find a Good Fit

Brenda M. Beckman, Delta College

Some decades ago there was a young woman who appeared destined for a successful career in higher education. She was extraordinarily intelligent, articulate, hard working, and tackled everything she did with impressive efficiency. She taught in an institution that decided early on to open its administrative ranks to women and she was an obvious choice to begin the process. She was appointed to a position of some considerable responsibility. She worked long and hard but never succeeded in doing a really effective job. She was in fact a terrible failure. It is difficult to say who was more distressed by the situation—the woman herself, the men who had appointed her, or the other women in the institution who had felt that if any woman could break into the administrative ranks successfully, she could. All parties were embarrassed by her lack of success and eventually she left the institution. Strangely, she took a different kind of administrative position elsewhere and later became very successful.

In reflecting on what had happened in this case, it became clear that there had been a serious mismatch between the young woman's values, workstyle, and interests and the needs of her first position. Ironically, these same factors contributed to her success in subsequent jobs. She was a detail worker, a person who liked to work alone. She preferred not to share ideas until all information was assembled. Being able to control what was happening was important to her. The needs of her first administrative post, however, were completely at odds with all these inclinations. The position needed a person who could help coordinate the activities of many different offices, someone able to cooperate with others in their decision-making in the early stages of program development while information was being accumulated. It required constant consultation and a willingness to share control with many other elements of the institution. As it became evident that she was not working out well in the job, she had relied increasingly on her habit of working long hours alone in her office poring over details. This of course exacerbated the situation.

This case and others like it triggered a series of conversations with administrators in many different kinds of jobs, and eventually led to a whole series of interviews conducted in an effort to find out how such unfortunate situations could be avoided. What kinds of things had helped administrators to make good career choices that worked well both for them and for the organizations that employed them? The information gathered began to suggest a simple process that could assist greatly those who were interested in designing successful careers. This process has been developed as a workshop which has been well-received in education, in business, in government agencies, and in industry. It has proved of particular help to women. Although the original design focused on employment activities, the same process has been adapted for use by retirees to help them develop rewarding retirement lifestyles.

Objectives

The workshop is designed to assist participants to recognize their own values, personality traits, and styles and relate these appropriately to career choices.

The workshop takes participants through a process for selecting suitable career fields and assembling a plan for developing the necessary knowledge, skills, and experience to enter and advance in the selected field. Participants will further develop a professional networking plan.

Lastly, the workshop is designed to enable participants to plan career shifts as personal and professional circumstances change.

Workshop Outline

Content	*Design*
I. Taking Stock: Values, Personality, Style. (25-30 minutes)	I. Mini-lecture on impact of these factors on job choice followed by opportunity for participants to list their own values, personality, and style.
II. Choosing the Field: Narrowing, Expanding, "Trying Jobs on For Size," Life Style Considerations. (25-30 minutes)	II. Mini-lecture and discussion on broadening horizons for career selections but within limits of life-style choices. Participants list options.
III. Building the Theoretical Knowledge Base: Observation, Education, Memberships and Subscriptions, The Interview Technique. (20-30 minutes)	III. Discussion, invite participant sharing. Participants outline knowledge-building plan.

IV. Creating Opportunities for Experience: Expertise Base, Experience Expansion, Breaking New Ground. (20-30 minutes)

IV. Discussion, invite participant sharing and peer advising. Participants outline experience-building plan.

V. The Résumé Process: Building, Updating, Using, Revising. (20-30 minutes)

V. Mini-lecture on résumé information accumulation and analysis process. Participants list information sources.

VI. Developing Networks: Mentors, Professional Contacts, Liaison with Related Departments. (20-25 minutes)

VI. Mini-lecture on network building and mentoring followed by discussion. Participants identify potential mentors and other professional contacts.

VII. Addressing Common Dilemmas: Professional Goals vs. Personal Needs, Examining Realities of Organizational Structure, Organizational Loyalty Concerns. (25 minutes)

VII. Mini-lecture discussion, invite participant sharing.

VIII. Fitting It All Together: Consolidation, Review, Return to "Go." (15 minutes)

VIII. General discussion of when and how to review steps I-VII.

I: Taking Stock

Procedure

Step 1: 10 minutes

Taking a case study approach, this can be presented with examples such as the one in the introduction. The general purpose is to help participants to be realistic about their own attributes and to recognize the importance of making career choices that will fit well with individual values, personality, and preferences for using certain operating styles. Alternatively, there may be a conscious choice to make personal style adjustments as needed by a particular job.

Step 2: 15 minutes

Discuss specific factors which each participant may wish to consider and encourage members of the group to add to the list. (I A)

Step 3: 5 minutes

Have each indivudual complete her own values, personality, and skills list.

I A: Taking stock

Values

Time with parents, spouse, children/work time demands
Nature of job/religious beliefs
Regular work schedule/unpredictable timetable
Planned time off/loss of personal flexibility
Controlled work environment/wide variety of externally controlled events
Working alone/preference for being part of team
Homebody/extended travel needs
Other . . .

Personality

Loner/gregarious
Risk taker/security
Need for completable tasks/open-ended activities
Need to be liked/willing to accept responses to unpopular decisions
Desire to be directly involved in detail/readiness to delegate
Operating without signposts/confident when undertaking new activities with no road map
Detail work and specific tasks/broad general activities
Other . . .

Style

Need to concentrate/willingness to tolerate interruption
Blunt, outspoken, direct/subtle, tactful
Firm/tendency to rigidity/flexible or easily dissuaded from decisions
Tendency to try to control outcomes/willingness to accommodate to different viewpoints
Other . . .

II: Choosing the Field

Procedure

Step 1: 5 minutes

General discussion of possible career moves within participants' present or anticipated fields, suggesting that they identify for themselves whether their inclination is to go more deeply into an area of specialization or into areas of greater generalization. Participants should list at least one possible career option of each type. (II A)

Step 2: 15 minutes

A "trying on for size" exercise designed to force consideration of a much larger range of occupational options than most people ever consider. This can be done as an individual exercise but if time permits can sometimes be more enjoyable and rewarding for participants if done in small groups of 3 or 4 people. (II A)

Step 3: 10 minutes

Individually or in discussion with others, participants should identify the life style considerations of at least three of the jobs identified in steps 1 and 2 and further categorize each consideration as positive, negative, or neutral. (II A)

II A: Choosing the field

Increased specialization options
    e.g., (1) general sales → marketing
         (2) student affairs → handicapped student services
Increased generalization options
    e.g., (1) medical benefits manager → personnel manager
         (2) faculty → dean
"Trying on for size" options
    Identify as many different jobs in your organization as possible from chief executive to janitor and try to visualize yourself doing each job. If it feels wrong, discard the thought immediately. If it feels interesting (even if you never considered it before) make a note of it.
    Note: If time permits this part of the exercise can be repeated for other types of educational, business, industrial, service, or governmental organizations. This can be a particularly useful exercise for the unemployed or retiree to promote some creative occupation/activity ideas.
List life-style considerations involved in the job of most interest to you from each of the above option categories such as:
    Does this job provide security?
    Does the job involve travel?
    Are long meetings involved?
    Is the work inside or outside?
    Is the income likely to be compatible with your needs?
    Are there unpredictable time demands?
    Would I like the kind of people I would have to work with?
    Is relocation required?
Identify each of the above considerations as positive, negative, or neutral.

III: Building the Theoretical Knowledge Base

Procedure

Step 1: 5 minutes

Participants should be asked to share some of the different jobs they have considered in II.

Step 2: 10-15 minutes

Through discussion, participants can be asked to suggest a range of options for building the necessary knowledge base to prepare effectively for the jobs identified in step 1.

Step 3: 5-10 minutes

Individual participants should be asked to list options appropriate to their own career choices. (III A)

III A: Building the Theoretical Knowledge Base

Possible options—
  Specific coursework
  General coursework
  Certificates or degrees
  Workshops
  Seminars
  Conferences
  Professional subscriptions
  Professional memberships
  Publications
  Observations
  Interviews
  Mentors
  Other . . .

IV: Creating Opportunities for Experience

Procedure

Step 1: 15 minutes

Through discussion, participants can be asked to share ideas for creating opportunities to gain experience for jobs identified in I, step 1.

Step 2: 5 minutes

Individual participants should be asked to list experience acquisition options appropriate to their own career choices. (IV A)

IV A: Creating Opportunities for Experience

Possible options—
  Observation of practice
  Volunteering
  Designing special project
  Requesting temporary or replacement assignment
  Creating own assignment to do things not now being done
  Offer assistance
  Assertive exploration
  Offering services to other organizations during vacation or leave
  Letting interest be known
  Other . . .

V: The Résumé Process

Procedure

Step 1: 20-25 minutes

A mini-lecture on the obvious and less obvious ways in which knowledge and experience have been acquired throughout life for both paid and unpaid work and some of the early, forgotten sources that can be used to jog the memory in preparation for drawing up a résumé. Three primary purposes of this segment are (1) to identify any gaps in knowledge and experience that may need to be filled before entering a career field or applying for a certain type of position; (2) to provide ready knowledge of and confidence in one's own knowledge and ability, to assist in the application and interview process; and (3) to have a constantly updated pool of relevant information to draw upon readily for résumé preparation as career opportunities for career entry, advance, or change occur. (V A)

Step 2: 5 minutes

Participants should list résumé information sources applicable to them. (V A)

V A: The résumé process

Sources of knowledge and experience:
  Girl/Boy Scouts

Church
Sporting activities
Military
Volunteer activities
Service clubs
Elective/appointive offices
Educational records
Correspondence
Avocational pursuits
  (see also III A and IV A)
Paid employment experience record
Other . . .

VI: Developing Networks

Procedure

Step 1: 10-15 minutes

A mini-lecture on the mentoring concept, the mentor selection process, and characteristics of a good mentoring relationship with clarification of the expectations each party should have of the other, followed by a brief explanation of networking. (VI A)

Step 2: 5 minutes

General discussion on mentoring and networking process.

Step 3: 5 minutes

Participants identify possible mentors and networking mechanisms suitable to their own needs.

VI A: Developing networks

Desirable elements for successful mentoring relationships:

Individual	*Mentor*
Initiate contacts	Position of power
Provide regular feedback	Respected in profession
on progress of career	Secure
Acknowledge benefits	Integrity
provided by mentor	Willingness to serve
Trust mentor	Prepared to give time

Be willing to risk
  making mistakes
	Provide access to people
	  and situation otherwise
	  not accessible

Shoulder own responsi- bilities in case of error	Allow individual to make mistakes

Avoid timidity in
  gaining access
	Provide support in both
	  success and failure

Make own decisions	Ready accessibility

Network building:
  Joining appropriate organizations
  Service on boards, commissions, councils, committees
  Publishing
  Correspondence with others in field
  Meeting follow-up
  Issue association or visibility
  Liaison with related units of inside and outside organizations
  Seek advice from other professionals

VII: Addressing Common Dilemmas

Procedure

Step 1: 5 minutes

Examples of common problems faced by professional people. (VII A)

Step 2: 15 minutes

General discussion of problems and sharing among participants of ways in which successful coping might occur.

Step 3: 5 minutes

Participants note the specific dilemma(s) that must be addressed in their own career situations and identify one or more possible strategies to handle the concern.

VII A: Addressing common dilemmas

  Needs of children
  Unsupportive spouses
  Ailing parents
  Own health problems
  Jealousy of coworkers
  Boss stifling career opportunities

Expectations of organizational loyalty, but no advancement opportunities within organization
Effects of stress
Sexual harassment
Racial prejudice
Other . . .

VIII: Fitting It All Together

Procedure

Step 1: 15 minutes

A review of the steps covered and the "plan of action" outcome of participants' notes. Emphasis on need for regular review of situation and development of new action plans as situations change. (VIII A)

VIII A: Fitting it all together

1. Clarifying personal characteristics.
2. Identifying positions of interest, and life style factors to be considered in relation to each.
3. Exploring needed knowledge and the means to acquire it for positions being considered.
4. Exploring experience needed for positions being considered, and means to acquire it.
5. Assembling résumé information and reviewing and identifying knowledge and experience relevant to specific positions, as well as identifying possible weak areas.
6. Developing plans to select possible mentor. Mapping professional network construction plan to strengthen professional position.
7. Directing attention to personal and professional problem areas that could hamper career advancement possibilities, and identifying possible measures to address problems.
8. Considering factors that should automatically trigger a review process designed to keep career moving in desired direction.

Criteria for Promotability:
When Doing a Good Job Isn't Enough

Krystal G. Paulsen, Upjohn HealthCare Services

Increasingly, organizations are offering more opportunities to serious career-minded women with managerial skills who are both competent and dedicated. Legislation has prompted many companies to accelerate opportunities for these qualified women, and yet women are not immediately demonstrating the ability to take advantage of these existing fortunate circumstances. Women are not advancing as quickly as men and probably will not do so until they understand that in most instances the organizations' informal relationships find their origins and function in male culture and male experience. Hennig and Jardim note in *The Managerial Woman*,

> If we think of the men who belong to these informal systems as the insiders: people who understand and support each other, the structure, and the rules; people who share common aspirations and dreams; people who grew up with similar backgrounds; who played together, learned together, competed together; and concurrently we think of how differently women grow up: their different orientations, expectations, aspirations and experiences—then we can begin to understand why in spite of the law, very little may really have changed for women.[1]

Other authors have addressed the same issue—notably Betty Lehan Harragan in *Games Mother Never Taught You* and Rosabeth Moss Kanter in *Men and Women of the Corporation*—that organizations are grounded in a male culture. But scrutiny shows that most of the techniques and skills wielded by male managers are generic in nature, and lack of recognition and familiarity with these techniques and skills is often what keeps women from being as successful as their male counterparts.

Experiential training can effectively increase women's awareness of how organizations—because they are grounded in the male culture and experience—require a success standard with which most women are unfamiliar, but to which they can become sensitized. Once sensitized, women managers can learn to analyze what criteria their organizations value for success and determine which of those criteria are generic and, therefore, easily modified and adopted for their own behavior.

What constitutes success criteria varies from organization to organization. But because of pressure to conform in our male-dominated organizations, close analysis can reveal what the criteria are—regardless of whether they are social, behavioral, appearance-related, attitudinal, educational, or experience-based. Examples of the criteria can be having line experience, having an MBA degree, using power effectively, reacting appropriately to criticism, playing the right office politics, dressing appropriately, being achievement-oriented, not being risk averse, delegating appropriately, maintaining assertiveness and/or visibility, or simply being friends with the right people. Only by closely analyzing her environment can a woman manager identify her organization's values, but she must first assume responsibility for assessing that environment herself—not often are these criteria overtly identified for her.

Objectives

One of the goals of this workshop is to help women gain the skills necessary to assess their environment. Because it is designed to duplicate a specific work environment, condition, process, or demand, simulation provides an opportunity for women to deal with problems and constraints occurring in the work world. As Waddell asserts (1982), simulation helps participants to:

- gain insight into their behavior
- gain insight into the perception of others
- develop skills to deal effectively with others
- develop risk-taking skills

all in an environment free from the consequences of real-life experiences.

Adapted to emphasize the need for identifying success criteria in an organization, this simulation provides an opportunity to discern the organization's covert success criteria for promotion. Job competence is not enough for the simulation participants to be rewarded by success—they must exhibit certain criteria to be recognized as successful and promotable. The simulation is effective in providing opportunity for:

- discovering environmental criteria
- getting actively involved in learning
- gaining immediate feedback
- discussing observed behavior
- adopting a broader perspective

Another goal is to help women practice newly identified skills in a risk-free environment. This simulation is the first step—it provides an opportunity to sensitize women to the need to identify their organization's existing success criteria. Coupling this with a video-taped role play provides women with the opportunity to actually practice the success criteria behavior for which they've recognized a need. The video-taping gives others the opportunity to observe and offer immediate feedback and multiple perspectives. Just as important, the participant can see for herself how effectively she communicated the necessary behavioral requirements. Her own feedback is real and immediate. She has the opportunity to practice and modify without the real-life risk inherent in doing so in her organizational environment.

Workshop Outline

Content		*Design*	
I.	Introductory Role Plays (20 minutes)	I.	Video-tape role play vignettes for review after simulation.
II.	Identification of Success Criteria (20 minutes)	II.	Group discussion of what makes managers successful.
III.	Simulation to Increase Awareness of Success Criteria (90 minutes)	III.	Give overview of simulation activities, divide group, give directions, run simulation, and discuss simulation events and outcomes.
IV.	Role Play to Incorporate Identified Success Criteria (60 minutes)	IV.	View video-taped vignettes, discuss and identify possible success criteria for vignettes, re-video tape to enact success criteria.
V.	Evaluation of Modified Behavior and Summary (30 minutes)	V.	Critique re-video-taped vignettes and evaluate for effectiveness of adapting to success criteria.

I: Introductory Role Plays

Procedures

A video-taped role play, completed before the simulation exercise, will provide a point of reference to which the class can return for evaluation after they've been sensitized to identifying operating success criteria. Use any manager-subordinate interaction of some substance (See I A). A five-minute encounter is sufficient. In the interest of time, you may only want to tape three or four interactions using different participants.

I A: Introductory role plays

Employee

You are reporting to your division manager about a project which is vital to the success of the organization. You received this assignment only yesterday and your instructions were:

1.   Prepare a draft of the document for approval by the manager.
2.   Meet with the manager today in her office to explain and/or improve the document.

You are well qualified and technically competent and are looking forward to this meeting because it concerns an area of special interest for you.

Manager

You are to meet one of the employees from your division in your office. She is to have prepared a document which is vital to the success of the organization. You expect the document to be in draft form as it will probably need editing and improvement.

You are proud of your division's record of productivity and its image of professionalism. To your knowledge, all the employees are competent in their field and you are looking forward to this meeting because the employee is one you really don't know well, but have heard excellent reports about her technical competence.

II: Identification of Success Criteria

Procedure

Direct the class, through discussion, to consider what it means to be successful. Focus on evaluating what makes managers successful. Questions to consider are:

- Have you been promoted or known someone who was promoted?
- Why were you or they promoted?
- What do you think is the basis for considering a person for promotion?
- Is promotability determined by competence alone?
- Have you ever been passed over for promotion and, if so, how did you feel?
- Did you consider whether you could do anything to influence your future chances for success? On what basis?

Evaluate whether any are aware of their need for competence in addition to acceptance by those who are most powerful and influential in their organizations.

III: Simulation to Increase Awareness of Success Criteria

The following simulation[2] adapted from Dodge and Ramsey (1981), provides an opportunity for learning to identify success criteria operating within an organization. Its goals are to:

1. Increase awareness of variable perspectives of success criteria.

2. Teach necessity for understanding management criteria for success behavior.

3. Lead to examination of whether and how women can gain positive visibility upon understanding an organization's multiple criteria for success.

Procedures

Step 1: 10 minutes
Give an overview of the simulation activities without identifying its goals.

Step 2: 60 minutes
Divide the group, give directions and run the simulation based on the guidelines in III A.

Step 3: 20 minutes
After the task is accomplished and the promotions announced, discussion can initially and specifically focus on whether plant managers became aware of the division managers' direction, concentrating on those plant managers who exhibited the success criteria of wearing the same color identification badge as their division managers. Members should be encouraged to share their feelings about this process.

As often happens in this exercise, the division manager is unable to assume that the plant manager meeting the success criteria of wearing the same color identification badge as herself is the same manager who is first to complete a square. Discussion should explore why the division manager makes the recommendation she does—on the basis of task performance (the first plant manager to complete a good square) or on the basis of exhibiting success criteria (the plant manager wearing the same color identification badge as the division manager).

The discussion can then be directed to identify what constituted "success" for the managers who facilitated operations. How was this made apparent? When faced with the reality of existing criteria, what can an employee do who doesn't exhibit the criteria? What choices are available? What is the consequence for women who perceive the criteria as being male? Can a woman adopt "male" behavior? What does this mean? *Should* a woman adopt male behavior? What is "successful" male behavior?

III A: Simulation to increase awareness of success criteria

Group size and organization:

Maximum of four groups of six people each per facilitator.

CEO
(Facilitator)

Division Manager	Division Manager	Division Manager	Division Manager
Plant Managers (5)	Plant Managers (5)	Plant Managers (5)	Plant Managers (5)

Materials:

Enough packets of pieces of squares so that each of the five participating plant managers can assemble a complete square.

Badges of different colors of construction paper for identification of each separate division manager and plant manager. Each plant manager should have a different color badge for identification, and one of the plant managers should have a badge the same color as that of her division manager.

Setting:

A separate work station for each participant sufficiently removed so that observation of other participants' work is at least difficult. Ideally, there should be a separate room for each team.

Process:

1.   The facilitator is the chief executive officer.

2.   Divide participants into groups of 6 people.

3.   The CEO chooses one person to act as division manager of each team of five plant managers.

4.   The CEO explains the general task to the entire group. Each team is to be given pieces to complete five squares. Each plant manager will be subject solely to the direction of the division manager to complete the task; plant managers cannot operate independently of the division manager and cannot exchange information between themselves without the division manager's direction. Promotion will be awarded to a plant manager from each team based on the division manager's recommendation; the CEO will in turn promote one of the division managers based on her team's performance. The division managers and plant managers are then separated and directions and identification badges are distributed to all.

5.   The CEO separates the division managers from the group, gives them their job descriptions (See Division Manager's Job Description), and explains

privately to the division managers that one of them is to be promoted to CEO— the division manager who first completes the task of producing five complete squares and who recommends a qualified replacement. The division manager is expected to recommend the plant manager who is first on the division manager's team to complete a square and who exhibits the success criteria of wearing the same color identification badge as the division manager. The CEO will recommend a division manager for promotion to CEO who meets both criteria successfully.

6. The CEO explains the team's task to the division manager. Each team, without verbal exchange, is to provide the necessary parts to each member so that each member can assemble a complete square. Each member is provided with a job description (See Plant Manager's Job Description) and a packet of parts but no one packet contains the necessary parts to complete the square. The parts must be traded between and among the members but members can talk only to the division manager who is responsible for directing the exchange of parts. The division manager is provided with a set of blueprints indicating how the pieces can be successfully assembled. The division manager is limited to transporting only one piece at a time and must direct the exchange so that the person who meets the success criteria, the one wearing the same color badge as the division manager herself, is also the person who is the first to assemble a good square.

7. After all the teams have completed their five squares and have assembled each, the CEO asks each division manager who her recommended replacement is. The CEO then determines which division manager is to be promoted to CEO.

What to expect:

1. CEO (Facilitator): She informs each division manager she is to be promoted and therefore needs to choose a plant manager to take her place. The person recommended must meet the success criteria as identified by the CEO *and* must be the first individual to complete a good square.

2. Division Manager: After being informed of her task, she must facilitate in a traditional vertical organizational structure the successful assembly of five squares. In doing so, she must assure that the first plant manager to complete a *good* square is also a plant manager who exhibits the success criteria as identified by the CEO so that person can be promoted to division manager. She has access to blueprints and can transport only *one* piece at a time.

3. Plant Manager: She is informed that upon the successful completion of the organization's task—the completion of five squares—

> one of the plant managers will be promoted. Each manager's eligibility for promotion is greatly enhanced if she is the first to complete a *good* square. She's entirely dependent on direction from the division manager in transporting pieces to successfully assemble all five squares and cannot independently interact with the other plant managers.

The objective of this exercise is to demonstrate how a variety of criteria are at work in determining successful behavior within an organization.

Typically, being identified as a promotable employee is more than a function of doing a good job. Through this exercise, participants will have an opportunity to experience a manager's efforts to control who succeeds and then attempt to identify what other criteria is considered necessary for success. By observing management's attempts to influence subordinates' successful behavior, participants can learn to direct their attention to analyzing what criteria, in addition to task accomplishment, are considered necessary for "success"—being perceived as promotable.

Division managers' job description

As division manager of Square, Inc., you are responsible for the productivity of five plants located across the U.S. mainland. The division's task is to assure that each of the five plants produces one 8.5 by 8.5 inch square, with no raw materials scrapped (i.e., no parts left over). Unfortunately, supplier shipping errors are common across the industry, which means your plants may not have the parts they need to complete their individual tasks. One plant may have some of what another needs, and vice versa.

Since the organization follows the basic principles of a traditional hierarchy, plant managers may be contacting you for information about what parts are available from which plants, and how they might obtain the parts they need. If they wish to contact you, they may do so via memo, or by signing up for an appointment on the communication board outside your office. If you wish to initiate contact with any plant, you may send memos to the individual plant managers.

Your busy schedule prevents you from visiting the individual plants, and your concern about establishing strong productivity records for your division prevents the transfer of the bulky, heavy production materials to your office in Oahu. The cost of transferring parts between the plants on the mainland is also high, so you are limited to initiating the transfer of parts between plants to one part at a time. You do have blueprints below indicating how the pieces need to be assembled in order to successfully complete five squares; you do not know at the onset what plant has which parts.

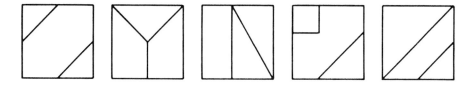

You have also been informed you are up for promotion to the CEO's position. You must recommend one of your plant managers as a replacement for you. The person you recommend must be the first plant manager on your team to successfully complete a "good" square. You must assure her that only a plant manager who exhibits the success criteria as designated by the CEO completes her square first. Your own promotion is dependent upon completing all five squares before any other division team.

Plant Managers' Job Description

As plant manager of one of Square, Incorporated's many production facilities, your mission is to produce a complete square, measuring 8.5 by 8.5 inches.

The organization is designed as a traditional hierarchy, which requires you to follow through the appropriate channels of communication. If you run into any serious production problems which prevent you from producing a square, you must refer your problem up through the organization's formal hierarchy to your division manager. You may send memos to your division manager or sign-up for a meeting with her on the communication board located near her office.

Due to their size and weight, it is very costly and time consuming for the organization to ship parts to the home office in Oahu. The cost of transferring parts between the five division plants on the mainland is also quite high.

Upon completion of the organization's task, you know one of the plant managers will be recommended for promotion to the division manager's position. Because completing a good square is dependent upon the division manager's direction, your success is greatly dependent upon her direction and influence in directing your task.

IV: Role Play to Incorporate Identified Success Criteria

Step 1: 40 minutes

Review the video-taped role plays done at the workshop's onset. Discuss what possible success criteria could be working in such a context and what behaviors do and don't reflect that criteria.

It may be helpful here to consider the points Sargent (1978) makes regarding positively perceived behaviors and attitudes in men and women (See IV A).

Step 2: 20 minutes

Retape the role plays and encourage the class to suggest for participants what may be helpful behavior and to reinforce behavior that fits the criteria at work.

IV A: Role play to incorporate identified success criteria

Strengths most men can develop further:
Strengths characteristic of women

Become aware of, accept, and express feelings

Regard feelings as a basic and essential part of life, as guides to authenticity and effectiveness for a fully functioning person, rather than as impediments to achievement

Accept the vulnerability and imperfections that are part of all persons

Assert the right to work for self-fulfillment, rather than only playing the role of provider

Value an identity that is not defined totally by work

Learn how to fail at a task without feeling one has failed as a person

Accept and express the need to be nurtured when feeling hurt, afraid, vulnerable, or helpless, rather than hiding these feelings behind a mask of strength, rationality, and invulnerability

Touch and be close to both men and women, minimizing any inhibition over the presence or absence of sexuality in such contact

Listen empathetically and actively but without feeling responsible for solving others' problems

Share feelings as the most meaningful part of one's contact with others, accepting the risk and vulnerability that such sharing implies

Build support systems with other men, sharing competencies without competition, and feelings and needs without dissembling

Personalize experience, rather than assuming that the only valid approach to life and interpersonal contact is objective

Accept the emotional, spontaneous, and irrational as valid parts of oneself to be explored and expressed as needed

Nurture and actively support other men and women in their efforts to change

Strengths most women can develop further:
Strengths characteristic of men

Learn how to be powerful and forthright

Become entrepreneurial

Have a direct, visible impact on others, rather than just functioning behind the scenes

State their own needs and refuse to back down, even if the immediate response is not acceptance

Focus on a task and regard it as at least as important as the relationships with the people doing the task

Build support systems with other women and share competence with them, rather than competing with them

Build a sense of community among women instead of saying, "I pulled myself up by my bootstraps, so why can't you?"

Intellectualize and generalize from experience

Behave "impersonally," rather than personalizing experience and denying another's reality because it is different

Stop turning anger, blame, and pain inward

Stop accepting feelings of suffering and victimization

Take the option of being invulnerable to destructive feedback

Stop being irritable, a "nag," and/or passive-resistant about resentments and anger

Respond directly with "I" statements, rather than with blaming "you" ones ("I'm not comfortable with that" rather than "you shouldn't do that.")

Become effective problem-solvers by being analytical, systematic, and directive

Stop self-limiting behaviors, such as allowing interruptions or laughing after making a serious statement

Become risk-takers (calculating probabilities and making appropriate tradeoffs)

Adapted from "The Androgynous Blend: Best of Both Worlds?" by A. G. Sargent, *Management Review* (October 1978), p. 62. Copyright 1978 by AMACOM, a division of American Management Association.

V: Evaluation of Modified Behavior and Summary

Critique the re-video-taped role plays by sharing feelings about the activity, about gaining insight into success criteria that may be hidden, and about the idea that each of us can, to varying degrees, assume some influence over our own success by identifying criteria and modifying our behavior to meet that criteria. An evaluation for the simulation exercise is available in V A.

V A: Evaluation of modified behavior and summary

Evaluation

Please respond to each item as realistically and accurately as you can.

1. How actively involved in the simulation did you feel?

___	___	___	___	___	___	___
1	2	3	4	5	6	7
Extensively			Moderately			Very little

2. How realistic did the simulation seem to you?

___	___	___	___	___	___	___
1	2	3	4	5	6	7
Very			Moderately			Not very

3. Does the simulation heighten your sensitivity to the problem women face in the business environment?

___	___	___	___	___	___	___
1	2	3	4	5	6	7
Very much			Moderately			Very little

4. Are the simulation instructions clearly stated?

___	___	___	___	___	___	___
1	2	3	4	5	6	7
Very			Moderately			Not very

5. Do you feel that the simulation is representative of a situation you might (or have) face(d)?

___	___	___	___	___	___	___
1	2	3	4	5	6	7
Very much			Moderately			Not very

NOTES

1. Hennig, M. and Jardim, A., *The Managerial Woman,* Pocket Books, New York, 1976, p. 13.
2. Paulsen, K. G. and Shull, C. A., "A Case for Experiential Training: Simulation for Professional Women," workshop simulation presented at the Midwest Conference on Women and Organizations, Western Michigan University, Kalamazoo, Michigan, May 26, 1982.

REFERENCES

Dodge, L. and Ramsey, V. "Exercise—Square, Inc." In T. Hall, J. Lewicki, D. Bowen, and Hall, F. *Experiences in Management and Organization Behavior* (2nd edition). Chicago: St. Clair Press, 1981.

Harragan, B. *Games Mother Never Taught You.* New York: Warner Books, 1977.

Kanter, R. *Men and Women of the Corporation.* New York: Basic Books, Inc., 1977.

Sargent, G., "The Androgynous Blend: Best of Both Worlds?" *Management Review,* October 1978, p. 62.

Waddell, G. "Simulation: Balancing Pros and Cons." *Training and Development Journal,* January 1982, pp. 80-83.

Reality Shock:
Where Did I Put My Rose-Colored Glasses?

Marie R. Hodge, Bowling Green State University

Reality shock occurs when rosy pre-employment expectations give way to organizational realities. Both the individual and the company lose, the former probably resigning, and the latter repeating the process of hiring and training at considerable cost to both. What should be done? The individual must be more realistic, the companies need to listen to "headhunters" to develop really "realistic job previews," and educational institutions need to tune in to the "real world."

Objectives

This workshop is designed to help women entering the world of work understand the realities of the work they will encounter in their first job. For a variety of reasons, individuals are looking at their future through "rose-colored glasses." Women (and men) have developed high expectations which recruiters have not disillusioned, for obvious reasons.

Initially, the workshop cannot disprove recruiters' "puffing" techniques. Through such a workshop, however, candidates will be encouraged to ask more perceptive questions in their interviews and visits to companies.

This workshop is designed to examine the concept of reality shock from the viewpoint of various professionals. Teachers, career counselors, trainers, as well as students, and entrants to the world of work should become aware of reality shock and understand the implications for both the individual and the organization.

The workshop is designed to address this awareness issue through both its content and process. Individuals sharing experiences, interactive exercises, and the contributions and expertise of the leader should develop this awareness. The workshop description which follows demonstrates activities to implement this goal of leader-group involvement.

As set up, the workshop is designed for 1½ to 2 hours, dependent on the size of the group. The activities could be divided into 2 sessions for a leader who wants to fit the activities into 2 class sessions. This would facilitate interim assignments to do reading and investigation of current attitudes.

For this workshop, the leader needs to understand organizations, their culture, and human resource needs. Career counseling experience is a "must" ingredient. Coupled with group discussion skills should be a sense of humor, the flexibility to allow diversions, and the control eventually to direct the group back to the workshop goals.

In a broader sense, reality shock is just one aspect of various concerns many of us in the human resources area share. Whether student, teacher, trainer, or recruiter, we each need to develop awareness of and strategies for effectively utilizing our human resources.

Workshop Outline

Content		*Design*
I.	Getting Acquainted (15 to 30 minutes depending on size of group)	I. Dyadic exercise to encourage interaction and involvement.
II.	Reality Shock (20 minutes)	II. Mini-lecture on reality shock, what it is, and what can be done about it.
III.	How to See Without Rose-Colored Glasses (30 to 50 minutes depending on size of group)	III. Completion of self-assessment instrument and discussion of results in groups of four to six.
IV.	Programs to Reduce Reality Shock (20 minutes)	IV. Distribution of instrument and discussion of importance.
V.	Setting Personal Goals (10 minutes)	V. Lecture-discussion on what individuals, educational institutions, and other organizations can do to reduce reality shock.

I: Getting Acquainted

Each participant should receive an agenda (workshop outline).

Procedure

Step 1: 5 to 10 minutes

Ask each participant to team up with a neighbor in the group and share information (name, occupation, place of residence, and reason for attending the workshop). The leader may pair up with the odd person if there are an uneven number of participants.

Step 2: 10 to 20 minutes

Ask each person to introduce the other person to the group as a whole.

II: Reality Shock

Material for a mini-lecture is included in this segment. In addition, depending on the background and experience of the leader, readings in Hall (1976) and Wanous (1980) are recommended. The current situation in your locale may be investigated by garnering information from your college placement office.

Lecture notes

Reality shock. What is it? Who is affected? How important is it? When does it occur? Is it fatal? What can be done about it?

You are ecstatic. You have a job. A real job—not part-time, summers, or holidays. Now you will be able to use what you have learned so painfully during those college years. All is well—you are eager to be challenged.

Six months later, you wonder why you needed a college eduation for what you have been assigned to do. You can't talk to your supervisor. He is not only lacking in sensitivity, but actually threatened by your gleaming new educational credentials. You could have handled this job four years ago. What has happened?

You are suffering from reality shock, the clash between your rosy view of your chosen career and your actual experience. Another way to put it—reality shock occurs when pre-employment expectations give way to organizational realities. Not only the job and supervisor may be involved but also your fellow workers and the larger climate—the corporate culture. No, it is not fatal to either you or your career!

Confronted with these happenings in your job, you wonder about the organization. Typically, first assignments tend to be easy, not too challenging because the organization wants you to start slowly, get a good understanding of your job before moving on to more important ones once you have shown your capabilities. Unfortunately for them, you may not be there next year to take their challenge. Hall (1976) reports that one company found their turnover rate the first year so high that they had to hire 120 people each year just to return 20. Finally, thinking (rightly) that the jobs might not be challenging enough, the company hired 30 people the next year and worked hard on upgrading the first-year jobs. At the end of the year, 25 people were still there and had far better first-year performances!

Another typical first-year assignment involves job-rotating training programs, often just observing situations rather than being a fully functioning, participating worker. Remember that rotating means going around in a circle.

While the opening scene related to the college graduate entering the permanent job market, the situation occurs as well at the MBA level. Recent research reported by Columbia University (1983) focuses on the MBA attrition problem. Early findings appear to revolve around formal orientation sessions, unrealistic "realistic job previews," and a lack of preparation for transition by MBA programs.

The cost to the individual is elusive. How can you measure disillusion, disappointment, frustration, and cynicism? The monetary loss may not be high, but time is money. And, a new job search may be costly, especially if a new job requires an employment agency's services. College placement services concentrate more on the placement of new graduates. And the individual involved has lost nine months, twelve, or however much time elapses prior to a decision to move on, wiser but older. Further complications arise if dual careers are involved, the location is not diverse enough for another job in the area, and so on.

The cost to the company is more measurable. Wanous (1980) reports the cost of this "premature" turnover at $6,000 for an insurance claims investigator, $24,000 for a field examiner, $31,600 for a sales person (with *below* average performance), and $185,000 for a sales manager. These replacement cost figures include acquiring a new person, training, and moving a present holder to another organization. The highest turnover rates are among newly hired employees.

What can be done about reality shock? Who should be responsible? Something, and everybody—specifically–the individual involved, the company accepting the person into their organization, and educational institutions preparing students. Each has a role to play in reducing reality shock.

III: How to See Without Rose-Colored Glasses

Step 1: 5 minutes

Each participant should fill out the "How to See Without Rose-Colored Glasses" questionnaire. (III A)

Step 2: 15 minutes

Form groups of four to six. Ask each group to discuss the individual responses and decide on a spokesperson to share specifics with the larger group.

Step 3: 15 to 30 minutes

Each group's chosen spokesperson should report on the group's discussion to the larger group.

III A: How to see without rose-colored glasses

1. Your first job _____.

2. Had you had experience in the area of your first job, perhaps an internship?

3. Was your first job what you studied in college?

4. Do you recall your expectations concerning the job?

5. What preview (after being hired) were you given prior to starting your position?

6. Once on the job, was it "as advertised"?

7. Was your first job structured or unstructured (ambiguous)?

IV: Programs to Reduce Reality Shock

It will be especially helpful if the leader knows the composition of the workshop participants, and selects from the following material those segments which are applicable to a particular group. Many of the following suggestions apply to college students, but other individuals should be able to relate to some of the suggestions. In addition, suggestions are made for trainers and human resource people in businesses and other organizations. Such people are really key to implement solutions to the problem.

Lecture notes

From the point of view of the individual

Individuals get little help in preparing for their professional careers. Few counselors in high schools know enough about today's careers; college counseling centers and placement services are more knowledgeable but rarely interact enough with students to be effective. College faculty advisors are usually conversant with their own teaching/research field and expertise, if you want to follow in their footsteps. Therefore, it will be up to you as an individual to learn your own strengths and weaknesses in order to have realistic aspirations in your career choice, as well as the company you enter.

The first step is to examine your values, what you really believe in. If you want to be of service to others, you will not want to join an organization that is highly competitive and money oriented. There are trade-offs to be made. If you want to advance in an organization and make money, you will devote both time and energy, really make a commitment. Engage in self assessment; set goals (a goal-setting exercise is included in the workshop). Because it is difficult to assess yourself objectively, first gather information without evaluating it. Ask for information about yourself from several sources—friends, family, teachers, former employers. Then, put it all together and you can probably see your values and your skills more clearly. The next step is to relate your values and your skills to those jobs that are available, and to be realistic. If you want a career in computers but refuse to take math, forget it. A sales job without being willing to travel might be unrealistic. Talk to people in the field; review your part-time work experience; query your parents and their friends; research the company you plan to interview with; take courses that help you develop your interpersonal skills—speaking, listening, writing, and interacting with other people. These skills are most frequently mentioned as lacking in employees in organizations.

From the point of view of an educational institution

Educational institutions especially need to address the issue of realilty shock. Probably the greatest reality shock would be the entry of many educational members into the "real world." Hall (1976) reported a dialogue between a group of professors and senior executives:

> An illustration of the standard organizational attitude toward new employees recently occurred in a dialogue between a group of business school professors and a group of senior executives. One distinguished-looking executive said, "You know, these students you send us are bright and eager enough, but they are so full of theory and impractical, wild ideas and skills that it takes us five years to train it all out of them." At this point an equally distinguished professor took a long, thoughtful puff on his pipe and replied, "Well, that's interesting to hear. But we are trying to increase it to ten!"

Let us not be disillusioned. Schools and universities are also cognizant of current economics. Most are willing to admit that although education is for life, making a living is such a large part of life, that both goals can and should be served. The current emphasis on internships is evidence of this. Involvement of alumni in externships—week-long working experiences—is growing. Faculties are examining their relationships to the community and the regions they serve. Professors consult, businesses seek advice, seminars are set up, continuing education serves adults. Silicon Valley owes as much to research scientists in that area as does Route 128 in Boston. Interdependence works, and will contribute to new reality realizations. The president of Bowling Green has just announced "BG Network" to interface our expertise at the university with organizations in Northwest Ohio.

If internships or co-ops are not available, short exposures such as films, field trips, campus visits by business speakers, shadow programs, and business education days are better than nothing. Another group that can be tapped to help is the counseling center or placement service. Encourage these offices to go beyond the usual "writing résumés" or "interviewing strategies" workshops. Workshops on corporate culture, role changes, risk-taking, coaching for the second interview, perceptions, and goal setting are just a few ideas to get all parties to a more realistic mind set.

Most agree that the most "realistic job preview" will be that given by recruiters in professional search firms. Such "headhunters" are hired by companies to recruit "the" person for the job that will be open. Obviously, the recruiter wants the best person for the job in question. He/she wants the candidate to know honestly and exactly what the potential job entails. Let's listen to what such recruiters might tell us.

Recommended activities for teachers

Develop a network of faculty who have had experience in business and industry. Such persons could have been in business or have been consultants.

Refer students to such persons; guest spots in your classes may be possible.

Utilize internships or externships at your school; if no program exists, start one. If this is not feasible, field trips, campus visits, shadow programs, etc., can encourage a better perception of jobs by students.

Work with your counseling center and/or placement services to develop workshops or mini-seminars on corporate culture, role changes, risk-taking, goal-setting, and preparations.

From the point of view of an organization

The recent recession has forced a fresh look at costs, particularly the largest costs in most organizations—those associated with employees at all levels. Reducing turnover can not only reduce costs directly but improve morale, build a better organizational climate, and improve human resource maintenance. This translates into increased productivity, which is the current goal. Dana Corporation has as their corporate culture goal, "Productivity Through People," and it has worked for them. Whether undergraduate or graduate, blue collar or white collar, a more challenging job will contribute to a more effective organization through more efficient employees.

Some specifics for those of you in an organization: realistic job previews by your interviewers is a first step; more challenging first jobs for those you do hire; better training for supervisors in performance appraisal so that new hires will know how they are doing on the job; management development that is more than a special one-time program; recognition that people grow best through being placed in challenging jobs—not just taking seminars. Management development should involve all management in the organization, not just the training department.

Recommended activities for trainers

Set up workshops for company interviewers to develop their understandings of the company, its culture, and the positions for which they will be recruiting.

Study your corporate culture for a profile of company values and objectives.

Matching up such values with those of students being recruited should improve your retention rate of new hires. Develop a program to exit interview those who do leave in the first 6 to 18 months with a view to identifying unrealistic job previews.

Work closely to prepare training programs for new hires that allow early misgivings in jobs when the new hires' perceptions question the need for the education they have just received. Better yet, try to convince management to put new college graduates and MBAs in challenging jobs.

V: Setting Personal Goals

Procedure

Step 1: 5 minutes

Distribute "Setting Personal Goals" Instrument (V A). If time allows, ask participants to complete. If not, urge them to do so following the workshop.

Step 2: 5 minutes

Not enough women set goals for themselves and this exercise addresses that issue, and gives a forward-looking aspect to a workshop somewhat devoted to looking backward. Urge them to use a similar instrument with their students or employees. Emphasize *USE.* Check your progress in one year, five years, whatever. Keep it in your vault—and put your rose-colored glasses there, too!

Remember each of you can make a difference. We all have to be innovative, creative, and think how to solve the problem. The person who deals effectively with "reality shock" will be more mature, more goal directed, more effective, and more likely, in his/her terms, to be successful. The organization hiring will be both more efficient and effective. And the educational institution will develop better understanding both of their students and the organizations which the students will be joining after graduation.

Finally, the leader of the workshop should encourage feedback from participants. The preceding workshop activities should have developed a climate of openness and sharing that will contribute additional suggestions not included in these materials.

V A: Setting personal goals

Step 1

Write a description of a successful "you." Jot down the first thoughts that come to mind; use descriptive phrases or adjectives; don't worry about complete sentences or polished prose. Brainstorm some ideas without evaluating them at this stage. Think in terms of outcomes or results—not activities (e.g., a bowling average of 180, a golf handicap of 10 or less, ownership of a specific business, or an income of $????). Push yourself to be long-range and comprehensive (a variety of dimensions). Ten years from now, how would a close friend or a colleague describe you in an ideal letter of recommendation? (use your own paper for this)

Step 2

Refine the ideas expressed in Step 1 by listing the important areas of concern or key dimensions (e.g., family, career, vocational, and personal skills), that will be important for you in determining success. Select 3-5 categories or areas of concern.

Step 3

Determine priorities for the above items by identifying the most important as 1, the second most important as 2, and so forth throughout the list. Write the five most important dimensions in the spaces below and describe how you will measure performance and/or judge results. Be as specific as possible while recognizing that not all indicators can be quantified.

For example (on your paper):

	Key Areas of Concern	*Measure of Performance*
1.	_____	_____
		_____
		_____
2.	and so on	

Step 4

For each of the key areas of concern that you have identified in Step 3, write several specific objectives for a relatively short time period—one year or less.

Key Areas of Concern   *Specific Short-Term Objectives*

REFERENCES

Career Center Bulletin, Vol. 4, Number 1, Columbia University, 1983.

Hall, D. T. *Careers in Organizations.* Pacific Palisades, California: Goodyear Publishing Company, Inc., 1976.

Wanous, J. P. *Organizational Entry—Recruitment, Selection, and Socialization of Newcomers.* Reading, Massachusetts: Addison-Wesley Publishing Company, 1980.

Dual Careers:
Impact on Individuals, Families, Organizations

Claire Scott Miller, RESOURCE: Careers

The world of work is changing. Consider these facts: Employment statistics demonstrate that more than half of the adult women in the United States are presently in the labor force. The projection is that by 1990, 70% of women aged 25-54 will be working.

Our family structure is also changing. Only 5% of all American families represent the traditional model with the husband as sole source of income, the wife at home, and two children under 18. In the last decade, women aged 25-34 (the usual child-bearing age) accounted for nearly half the increase in female workers entering the labor force. In 1970, there were 3 million multi-earner families and by 1980, there was an enormous increase to 28.5 million.

As women increasingly enter the workforce, they also choose to marry and they continue to join with working partners. For many couples, two careers are an economic necessity; for others the reason is psychological, a need to avoid what Abraham Maslow once called, "neurosis as a failure of personal growth." Work for women, as for men, is becoming central to their identity.

Dual-career couples look at managing their careers as serious business. New lifestyles have emerged as traditional roles and values have been questioned. In addition to separate work roles, two-career couples are defined by their lifestyle, which is designed to support, encourage, and facilitate—not just tolerate—the career and pursuits of both members (Hall and Hall, 1979). Not only do two-career couples strive to complement one another, they view their work, career, and family life as part of a total whole. Career goes beyond the narrow occupational limits to encompass the person's total life space (Wolfe and Kolb, 1980).

The changes in the family structure and the workplace have implications that affect each other. As educators and trainers, we need to be aware of these changes and proactively assist students (our future professionals) and organizations adapt to the change.

One model looking at dual-career issues was developed by RESOURCE: Careers, a career development and referral service. Recognizing the realities of the changing employment market and the emergence of the dual-career family, RESOURCE: Careers, through a grant from The Cleveland Foundation, conducted a comprehensive survey of 167 organizations and 400 dual-career couples in N.E. Ohio.

One of the significant findings of the RESOURCE: Careers survey demonstrated that attitudes are changing; organizations are aware of these changes and respondents indicated a need for programs to assist them in implementing change. Dual-career issues such as child care, time and stress management, maternity/paternity leave are obviously important to couples trying to combine work and family responsibilities. These have become bottom line issues for corporations, affecting recruiting, relocation, employee benefits, policies, and practices. Employee retention, productivity, and the effects on company profits are critical concerns. The more a person's work life and family life complement, rather than conflict with, one another the more productive will that individual be.

The following highlights how the Dual Career Project was organized, the methodology used, how data was gathered, corporate and couples' survey findings, implications and suggested action plans for teachers and trainers.

Methodology

The objective of the Dual Career Project was to gather information from dual-career couples and organizations and then to present programs to assist in meeting the stated needs. The project was conducted in two phases.

Phase I—Information gathering

Information about dual-career issues and the effect on corporations (i.e., recruiting, relocation, retention, benefits, policies, and practices) and individuals (i.e., time and stress management, child care, career development) was gathered both nationally and locally in Northeastern Ohio. National information was gained from periodicals, papers, and current research work on dual career couples and adult development. A Task Force was developed with representatives from industry, banking, health care, social service, higher education, and public education (from whence our future dual-career couples will come). The charge to the Task Force was to generate ideas and to provide support from the business community.

Phase II—Program implementation

After analyzing the results of the organizational and dual-career couples' survey findings, programs were developed to respond to the specific needs uncovered in the surveys. The program stage emphasized results-oriented activities.

Data gathering

Information on dual-career issues was obtained through two surveys conducted in Northeastern Ohio. One survey examined corporate issues, poilicies, and attitudes concerning dual-career couples as perceived by their human resource professionals. The second survey dealt with two-career issues from the perspective of the couples themselves. Data for the two surveys were collected during the period Fall 1982-Spring 1983.

The corporate survey was conducted via a telephone appointment to a respondent within the human resource department. A twenty-member corporate interviewing team was developed and trained in phone survey techniques. The organizations interviewed ranged in size from those with five employees to those with more than 100,000. Their activities were representative of those in the Northeastern Ohio region. The survey included responses from 156 organizations.

TABLE 1

Industry Representation of Organizations by Percent

Manufacturing	= 40
Health Care	= 19
Services	= 23
Utilities	= 5

Major questions addressed in the organizational survey included:

- Are recruitment practices, productivity, and profits affected by the problems of two-career families?

- Are companies experiencing resistance to transfers, and do they recognize the special needs of two-career families?

- What specific steps are corporations taking to retain dual career employees and to help them be more productive?

- How satisfied are corporations with formal or informal programs initiated?

- What further steps would corporations like to take to address these complex issues?

The couples survey was completed by 392 Northeastern Ohio dual career couples, or 784 individuals representing a variety of careers.

Career was defined as "attitudinal on the part of the individual, encompassing any lifelong work characterized by strong commitment, personal growth, and increasing levels of responsibilities" (Catalyst, 1980). Jobs were not classified as "career" or "noncareer"; instead, responding dual-career couples were those who agreed with this definition.

TABLE 2

Industry Representation of Individuals by Percent

Manufacturing	= 28
Services	= 25
Health Care	= 12
Utilities	= 5

Questionnaires were distributed at professional meetings and seminars, and were sent by request to those responding to announcements in selected magazines and newspapers, and on television and radio stations.

Major questions addressed in the couples' survey included:

- What are the social, economic, and demographic characteristics of two-career couples?

- How are couples balancing the demands of individual effectiveness in business careers with responsibility to spouse and children? Which is most important?

- How are couples dealing with relocation?

- How are they dealing with child care?

- How satisfied are they with their careers, with their marriages, and how they are combining the two?

The response to the surveys was overwhelming and demonstrated the interest in the dual career issue from both organizations and individuals. The initial target for organizations was 50 with an actual 156, a 321% increase over expectations, and the target for couples was 200 with an actual 392 or 196% increase.

Corporate Survey Findings

At the beginning of the corporate/organizational survey, four issue statements about dual career concerns were given. Responses to these indicated the tone and were the basis for the following results on relocation, parenting, policies, and practices.

- Sixty-six percent (66%) of the organizations are concerned about dual-career issues.

- Fifty-three percent (53%) of the organizations feel that they lack the resources to deal with the problems of dual-career families.

- Seventy percent (70%) do not see their involvement in the problems of dual-career couples as an invasion of privacy.

- More than sixty-six percent (66%) feel that the problems of dual-career families have not yet affected their operations.

Relocation

More than 50% of the organizations surveyed indicated that they transfer employees. Of the organizations that transfer employees, 42% report an increase in employee resistance to transfer. The reasons for resistance were cited as financial, and the spouse's reluctance to move. More than 66% of the organizations expect to see an increase in employee transfers involving dual-career couples within the next five years. Currently, assistance to relocated employees is primarily financial, including moving costs, interim living, and mortgage differential. Assistance to the spouse in obtaining a job in the new location (i.e., job search strategy, contacts, résumé assistance) is seldom provided.

TABLE 3

Relocation

Transfer	Resistance	More Dual Career Transfers
50%	42%	66% +

Parenting

While more than 75% of the organizational respondents indicated that parenting responsibilities fall primarily on women, they feel in the same proportion that men are increasingly sharing in the parenting responsibility. More than 75% do not see a problem in combining parenting with a career for either men or women. Regarding paternity and maternity leaves, virtually all organizations provide maternity leaves, but only 7% provide paternity leaves, with over 33% of the organizational respondents favoring paternity leaves. In the area of child care assistance, almost 30% favor on-site child care, but fewer than 3% of the companies provide it. Only one organization reports providing subsidies for child care, yet almost 20% favor it. Nearly 50% of the respondents favor monetary support of community-based child care, with only 12% providing this support. The largest response, 75%, favor child-care services.

Policies and practices

Currently, more than 50% of the respondents favor a "cafeteria" approach to benefits with only 12% of the organizations offering this approach. Cafeteria benefits refers to a flexible, coordinated approach to a benefits program which allows the employee to select from a range of benefits those most appropriate to his or her needs (Catalyst, 1981). Over 30% of the organizations favor flexible working hours, but the same percent does not provide them. Regarding nepotism, more than 75% of the organizations do not have a policy that forbids a spouse from working for the same company, but more than 60% say they cannot work in the same department or function.

TABLE 4

Organizational Policies and Practices

	Childcare Assistance by Percent	
	Favor	Provide
On-Site Child Care	30	3
Child Care Information and Referral	75	33
$ Community Child Care	50	33
	Benefits & Policies by Percent	
Flextime/Cafeteria Benefits	66	33
Flexible Workplaces	33	11
Maternity Benefits	100	100
Paternity Benefits	53	7

Couples Survey Findings

The participants

The bulk of the participants responding to the survey were between the ages of 25-54 with the largest single category being 25-34 (47%). The participants were well educated with 84% having college degrees and over 40% with post-graduate degrees. Individual income clustered in the $15,000-$29,000 (45%) and $30,000-$49,000 (34%) categories. More than 69% of the couples have combined incomes in the range of $30,000 to $100,000. Respondents have been in their chosen careers an average of 8.6 years and in their current position an average of 2.6 years.

Relocation

More than 40% of the men and women have relocated as a result of their own job transfers, but an almost equal number, 37%, have refused a transfer. Family-related factors (spouse refused to move, spouse's job) were cited as the reason for refusal by the majority of respondents. More than 90% of the couples believed that companies should provide some form of assistance to spouses asked to relocate. The form of spouse assistance ranked as most helpful was the making of informal job contacts; job counselling ranked second. Couples see themselves as an "economic unit." When asked about relocation, the number one response (38%) was that a couple would move "only if the net gain to family is irresistable."

TABLE 5

Demographic Description of Respondents

Who are the couples?
- 47% are 25-44 years old
- 84% are college graduates
- 40% are post graduates

Individual income levels	Years in career/current position	
	Career	Position
• 45% = $15,000-$29,999		
• 34% = $30,000-$49,999	8.6 years	2.6 years

Couple concerns

Considering career, family, and outside interests and friends, family was the number one concern by more than 65% of those responding. Projecting ten years ahead, family remains at about 65%, but career loses almost 8% to outside interests and friends. Competitive feelings with one's spouse over career advancement was almost negligible and about 60% report that both careers in the family are equally important.

TABLE 6

Couple Concerns

Most Important Area Now By Percent	Most Important Area in 10 Years By Percent
65 = Family	65 = Family
30 = Career	22 = Career
4 = Outside Interests	12 = Outside Interests

Parenting

Generally, the respondents believe that being part of a two-career family has a positive impact on children. More than half of the couples have children, just under 25% plan to have children in the future, 12% have decided not to have children and the remainder have not decided or are in conflict over the decision.

Both men and women were usually working when the first child was born. Emphasizing the importance of their careers, 71% of the women took pregnancy leaves of six months or less. Couples are generally satisfied with their current child-care arrangements, with approximately 45% of the couples reporting an equal division of child-care responsibilities and about 50% reporting that the mother has most or all responsibility.

Integrating career and family

Being part of a dual career family has its advantages. Higher income was ranked as the most important advantage, "growth" was ranked second, and more security and autonomy for both virtually tied for third. But it has its disadvantages too. There is too much to do, couples don't have enough time together, and there is not enough leisure time.

Career satisfaction

Survey respondents were generally satisfied with their careers: on a one-to-seven scale, where seven corresponds to "very satisfied," more than 66% of the women and nearly 75% of the men rated career satisfaction at 5 or better. In general, as income increases, reported career satisfaction tends to increase.

Implications

Although organizations and dual-career couples face a number of issues, the resolution of many of these is beyond the scope of either the organization or the couples themselves, and is instead bound up in the slow moving process of cultural evolution. We are in the midst of change. What we do know is that the way businesses and families have operated in the past is not how they will operate in the future.

The couples that responded, well-educated and fast-tracked, responded that their number one priority was family. This remains constant ten years into the future, with career losing ground to outside interests and friends. Organizations need to be aware of these values as they develop and implement programs and practices to maintain productivity.

Relocation

While more than half of the organizations surveyed transfer employees, in general, the couples surveyed have a negative view of relocation. This is supported by the organizations, over 71% of whom report that resistance to relocation has increased or remained unchanged, compared to 29% reporting less or no resistance.

The reasons for couples' negative views are evident: the family is seen as more important than career and the family does not necessarily benefit from a transfer. Couples look at themselves as an "economic unit." A promotion that includes a relocation may be turned down if it means one spouse will not have a job. With only one income guaranteed in the new location, the couple's ability to secure a comparable home and mortgage may be affected.

An organization seeking to decrease resistance to relocation needs to address these "negatives." While remaining responsive to direct financial issues (e.g., moving expenses, help with house sale), organizations need to attend more to the indirect financial and career path problems which occur because one member of a couple leaves a position due to a spouse transfer.

Career assistance for the spouse of a transferee was reported as routinely provided by fewer than 25% of the organizations, but over 90% of the individuals surveyed believe that the spouse should receive assistance.

Parenting

Parenting duties were shared by couples, although womens' traditional role is still the norm in the majority of couples. Paternity benefits, while seldom available, would assist couples in initiating shared parenting. Sixty-six percent of the organizations support this by indicating they favor paternity benefits.

Emphasizing the importance of their careers, an overwhelming majority of women (71%) were back on the job six months or less after the birth of their baby. To make this transition even more successful, women and men indicated they did not seem to suffer, with 75% maintaining their positions or receiving a promotion within one year after maternity leave.

Policies and practices

Techniques to facilitate the combination of career and family include policies for flextime, the availability of part-time hours, "cafeteria benefits," and child-care policies. Flextime is supported by a majority of organizational respondents (66%), but was only offered at 33% of the organizations. Both men and women commented that part-time hours would be helpful at different stages in their career—when their children were infants, when pursuing further education, preparing for retirement, or caring for elderly parents.

The large discrepancy between the existence of a policy and an organization's favorable view of a policy was evident with on-site child care. Thirty percent favor on-site child care but only 3% of the organizations provide it. A benefit provided by a larger proportion of organizations is child-care information and referral. The climate appears ready for an increase in this area with 75% of the organizations indicating they favor this for their employees.

Action Plan: Organizations

The organizations surveyed recognize we are living with a changing economic and world climate and a changing work force. They support this by indicating they favor a variety of new approaches to running business, such as "cafeteria" benefits, flexible hours and places, child-care assistance. Attitudes are changing; organizations are aware of these changes and respondents indicated a need for programs to assist them and their companies in implementing change.

The survey results support the value of instituting a needs analysis within the organization to explore employees' career and dual career concerns. The interplay between the individual and the organization entails two processes: acculturation, the influence of the organization on the individual, and innovation, the influence of the individual on the organization. The relationship between the individual and the organization is a process which takes place over time and changes with changing career needs (Schein, 1980). Individuals need to take the initiative in assisting organizations to respond to change proactively. Dual-career couples (fast-tracked, well-educated professionals) indicated family was their number one concern. Awareness of this and receptivity to creative ways of integrating career and family life—working parent seminars, flexible time and work places, part-time professional positions—could have positive effects for the employee and may save the company money in increased productivity. The more employees' work and family life complement one another rather than conflict, the more productive they will be.

Relocation

Are relocations always necessary? Given the expense of relocation and the incidence of turn-downs and the possible loss of an employee, perhaps other methods of career pathing and management development should be considered. A few organizational respondents indicated they have developed in-house career development programs to provide challenging assignments as options to relocation. When relocation occurs, the couple should be considered as an "economic unit," with spouse assistance in the form of job referral, career counselling, and résumé preparation included.

Recruiting and retention

If an organization does not take steps to react to the changing environment, other organizations will. Policies more in step with the changing work force will give the progressive organization the edge in recruiting and help in retaining valuable employees. Line managers need to be educated about the changing workforce, including the fact that the dual-career family has emerged as the dominant family type.

Pregnancy and maternity/paternity leaves

Statistics indicate that women are increasingly delaying childbirth in order to establish their careers; therefore, at the time of maternity leave, they are often in responsible management positions. In addition, the survey indicated an increasing number of men are interested in more fully sharing parenting responsibilities. Time and money invested in a valuable employee could be saved by consideration of paternity leave in addition to maternity leave.

Alternative work schedules

The standard five-day, forty-hour week work schedule is only one option. Other choices available to employers include flextime, shared jobs, work sharing, permanent part-time positions, work from home, or short, project-oriented assignments. A company could also identify part-time jobs that would be available as pass-through positions. Both men and women indicated an interest in part-time hours during some part of their career.

Child care

Employees' child-care arrangements can affect their job performance. There are a variety of child-care resources available and already working: information and referral, subsidies to child-care centers, on-site child care to name a few. Organizations that provide such assistance can benefit by tax incentives, and by the reduction of employee tardiness or missed work days due to unreliable child care.

Flexible or "cafeteria" benefits

Dual career couples may not need identical comprehensive coverage from two different employers, or the same benefit package during the span of their careers. It might be more cost effective to the organization for the employees to select the relevant benefits for their needs at different stages in their career. For example, a young couple might choose child-care credits, while another couple might focus on retirement benefits or a company stock option.

Action Plan: Individuals and Couples

Dual career couples, like organizations, indicated that attitudes toward work and family have changed; however, behavior still follows traditional male and female roles. This conflict creates a potential source of stress in the individual, the family, and the organization. Everyone wants to be perceived by his or her employer as a productive and valuable employee. Survey respondents indicated that productivity can be directly related to the stress created from the difficulty in handling the combination of family and work schedules, child care, household responsibilities, and career advancement. Time management was identified as a major issue.

Managing lifestyles

Effectively managing the new emerging lifestyles is a challenge which can be facilitated by the identification and use of community resources. Taking the initiative to increase employer awareness, i.e., making them aware of and sensitive to the complex roles being played by the employees, may lead to increased productivity on both sides.

Relocation

When considering relocation issues, dual-career couples are urged to be proactive. Couples are encouraged to discuss what impact a relocation would have on a family, career, and quality of life. A major concern when dual-career couples were asked to relocate was the continuation of the spouse's career in the new area. Couples indicated that although organizations did not have formal spouse assistance programs, if they asked for assistance it was usually made available.

Career and life development

A career should be looked at as a life-long process that will vary as one progresses through the stages of adult development. Both husband and wife may not be in the same stage at the same time; spouses are encouraged to support each other as they both continue to grow and change. Career development involves one's whole life, not just one's occupation (Wolfe & Kolb, 1979).

Action Plan: Teachers and Trainers

Young men and women need realistic information about the compromises involved in combining career and family life. This can be accomplished by integrating speakers, case studies, role models, and discussions into courses.

Speakers

To bridge the gap between the classroom and the world of work, representatives from various career areas can be invited into the class to talk about managing career and family. Sources of speakers can be local businesses, corporate recruiters, and alumni. The format could consist of a panel with different couples representing various stages (e.g., young college graduates newly married; a professional couple with small children; a couple who have decided not to have children; a couple with older teenage-college children). Areas they can cover include how they manage their time; household responsibilities; issue of relocation if one receives a transfer; decision to have children; who takes care of children; alternate work schedules (i.e., shared jobs; part-time; flexible hours). Another method—an alternate to the panel format—would be to highlight a different issue that working couples commonly face (e.g., relocation, child care) each class session. In selecting speakers, be aware of role alternatives, such as the husband who elects to care for the baby while the wife continues in medical school.

Case studies

The case study method can assist students in looking at different issues dual-career couples face, coming up with possible solutions, and discussing the suggestions. Case studies are available on relocation, decision to have children, child-care options, nontraditional careers, and role identification (RESOURCE: Careers).

Role models

To complement the case studies, students can arrange to contact a dual-career couple and spend time with them throughout a typical working day in a "shadowing" experience. This will give the student first-hand experience on how couples manage work and family life, as well as give them an opportunity to interview the couples about their style of integrating career and family. To broaden the experience, each student would be encouraged to report back to the class suggestions from their particular couple. Hopefully, this would illustrate that there is no set blueprint, but alternatives from which to choose.

Discussion

Various exercises can be devised as catalysts for discussion. Some of these are myths and facts about dual careers; role inventory and coping with role conflict; time management exercises; decision making; identification of issues facing dual career couples; adult and career development; and the impact on organizations. Students are urged to look at the issues not only as individuals but also from the perspective of future managers—how will they relate to the concerns of their employees.

Workshops

Manufacturing, health care, service industries, and educational institutions have all conducted workshops for managers about the changing workforce and family. An understanding of these changes provides greater insight into the concerns of their workers.

To assist with recruiting, workshops for recruiters about how to recruit dual career couples and implement a spouse assistance program have proven valuable. Contacts at the companies can develop into a consortium of employers to assist each other in locating jobs for relocated spouses. Organizations have also sponsored workshops for employees on preparing for relocation.

Working parent seminars

Recognizing the importance of time to working parents, seminars during the lunch hour have been held at companies covering topics such as: Managing Career and Family; Finding Quality Child Care; Child Care Tax Credit Act; Time Management; Stress Management; Career and Pregnancy; Career and Family. Speakers representing community resources can provide further advice to working couples about what is available in their area. The seminars also provide a network of working parents to share their concerns and offer support.

Conclusion

As has been identified, the world of work and our family structures are changing. An awareness of these changes and a personal exploration into what this means to students as individuals, as part of a family, and as part of an organization is essential. "The integration of business and personal life can only strengthen the family and make the corporation more vigorous and useful in the community" (Greiff and Munter, 1980).

Within organizations, there are a variety of programs and policies that can be implemented to foster compatibility, rather than conflict, between the employees' work and home life. Policies affecting alternate work schedules and places, flexible benefits, maternity/paternity leaves, child care, recruiting, and relocation are being examined by more and more companies. There is honest interest in these new approaches because many actually demonstrate bottom-line cost effectiveness.

REFERENCES AND SUGGESTED READINGS

Alter, J. *A Part-Time Career for a Full-Time You.* Boston: Houghton Mifflin, 1982.

Applegath, J. *Working Free . . . Practical Alternatives to the 9 to 5 Job.* New York: AMACOM, 1982.

Badan, C. *Work and Family—An Annotated Bibliography 1978-80.* Wheelock College Center for Parenting Studies, 1981.

Berk, A. "Modern Woman's Double Life." *Newsweek,* September 29, 1980, p. 10.

Bird, C. *The Two-Paycheck Marriage: How Women at Work are Changing Life in America.* New York: Rawson & Wade, 1979.

Bohen, H. *Balancing Jobs and Family Life—Do Flexible Schedules Help?* Philadelphia: Temple University Press, 1981.

Bryson, R., Bryson, J. B., and Johnson, M. F. "Family Size, Satisfaction, and Productivity in Dual Career Couples." *Psychology of Women Quarterly,* 1978, 3(1), 67-77.

Cardwell, J. W. "The Other Side of Relocation-Relocating the Spouse." *Personnel Administrator,* Sept. 1980, 53-56.

Catalyst. *Two-Career Families: A Bibliography of Relevant Readings.* 1980.

Catalyst Career & Family Center. *Corporations and Two-Career Families: Directions for the Future.* 1981.

Cecere, L. "Dual Careers Make for Marriages on the Run." *The Cleveland Plain Dealer,* July 25, 1982, p. 1C.

Cohen-Hagar, S. "Breastfeeding and Work: Can Women Manage Both?" *The Tampa Tribune-Times,* Feb. 28, 1982, p. 1G.

Collins, G. "Paternity Leave: A New Role for Fathers." *The New York Times STYLE,* Dec. 7, 1981, p B18.

Cooley, M. *Checklist for a Working Wife.* Garden City, NY: Dolphin Books, Doubleday & Co. Inc., 1979.

Edgerton, J. "Two-Income Tactics." *Money,* Feb. 1982, p. 47.

Evans, L. "Spouse Placement: Relocating a Dual-Career Family." *Maturity,* May/June 1980, p. 51.

Friday, N. *My Mother, Myself.* New York: Dell Publishing, 1977.

Friedman, D. "Where His Career Leads, Would You Follow?" *Working Woman,* June 1981, pp. 74-78.

Gilmore, C. B., and Fannin, W. R. "The Dual Career Couple: A Challenge to Personnel in the Eighties." *Business Horizons,* May/June 1982, pp. 36-41.

Gottschalk, E. C. "Firms Increasingly Help Spouses of Transferred Employees Find Jobs." *The Wall Street Journal,* Jan. 21, 1982, p. 29, ed. 4.

Grady, S. "One Job, Two Careers." *Working Woman,* May 1981, pp. 79-84, 108.

Gray, B., Loeffler, D., and Cooper, R. *Every Woman Works.* Belmont, California: Lifetime Learning Publications, 1982.

Greiff, B. S., and Munter, P. K. *Tradeoffs—Executive, Family and Organizational Life.* New York: Mentor Book—New American Library, 1980.

Gruber, I. "The Dual Career." *Women's Work,* May/June 1979, pp. 15-17.

Hall, F., and Hall, T. *The Two-Career Couple.* Reading, Mass.: Addison-Wesley, 1979.

Hoffman, M. "Business Begins to Address Needs of Dual-Career Families." *The Christian Science Monitor,* August 27, 1981, p. 17.

Hortsmann, V. "Beyond Nine to Five." *Working Woman,* May 1982, pp. 97-98.

Hunter, B. "Relocation." *Working Woman,* Feb. 1982, p. 16.

Jones, W. M. *Two Careers—One Marriage.* New York: AMACOM, 1980.

Kahnweiler, J. B., and Kahnweiler, W. M. "A Dual-Career Family Workshop for College Undergraduates." *The Vocational Guidance Quarterly,* March 1980, pp. 225-29.

Kamerman, B. *Parenting in an Unresponsive Society: Managing Work and Family.* New York: The Free Press-Division, McMillan Publishing Co. Inc., 1980.

Katz, L. C. "When Mother Goes to Work." *Parents,* Feb. 1982, p. 100.

Kuzmack, L. G., and Salomon, G. *Working and Mothering—A Study of 97 Jewish Career Women with Three or More Children.* New York: National Jewish Family Center—The American Jewish Committee, 1980.

Lee, N. "The Dual-Career Couple: Benefits and Pitfalls." *Management Review,* Jan. 1981, pp. 46-52.

Levinson, J. *The Season's of a Man's Life.* New York: Ballantine Books, 1978.

Longshore, S. J. "How Working Mothers Work It Out." *Redbook,* May 1980, p. 27.

Loudis, C. R. *Summary of Results: Analysis of the RESOURCE Survey on Working Mothers.* Research paper, March 19, 1980.

Louis Harris and Associates, Inc. *Families at Work: Strengths and Strains.* General Mills Study, 1981.

Meier, S. *Job Sharing—A New Pattern for Quality of Work and Life.* Chicago: W. E. UpJohn Institute for Employment Research, 1978.

Norris, G., and Miller, J. *The Working Mother's Complete Handbook.* New York: Sunrise Book, E. P. Dutton, 1979.

Office of the Governor of North Carolina, *Helping Working Parents: Child Care Options for Business.* Department of Human Resources, 1981.

Ogden, W. *How to Succeed in Business and Marriage.* New York: AMACOM, 1978.

Olds, S. W. *The Mother who Works Outside the Home.* New York: Child Study Press, 1975.

O'Toole, P. "Moving Ahead by Moving Around," *Savvy,* April 1982, p. 37.

Price, J. *How to Have a Child and Keep your Job.* Martin's Press, 1979.

Raffel, D. "Benefits, Cafeteria-Style Plans." *Working Woman,* Dec. 1981, pp. 28-29.

Rapoport, R., and Rapoport, R. *Working Couples.* New York: Harper Colophon, 1978.

Report from the Editors of Better Homes & Gardens. *How Work is Affecting American Families,* 1981.

RESOURCE: Careers. *Report of the Dual Career Project,* 1983.

Rice, F. *Working Mother's Guide to Child Development.*New Jersey: Prentice-Hall, 1979.

Rice, G. *Dual Career Marriage Conflict and Treatment.* New York: The Free Press, 1979.

Riechers, M. "When You Both Work." *Women's Work,* May/June 1978, pp. 5-10.

Sachs, S. "Jobs and Marriage Don't Always Mix." *The Cleveland Press,* March 7, 1982, p. 03A.

Schein, H. "The Individual, the Organization, and the Career: A Conceptual Scheme." In Kolb et al. (Eds.), *Organizational Psychology: A Book of Readings,* 3d ed., pp. 498-514. New York: Prentice-Hall, 1979.

Sheehy, G. *Passages.* New York: E. P. Dutton & Company, Inc., 1976.

Shore, L. A. "Dual Careers Lead to Cleveland." *Northern Ohio Business Journal,* September 1982, pp. 70-71.

Strauss, N. "The Dual-Career Phenomenon: Is It a Threat to Corporate Relocation?" *Mobility,* Nov./Dec. 1981, p. 34.

Trunzo, C. E. "Mixing Children and Jobs." *Money,* Nov. 1980, pp. 80-84.

U. S. Department of Labor. *Children of Working Mothers*. Bureau of Labor Statistics, 1977.

_____. *Community Solutions for Child Care*. Office of the Secretary Women's Bureau, Aug., 1979.

_____. *Marital and Family Characteristics of Workers 1970 to 1978*. Bureau of Labor Statistics, April 1979.

Wolfe, M., and Kolb, A. "Beyond Specialization: The Quest for Integration in Midcareer." In C. B. Deer (Ed.), *Work, Family, and the Career*, pp. 239-65. Praeger Special Studies, 1980, p. 240.

_____. "Career Development, Personal Growth, and Experiential Learning." In Kolb et al. (Eds.), *Organizational Psychology: A Book of Readings*, 3d ed., pp. 535-63. New York: Prentice-Hall, 1979.

Motherhood and the
Career-Minded Woman[1]

Dorothea Nuechterlein, Valparaiso University

We might as well face the facts: American men have seldom had to choose between, on the one hand, achieving all the occupational success of which they are capable, and, on the other hand, becoming successful parents.

Women must.

This disparity in the opportunity structure has grown as increasing numbers of women have entered the labor force. It has been the basis of much conflict within individual women, between husbands and wives, and throughout segments of our society.

It is especially difficult for professional women: those whose commitments to their work are long-term, based on intensive training and increasing responsibility, and whose reasons and rewards for their labors are personal as well as financial.

This paper explores some of the changes in outlook that have come about in our society; how opinions are being formed within today's young adult educated population; and the career woman's double bind. It concludes with a possible strategy for the future.

Historical Background

Several historical factors have produced the climate for change in American women's roles today. For one thing, the United States has had since its beginning a proclaimed allegiance to the principle of equality. Although many persons and groups were excluded from this ideology in the early period, the contradictions between the ideal and the real have brought pressures to bear on government and governed alike, until the rights and privileges of citizenship have been offered to most residents of the land.

While the ballot is primary in a democracy, education is the tool that forges unity and commonality. There can be no doubt that our system of compulsory

153

universal education creates the basis for a practical equality among the races and between the sexes in this country. At every level, those who study the same subject matter receive the same training. Today's college woman—who is now part of the majority sex on most campuses—is prepared equally with her male counterpart to make a meaningful contribution to the world of work.

Despite lingering questions as to whether capacities in certain subject areas or forms of reasoning vary somewhat by sex, few today would suggest that women students are less able than, or are intellectually inferior to, men. Furthermore, it is a given in advanced technological, bureaucratic societies that occupational roles are assigned by ability and achievement, not by ascribed characteristics. Rationality insists that race, background, sex, or religious persuasion are not sufficient cause to deprive society of the competence and skills of talented individuals.

Secondly, the extension of the life span during this century for everyone, but especially for women, has had an enormous effect on role choice. A female born today can expect to live nearly eighty years. Even she who doesn't marry until she graduates from college, and then is financially able to remain at home until her children are of college age, is likely to face a third or more of her anticipated lifetime still ahead when her child-bearing and -rearing days are over. Given the price tag on education, it is hardly surprising that many of these women hope to achieve some return on that investment by finding gainful employment.

It is well-documented that the stay-at-home mother is becoming continually less common. Although "immediate financial need" is the reason employed mothers often give for their choice, their other primary motivation relates to expanded longevity: active motherhood simply takes too small a bite out of one's lifetime to remain the sum and substance of her existence. In view of the fact that time away from the work world so negatively affects one's future participation in it, and in light of studies which fail to show any significant differences between children of employed vs. unemployed mothers, the trade-off hardly seems necessary to many.

A further inducement to work comes from the divorce/widowhood statistics: women can by no means assume they will be financially taken care of forever. The Displaced Homemaker, she who is left behind by death or desertion and robbed of the only way of life she has ever known, is largely responsible for the distressing figures on female-headed households trying to exist below the poverty level. Even the woman who prefers not to work at all throughout her marriage is undeniably more secure if she is at least prepared to do so should the need arise.

A third factor has emerged in the past two decades which is perhaps most instrumental in influencing women's move from the buying to the selling side of the marketplace. Throughout most of history, as Freud pointed out, anatomy has been destiny. Once a woman reached physical maturity, she was very largely tied to her biological reproductive capacity. With the shorter life span and the higher fertility rate typical of former times and still prevalent in many parts of today's world, the representative female in most societies could expect to spend the greater part of her adulthood in mothering. Even if she did not, she was *potentially* pregnant at all times. It is small wonder, then, that the division of labor was so often defined along sex lines, which were consequently seen as inherent or even God-given.

That state of affairs simply no longer exists in modern America. The contraceptive revolution has changed the very nature of reproduction. For the first time in history, humans have nearly unconditional control over their generative powers and processes. Whatever one's personal views on the consequences of the separation between sex as procreation and sex as recreation, that is the situation that exists today. Most Americans can, if they desire, choose both whether and when to bring children into the world. That they do not always exercise that choice, as the concurrent rise in illegitimacy would indicate, does nothing to detract from the fact that no woman need be barred or dissuaded from participation in any of men's roles simply on the basis of possible pregnancy, as once was true.

Taken together, then—an ideal of equality which permeates the identical education afforded the sexes, a lengthened life which decreases the proportion of years needed for child care, and control over the one physiological fact that had created the major barrier to wider participation—the old assumption that every woman's place is in the home is no longer tenable.

Changing Attitudes

One of the traps social analysts must avoid is the temptation to look at the future strictly through eyes attuned to the past and the present. We cannot predict future knowledge, of course; that knowledge may bring about philosophical upheavals or technological alterations; social arrangements are often created out of the cloth woven from new ideas and products. As the nineteenth-century feminists could not foresee the great transformations that have occurred in women's lot (what they foresaw is not quite what happened), so today's visionaries cannot be certain of what lies ahead. Yet we do know that we are in a transition stage. The old foundations for male/female relationships have shifted and the former rules no longer apply in their entirety. Where are we really going, and how shall we get there?

In the past half dozen years I have conducted a small-scale research project among undergraduates that points to a growing common viewpoint between young males and females regarding egalitarianism within the home. By means of an attitude inventory developed in the 1950s and modified during the last decade, students are asked to state their expectations regarding possible future marriage roles; then they go over the same list, guessing how their opposite-sex peers would respond. The ten statements used (See Appendix) deal with such items as whether financial decisions will be made jointly, whether child care and other household responsibilities should be shared, and whether the wife should combine motherhood and career.

In a dozen classrooms, totalling 500 students on two campuses in different North American countries, I have found three consistent patterns. (1) Comparing female responses with male guesses, the men prove to be remarkably accurate. In fact, it is not unusual to find on selected items that males will guess the females to be more liberal (liberated?) than the women's statements would suggest. For example, one item asks whether it would be undesirable for the wife to be better educated than the husband; females are often more ambivalent about that possibility than males expect them to be (and, in fact, than males often answer themselves). Occasionally, the males will guess a trend in the wrong direction, such as with a statement concerning husbands being mainly providers for and discipliners of children; the women seem to expect their mates to have a more complete relationship with their children than the guessers would believe. On the whole, though, there is an overwhelmingly correct assessment of female attitudes by males.

(2) This is not true the other way around; females are usually quite mistaken about male attitudes on most of the given items, with only a few trends in the right direction. An example here is that most young males seem to support the idea that if both partners work outside the home, both should share responsibility for work inside as well; however, barely half the women guess that men will feel that way. Few males state opposition to wives combining motherhood and career, but females expect otherwise. On several other points, such as whether the husbands should devote their weekends to R & R (Rest and Recreation) or whether money decisions should be made jointly, most classes have shown women assuming men will take conservative positions, whereas in fact males often feel quite strongly on the nontraditional side. Thus, females have been much less successful in speculating about male attitudes.

(3) The most significant comparison is that between the attitudes of both sexes. On nearly every issue there is extraordinary consensus among the students surveyed, with males at times expressing more liberal attitudes than do their female counterparts. Of course this is an impressionistic study, done without scientific controls, asking respondents to project attitudes into the future. We all know that what we say is not necessarily what we do. Yet, since every replication largely confirms those preceding it, the suspicion emerges that present-day North American collegians indeed share many expectations concerning possible equalization in marriage roles, but only the males realize it.

Students are always astonished at the results of this little exercise. After the men declare that it proves their natural superiority, we discuss such things as the role of the women's movement in recent years, which has provided a platform through which the wishes of many women have been made known. This has created a stereotypical picture, which explains why so often the men assume women to be more liberal than they are. Men have no such vehicle for expressing the fact that they have been responding favorably to women's needs and have begun to change their own opinions. While men know what women-in-general think about many relationship issues, women have little opportunity to determine the views of men-in-general. Thus younger men, it seems, are saddled with stereotypes based on views that may have been accurate previously, but that appear to be going out of date.

If it is true that young men's ideas on marital equality are converging with those of young women, how have they gotten that way? I went back to the original article on marriage roles by Marie Dunn, published in 1960, which found that role expectations had already begun to evolve at that point. While most retained the traditional conception of the division of labor (husband working outside the home, wife inside it), most agreed that if the wife did go out to work the homemaking duties should be shared. Both sexes felt child care and major decisions should be joint ventures. Above all, they believed firmly in equal access to higher education. Education is, after all, the supreme individualizing experience, and the Fifties high school generation became the first to participate in mass college enrollments. Dunn thus expected that the trend in American family life would continue to develop in an egalitarian direction.

College students of the Fifties are the parents of college students of the Seventies and Eighties. It seems reasonable to suppose that, as parents, those mid-century adolescents, with their leanings toward family equality, passed those values on to their children. Even women whose husbands did not, in fact, treat them equally could socialize their sons in the new ways of thinking. As women have increasingly gone out to work, especially in higher level positions, they have served as role models for both sons and daughters. At any rate, educated youth of today seem to assume that woman's place is where she wants it to be.

Practical Adjustments

Early leaders of the present feminist movement claim that they did not intend a polarization between women's selfhood and the family; they wanted transformation, not extinction, of family roles. Betty Friedan's *Feminine Mystique* (1963) was the image of all women, regardless of their individual talents or preferences, as being totally fulfilled and satisfied in their roles as wives, mothers, and servers of others' needs; the boundaries had become so petrified that many women could no longer live and breathe within them.

Subsequently, Friedan (1981) speaks of a feminist mystique, which she labels the attempt by extremists to deny women's needs for love and personal relations. But both women and men look to the family for security, love, and roots in life, and both sexes must work together in living out their equality before further progress can appear. There can be no going back to the old ways, because as women changed their own lives, it became possible for men to do the same. They are no longer burdened with the demand to always be strong enough (emotionally, financially) for two; increasing egalitarianism has brought a sharing of both strengths and weaknesses, enabling both sexes to be more complete in themselves. Just as dependency is no longer the only image that fits womanhood, John Wayne is not the role model all men are expected to emulate.

Not all men are happy with the change, as it requires giving up being catered to as the center of their universe. The transition has been especially difficult for those who were brought up under the old set of rules, and those who are unsure of their women's love. The benefits, however, include both the economic cooperation often so necessary in these times, as well as a fuller participation in their children's lives. Men and women both may discover anew that they are indeed dependent upon one another—for security, love, and intimacy, those qualities that bring delight and meaning to our lives.

Columbia University sociologist William Goode doubts if women will ever give up their new sense of self-respect and freedom.

> Males will stubbornly resist, but reluctantly adjust; because women will continue to want more equality and will be unhappy if they do not get it; because men on the average will prefer that their women be happy; because neither will find an adequate substitute for the other sex; because neither will be able to find an alternative social system. (Quoted in Friedan, 1982, p. 155.)

Having always taken their superiority for granted, Goode suggests, makes it difficult for men to recognize the unearned advantages they have always held. These are now threatened, as women become competitors for desirable jobs which were previously assumed to be for men only. Furthermore, the skills and qualities now in demand in many top-level positions include the intuitions and sensitivities to others' needs once thought to be feminine qualities, which men have heretofore often been obliged to repress.

It is imperative, then, that the sexes work together in learning to adjust to the new social arrangements which history and upheaval have brought about. The abstract polarization between equality and family does not seem prevalent in everyday life for most people, as women together with their men work through the practical questions of employment, child care, home tending, and decision-making. If this is true—and I see this adjustment process in the lives of my own friends and acquaintances—then the students who have responded to my survey have already begun to prepare themselves for realistic adult roles and relationships with one another. Any of us, man or woman, should be able to find a place both in and out of the home.

Confronting the Dilemma

Major problems remain. We are not, after all, totally autonomous beings. It is one thing to strive for and even achieve equality in the intimate one man/one woman relationship, and quite another to sustain that when the surrounding social structure has little flexibility in allowing for personal rearrangements.

To return to the problem posed at the beginning of this paper, there is an implicit sex bias in our system of allocating upper-level positions in the occupational formation. Certainly, women are now legally entitled to compete for any station they wish; however, they must conform to the standards developed when such opportunities applied only to men. There are two difficulties here: first, in the good old days it was more or less assumed that the professional man had someone at home handling such details of life as children, food preparation, and social obligations. Unfortunately, the working woman doesn't have a wife, as the saying goes—quite often she has to shoulder the lion's share of the homefront burdens in addition to her paid duties.

That double load has in the past often been seen as acceptable, because women's work was viewed as marginal and momentary: before marriage, during hard times, in case the marriage went badly. Paid labor was thought of as temporary, even when it was not. Some women have always worked, but most were at the bottom of the heap in responsibility and reward, with limited commitment to their outside labor. They might have two jobs to perform, but at least their nights and weekends were free for the second.

The crunch has come with the increased flow of women into professional and career positions. Such work does not neatly fit a time clock. There are goals to reach and tasks to perform, in whatever ways and however long they take. A wife/mother in this situation may play both roles fully only by becoming Superwoman, at risk to either her health, her advancement, or her relationships. It seems, though, that when two super-achievers are married to one another, it is the woman's career that must be most flexible. As Caroline Bird puts it, "Couples say they regard themselves as equal partners, but most of them don't act that way" (1979, p. 57).

"Well," one might counter, "that is hardly the fault or responsibility of the employer," and to be sure the personal arrangement made between a woman and her man can go a long way toward alleviation of the dual burden. However, even the rare woman who gets splendid cooperation from her husband and is able to devote time and energies to career-advancing extras—traveling, publishing, meetings—is often perceived as being a typical overburdened female. Sometimes a boss "protects" her by withholding special opportunities, thereby stunting her potential. Other bosses, perhaps wary of being accused of showing any signs of favoritism, push such a woman to the limit, almost insuring her failure in either home life or career.

The second problem with the male model for job success is much more serious. Women are not men. Their life cycles and biographies are not identical to those of men. This goes beyond simple individuality, such as the fact that men are not exactly alike, either. For we must again confront the biological fact: women, not men, bear children, and the cost of doing so may have substantial consequences in terms of their work life.

Seniority is an important principle in our employment hierarchy, and time lost often cannot be made up, especially if it extends over months or years. The woman who goes back to her job immediately after childbirth is regarded by many—often even herself—as a bad mother, but the one who takes a leave of absence or quits altogether for a while is not considered serious about her work. Then when she attempts to return, she normally starts back at or near the bottom, far behind men of her age, competing with the younger "comers" of both sexes.

There is no way, naturally, to evaluate the experience or wisdom one might gain from motherhood to determine how it might contribute to one's participation in the wider sphere. (There is a great deal of condescending lip service paid to the idea of the social utility of women's work in raising the next generation, but when it comes to some means by which to channel that usefulness into larger service, the show of solicitude rapidly vanishes.)

The decline in fertility among working women can be partially blamed on the recognition of the economic and status deprivations they will face if they choose to have children. Yet the costs of not doing so are significant, also. Women who choose not to be parents miss something which cannot be duplicated in any other way—and so do men. For obviously, if women choose not to become mothers, men will involuntarily be prevented from becoming fathers. As mating patterns in this country have become increasingly homogamous, the option for men to marry "downward," selecting less career-minded partners to carry their children, has become less attractive than when that solution was used earlier in the century when the first wave of "career women" either remained single or chose childlessness.

What's to be done? The extremists say that women may be exploited and disadvantaged, unfortunately—but life is tough. Someone has to take care of the children, and since women are there from the beginning it "naturally" is their lot to see the job through. Finding some way of making that experience pay off on the opportunity ladder would be unfair, however, since *men* would then be disadvantaged. (We might notice that from this perspective, certain unfairnesses appear to be more unfair than others, depending on who is standing in which spot.) People have to be "qualified," which means they have to accomplish things, which means they have to spend their time and talents producing ideas and plans, not babies. And anyway, aren't there studies showing differences in hormones and aggression and such and doesn't that maybe show that females are less suited than men to high level competition—especially considering PMT (premenstrual tension) and all?

I prefer the positive approach. It is utopianism, of course, to say, "Suppose we could redesign the universe?" But suppose we could? Social arrangements are human inventions, after all. Our contemporary patterns evolved over a long period of history, but their present existence does not prove that they are unalterable. While we cannot literally rip everything out and start afresh, creating ideal sketches can help us to see possible modifications in existing structures.

For a start, my vision would get rid of the notion of someone standing behind the company fellow keeping the home fires burning. That model is outmoded;

it does not apply even to many men today. If the assumption were rather that each worker also has major responsibilities in the private realm, there might be fewer stress-related health problems, along with providing more equivalency in the job market.

Instead of using men as the center of the universe and determining how nearly women can duplicate their strengths, I think we could do much more than we are at present to reevaluate positions and the qualities needed to fulfill their requirements. The current gerontological advance in our society is already leading to questions about the relative values of youth and age, experience and wisdom. Length of service does not always equate with loyalty; creativity is at times more valuable than factual knowledge. There are too many workers chasing too few openings, so there should be a buyer's market on the employment scene; but all the guidelines for hiring and promotion seem to be leftover from bygone days when persons were less plentiful than positions, and those guidelines tend to work against the advancement of women.

We might also explore, at least on a temporary basis, the possibility of assigning certain portions of the hierarchy in any given field according to sex, so that males would compete with one another, leaving females to do the same. That suggests quotas, I know, which many reject because they seem to violate the rules of fair competition. But we already have a discriminatory system in effect. It is stratified by layers, with males dominating most of the upper levels and the most prestigious occupations. My scheme, or something like it, would allow for parallel paths up the career ladder.

The career-minded woman's dilemma touches us all, to some degree, as it does our children. Certainly we cannot change the situation overnight, and our options are not without limits. But change we will. One definition of an autonomous being is the individual who attempts to influence and control social forces, rather than simply being influenced and controlled by them. We can do that best, it would seem, on a collective basis. Perhaps individually we are better at seeing insurmountable problems than we are at discovering stepping stones to solutions. Our challenge—our "place"—is to work together to see to it that woman's dilemma does not become our common defeat.

Implications for Teachers and Trainers

Both men and women must face squarely the problem of family/career conflict. Educational institutions and other organizations have an obligation to foster discussion of this issue—schools because they supposedly prepare students for the "real world," employers because they are a large part of that world. It is easy for individuals, especially the young, to assume that somehow "everything will work out," or even to be oblivious to the practical difficulties they may encounter as they take their places in adult society.

The past two decades have brought an abundance of research and writing on this matter; the attached list is a mere sample of resources that could be used in raising some of the questions that need to be dealt with. In particular one should help both sexes confront—through active discussion—the assumptions they hold, often subconsciously, to see if the pictures in their heads are compatible with reality. One might ask:

1. What is the nature of competition between men and women? Does it differ from that within one sex or the other?

2. Do males and females possess differing skills? If so, how can equality in the job market be achieved? If not, why do differential wage and opportunity levels exist, and what can be done to eradicate them?

3. What are the true costs of parenthood in dual-career families? Can those costs be shared equally between the father and the mother?

4. Given the historical division of labor (man outside, woman inside the home), is it realistic to suppose that couples will be willing to change to a shared-outside, shared-inside pattern? If one partner is willing and the other is not, how might the conflict be resolved?

Solutions to these and other questions are not obvious, but the problem must be faced. There is too much at stake, for the larger social order as well as for private persons and family units, to do otherwise.

Appendix

Marriage Role Expectation Inventory

Please complete the inventory below twice, answering first on the basis of your own feelings, then answering the way you think typical members of the opposite sex on this campus would feel. Mark your own feelings in the column which corresponds to your sex, and your guesses about the opposite sex in the remaining column.

Mark SA for strongly agree, A for agree, U for undecided, D for disagree, and SD for strongly disagree.

In my marriage I expect that . . .

FEMALE FEELINGS   MALE FEELINGS

_____   1. if there is a difference of opinion, the husband   _____
                will decide where to live.

_____   2. the wife's opinion will carry as much weight as   _____
                the husband's on money matters.

_____   3. it would be undesirable for the wife to be better   _____
              educated than the husband.

_____   4. the wife will combine motherhood and career if   _____
              that proves possible.

_____   5. the husband will be the "boss" who says what is   _____
              to be done and what is not to be done.

_____   6. the husband will leave the care of the children   _____
              entirely up to the wife when they are babies.

_____   7. if the wife prefers a career to having children,   _____
              we will follow that choice.

_____   8. the husband and wife will share responsibility for   _____
              housework if both of us work outside the home.

_____   9. the husband's major responsibility to our children   _____
              will be to make a good living, provide a home,
              and make them obey.

_____   10. weekends will be a period of rest for the husband,   _____
              so that he will not be expected to assist with
              cooking and housekeeping.

Please indicate your own sex by circling below:

Female   Male

NOTE

1. An earlier version of this paper appeared in *The Cresset,* 1982, 45, 4-10.

REFERENCES AND SUGGESTED READINGS

Barnett, R., and Baruch, G. "Toward Economic Independence: Women's Involvement in Multiple
    Roles." In D. G. McGuigan (Ed.), *Women's Lives: New Theory, Research and Policy,* Ann Arbor:
    University of Michigan Center for Continuing Education of Women, 1980, pp. 69-83.

Berch, B. *The Endless Day: The Political Economy of Women and Work.* New York: Harcourt Brace
    Jovanovich, 1982.

Bernard, J. "Changing Family Life Styles: One Role, Two Roles, Shared Roles." In L. K. Howe (Ed.), *The Future of the Family*. New York: Simon and Schuster, 1972, pp. 235-46.

_____. *The Female World*. New York: Free Press, 1981.

Bird, C. *The Two-Paycheck Marriage*. New York: Rawson, Wade, 1979.

Chafe, W. H. *The American Woman: Her Changing Social, Economic, and Political Roles, 1920-1970*. New York: Oxford University Press, 1972.

Colwill, N. L. *The New Partnership: Women and Men in Organizations*. Palo Alto: Mayfield, 1982.

Crosby, F. J. *Relative Deprivation and Working Women*. New York: Oxford University Press, 1982.

Degler, C. N. *At Odds*. Oxford: Oxford University Press, 1980.

Dunn, M. S. "Marriage Role Expectations of Adolescents." *Marriage and Family Living,* 22 (May 1960): 99-111.

Friedan, B. *The Feminine Mystique*. New York: Dell, 1963.

_____. *The Second Stage*. New York: Summitt, 1981.

Giele, J. Z. *Women and the Future: Changing Sex Roles in Modern America*. New York: Free Press, 1978.

Hall, F. S., and Hall, D. T. *The Two-Career Couple*. Reading, MA: Addison-Wesley, 1979.

Kessler-Harris, A. *Women Have Always Worked: A Historical Overview*. Old Westbury, NY: Feminist Press, 1981.

Lott, B. *Becoming a Woman: The Socialization of Gender*. Springfield, IL: Thomas, 1981.

Peck, E. *The Baby Trap*. New York: Pinnacle, 1971.

Rothman, S. M. *Woman's Proper Place*. New York: Basic, 1978.

Sochen, J. *Herstory: A Record of the American Woman's Past*. Palo Alto: Mayfield, 1981.

Stromberg, A. H., and Harkess, S. *Women Working: Theories and Facts in Perspective*. Palo Alto: Mayfield, 1978.

Veevers, J. E. "The Life Style of Voluntarily Childless Couples." In L. E. Larson (Ed.), *The Canadian Family in Comparative Perspective*. Scarborough, Ont: Prentice-Hall, 1976, pp. 395-411.

The Impact of Perceived Career Interruptions on Individuals and Organizations

Linda Ellison Sugarman, The University of Akron

According to Department of Labor Statistics (1982), 53 percent of all women are now in the labor force. In 1980, in the age group 25-54, almost 64 percent of women were in the work force, and of those younger aged women 20-24, 69 percent were in the work force. It has been predicted by the Urban Institute, Washington, D.C., that by 1990, 75 percent of the married women will be in the labor force as compared with 50 percent in 1979. According to *U.S. News and World Report* (5/3/82) the 1980 census showed that 46 percent of women with children under 6 were in the labor force compared to 31 percent in 1970. More women are entering the labor force and more of them are choosing business as a career. The *Chronicle of Higher Education* (9/17/79 and 1/15/81) shows that the proportion of business bachelor degrees awarded to women increased from 9.7 percent in the year 1971-72 to 30.7 percent in the 1978-79 year, and that trend appears to be continuing.

When business organizations were predominantly male, one could expect that a man entering a business career would progress through a rather stable and continuous career pattern. Now that women make up a larger and larger proportion of supervisory, managerial, and executive levels in business organizations, we can no longer expect that all career business people will have continuous career patterns. Many working women, because of "stopping out" for motherhood, will not progress in a stable and continuous career pattern. This paper will present findings from data collected in a study related to career interruption expectations of female business majors.

Recent Research

A review of the related literature indicates that most working women anticipate careers, marriage, and children. A study by the Catalyst Organization, *Corporations and Two-Career Families: Directions for the Future* surveyed two-career families to determine how many families were planning to remain childless. The study found that only 17 percent of these two-career families anticipated not having children.

In Harmon's (1981) study of women, only 8 percent of the women surveyed expected to remain single. Of those who were married or anticipated marriage, 84 percent anticipated marriage and children. In rating the relative importance of family and career, only 10 percent of those surveyed by Harmon rated career as more important than family, while 55 percent rated their importance equally. Forty percent of the women in Harmon's study expected to work with time off to raise a family. Only 2 percent of Harmon's respondents expected minimal employment during their lives. The Harmon study was a follow-up on an earlier study and shows a large increase over the earlier 1968 study in the number of women who planned to work all their lives. Forty-seven percent planned to work most of their lives as opposed to only 27 percent in the earlier study.

The Study

With more and more women choosing business as their field, what expectations do today's women have of their careers and their lifestyles? A questionnaire designed to discern career and career-interruption expectations of women students in business was distributed by the author at an urban midwestern university. This questionnaire was distributed to Junior and Senior women majoring in business disciplines and to Sophomore women enrolled in Principles of Accounting. Questionnaires were mailed to all declared women business majors, and 350 usable questionnaires were returned to give a response rate of 85 percent. An additional 128 questionnaires were returned by women enrolled in Principles of Accounting classes who indicated they intended to major in business but had not officially done so.

Plans after graduation

The following questions were included in the study:

Question: Immediately after graduation, I intend to:

> a. enter full-time employment
> b. enter part-time employment
> c. go to graduate school
> d. I do not intend to seek employment

Table 1 shows that 78.5 percent of the College of Business Administration women intend to seek full-time employment after graduation or are already employed fulltime. If we break this down by age, we find that 87.7 percent of the women College of Business Administration students under 25 (traditional-age college women) intend to seek full-time employment immediately after graduation.

TABLE 1

Cross Tabulation of College of Business Administration Women
by Age and Immediate Plans After Graduation

Count Row Pct Col Pct Tot Pct	No Response	(A) Full-Time Employ-ment	(B) Part-Time Employ-ment	(C) Grad School	(D) Not Intend-ing to Seek Employment	Combina-tion of A, B, C	Row Total
Under	3	285	6	16	3	12	325
25	0.9	87.7	1.8	4.9	0.9	3.7	68.0
	100.0						
		76.0	40.0	59.3	50.0	23.1	
	0.6	59.6	1.3	3.3	0.6	2.5	
25-29	0	46	1	5	2	26	80
	0.0	57.5	1.3	6.3	2.5	32.5	16.7
	0.0	12.3	6.7	18.5	33.3	50.0	
	0.0	9.6	0.2	1.0	0.4	5.4	
30-34	0	24	4	5	0	5	38
	0.0	63.2	10.5	13.2	0.0	13.2	7.9
	0.0	6.4	26.7	18.5	0.0	9.6	
	0.0	5.0	0.8	1.0	0.0	1.0	
35-39	0	14	1	0	1	6	22
	0.0	63.6	4.5	0.0	4.5	27.3	4.6
	0.0	3.7	6.7	0.0	16.7	11.5	
	0.0	2.9	0.2	0.0	0.2	1.3	
40-49	0	4	3	1	0	3	11
	0.0	36.4	27.3	9.1	0.0	27.3	2.3
	0.0	1.1	20.0	3.7	0.0	5.8	
	0.0	0.8	0.6	0.2	0.0	0.6	
50 and	0	2	0	0	0	0	2
over	0.0	100.0	0.0	0.0	0.0	0.0	0.4
	0.0	0.5	0.0	0.0	0.0	0.0	
	0.0	0.4	0.0	0.0	0.0	0.0	
Column Total	3	375	15	27	6	52	478
	0.6	78.5	3.1	5.6	1.3	10.9	100.0

TABLE 2

Cross Tabulation of College of Business Administration Women by Age and Reason for Career Interruption

Count Row Pct Col Pct Tot Pct	No Response	(A) Continuous	(B) Marriage	(C) Child Rearing	(D) Further Education	(E) Terminated with Marriage	Total
Under	2	84	19	203	16	1	325
25	0.6	26.8	5.8	62.5	4.9	0.3	68.0
	66.7	42.2	90.5	86.4	84.2	100.0	
	0.4	17.6	4.0	42.5	3.3	0.2	
25-29	0	51	1	25	3	0	80
	0.0	63.8	1.3	31.3	3.8	0.0	16.7
	0.0	25.6	4.8	10.6	15.8	0.0	
	0.0	10.7	0.2	5.2	0.8	0.0	
30-34	0	31	0	7	0	0	38
	0.0	81.6	0.0	18.4	0.0	0.0	7.9
	0.0	15.6	0.0	3.0	0.0	0.0	
	0.0	6.5	0.0	1.5	0.0	0.0	
35-39	1	20	1	0	0	0	22
	4.5	90.9	4.5	0.0	0.0	0.0	4.6
	33.3	10.1	4.8	0.0	0.0	0.0	
	0.2	4.2	0.2	0.0	0.0	0.0	
40-49	0	11	0	0	0	0	11
	0.0	100.0	0.0	0.0	0.0	0.0	2.3
	0.0	5.5	0.0	0.0	0.0	0.0	
	0.0	2.3	0.0	0.0	0.0	0.0	
50 and	0	2	0	0	0	0	2
over	0.0	100.0	0.0	0.0	0.0	0.0	0.4
	0.0	1.0	0.0	0.0	0.0	0.0	
	0.0	0.4	0.0	0.0	0.0	0.0	
Column	3	199	21	235	19	1	478
Total	0.6	41.6	4.4	49.2	4.0	0.2	100.0

Duration of work life

Question: I expect my work life to be:

  a. continuous
  b. interrupted for marriage
  c. interrupted for pregnancy and/or child rearing
  d. interrupted for further education
  e. terminated with marriage

Forty-one percent of the College of Business Administration women expect their work life to be continuous, but of the traditional age group, only 26 percent expect this to be so. Sixty-two percent of those in the under 25 age group expect to interrupt their careers for pregnancy and/or child rearing. In the 25-29 age group, 31 percent expect to interrupt their careers for pregnancy and/or child rearing. In the 30 and over age groups, many have finished their families and do not need to interrupt their careers for this reason. Only one student out of 478 expected her career to terminate with marriage (Table 2).

Length of anticipated interruption

Question: If you expect your work life interrupted, indicate length of interruption:

  a. none to less than one year
  b. one to two years
  c. two to five years
  d. six to nine years
  e. ten to fifteen years
  f. 16 years or more

Forty-one percent of the College of Business Administration women indicated that they expected that their careers would be continuous. Of those who expected to interrupt their careers, over 50 percent expected to interrupt their careers for more than one year; 19 percent expected to interrupt their careers for more than 5 years. In the age group under 25, the number indicating they would interrupt their careers rises to 64 percent. In this under 25 age group, almost 28 percent of the respondents expect to interrupt their careers for more than 5 years (Table 3).

Marriage and motherhood

Question: a. I am presently married

  b. I am presently not married but would like to be married within the next 5 years

TABLE 3

Cross Tabulation of College of Business Administration Women by Age and Length of Perceived Career Interruption

Count Row Pct Col Pct Tot Pct	None to Less Than One	One to 2 Years	Two to 5 Years	Six to 9 Years	Ten to 15 Years	16 and Over	Row Total
Under 25	115 35.4 48.7 24.1	37 11.4 80.4 7.7	83 25.5 83.8 17.4	35 10.8 92.1 7.3	44 13.5 91.7 9.2	11 3.4 100.0 2.3	325 68.0
25-29	54 67.5 22.9 11.3	7 8.8 15.2 1.5	12 15.0 12.1 2.5	3 3.8 7.9 0.6	4 5.0 8.3 0.8	0 0.0 0.0 0.0	80 16.7
30-34	34 89.5 14.4 7.1	1 2.6 2.2 0.2	3 7.9 3.0 0.6	0 0.0 0.0 0.0	0 0.0 0.0 0.0	0 0.0 0.0 0.0	38 7.9
35-39	20 90.9 8.5 4.2	1 4.5 2.2 0.2	1 4.5 1.0 0.2	0 0.0 0.0 0.0	0 0.0 0.0 0.0	0 0.0 0.0 0.0	22 4.6
40-49	11 100.0 4.7 2.3	0 0.0 0.0 0.0	0 0.0 0.0 0.0	0 0.0 0.0 0.0	0 0.0 0.0 0.0	0 0.0 0.0 0.0	11 2.3
50 and over	2 100.0 0.8 0.4	0 0.0 0.0 0.0	0 0.0 0.0 0.0	0 0.0 0.0 0.0	0 0.0 0.0 0.0	0 0.0 0.0 0.0	2 0.4
Column Total	236 49.4	46 9.6	99 20.7	38 7.9	48 10.0	11 2.3	478 100.0

TABLE 4

Cross Tabulation of College of Business Administration Women by Age and by Marriage Intentions

Count Row Pct Col Pct Tot Pct	No Response	(A) Presently Married	(B) Next Five Years	(C) After Five Years	(D) Will Not Marry	Row Total
Under 25	1 0.3 25.0 0.2	31 9.5 25.8 6.5	194 59.7 84.3 40.6	86 26.5 91.5 18.0	13 4.0 43.3 2.7	325 68.0
25-29	0 0.0 0.0 0.0	41 51.3 34.2 8.6	27 33.8 11.7 5.6	5 6.3 5.3 1.0	7 8.8 23.3 1.5	80 16.7
30-34	2 5.3 50.0 0.4	27 71.1 22.5 5.6	6 15.8 2.6 1.3	0 0.0 0.0 0.0	3 7.9 10.0 0.6	38 7.9
35-39	1 4.5 25.0 0.2	12 54.5 10.0 2.5	2 9.1 0.9 0.4	3 13.6 3.2 0.6	4 18.2 13.3 0.8	22 4.6
40-49	0 0.0 0.0 0.0	7 63.6 5.8 1.5	1 9.1 0.4 0.2	0 0.0 0.0 0.0	3 27.3 10.0 0.6	11 2.3
50 and over	0 0.0 0.0 0.0	2 100.0 1.7 0.4	0 0.0 0.0 0.0	0 0.0 0.0 0.0	0 0.0 0.0 0.0	2 0.4
Column Total	4 0.8	120 25.1	230 48.1	94 19.7	30 6.3	478 100.0

TABLE 5

Cross Tabulation of College of Business Administration Women by Age and by Motherhood Expectations

Count Row Pct Col Pct Tot Pct	No Response	(A) Presently Mother	(B) Next Five Years	(C) After Five Years	(D) Never Expect to be a Mother	Total
Under 25	2 0.6 50.0 0.4	6 1.8 8.1 1.3	54 16.6 62.1 11.3	227 69.8 93.8 47.5	36 11.1 50.7 7.5	325 68.0
25-29	2 2.5 50.0 0.4	20 25.0 27.0 4.2	26 32.5 29.9 5.4	15 18.8 6.2 3.1	17 21.3 23.9 3.6	80 16.7
30-34	0 0.0 0.0 0.0	18 47.4 24.3 3.8	7 18.4 8.0 1.5	0 0.0 0.0 0.0	13 34.2 18.3 2.7	38 7.9
35-39	0 0.0 0.0 0.0	19 86.4 25.7 4.0	0 0.0 0.0 0.0	0 0.0 0.0 0.0	3 13.6 4.2 0.6	22 4.6
40-49	0 0.0 0.0 0.0	9 81.8 12.2 1.9	0 0.0 0.0 0.0	0 0.0 0.0 0.0	2 18.2 2.8 0.4	11 2.3
50 and over	0 0.0 0.0 0.0	2 100.0 2.7 0.4	0 0.0 0.0 0.0	0 0.0 0.0 0.0	0 0.0 0.0 0.0	2 0.4
Column Total	4 0.8	74 15.5	87 18.2	242 50.6	71 14.9	478 100.0

   c. I am presently not married but would like to get married sometime after the next 5 years

   d. I do not intend to marry or remarry

Only 6.3 percent of the total respondents indicated they would never marry or remarry. In the under 25 age group, only 4 percent indicated no intention of marriage or remarriage (Table 4).

Question: a. I am presently a mother

   b. I would like to be a mother within the next 5 years

   c. I would like to be a mother someday but not within the next 5 years

   d. I never intend to become a mother

According to Table 5, 16 percent of all the women surveyed are mothers and another 69 percent expect to be mothers someday. The largest percentage of this group appears to be postponing motherhood until at least their late 20's; perhaps to get a good start in a career.

Career goals

Question: My career goal is _____ (indicate highest position you ex-
            pect to attain).

The responses to this question were classified as follows:

Did not or could not respond	21.5%
Top management	6.5%
Middle management	14.6%
Lower management	15.7%
Staff other than CPA	9.2%
CPA	15.0%
CPA Partner	4.0%
Have their own business	7.9%
Other	2.5%
Have a good job	2.5%

The responses to this question indicated that the career expectations of this group will come after they have put in a number of years establishing themselves in their career.

Impact of Findings

The author believes that this type of career interruption pattern will have significant impact not only on an individual woman's career but on the business organization as a whole as "mid-level" women "stop out" of their careers and leave the corporation for a time. Many women expect to "stop out" of their careers and then later step in and resume them. The reality of the workplace at this point is such that this may be difficult to accomplish. Reentry at other than initial entry-level jobs is often difficult, if not impossible.

The corporate organization is aware of the demands of parenting. Many organizations expect a total full-time commitment to the corporation at certain levels of employment. Children can impact on an individual's career. In the Catalyst survey, more than 40 percent of the corporate respondents indicated that certain positions in their firm could not be attained by a woman who combines career and parenting. Thirty-five percent of the corporate respondents indicated that this was also true of a man who combines career and parenting.

Conclusions

If the business organization expects to benefit fully from the potential of all its workers, it must accommodate itself to new career patterns. More options need to be available to women so that they will not have to totally interrupt their professional careers but need only "stop out" of the full-time job market for a time or reduce their weekly commitment, thus enabling them to remain current.

Some of the possible solutions to the career interruption problem include:

1. part time jobs should be available to the professional woman who needs to spend time with her family;

2. per diem work should be made available to women who cannot work a five- or six-day week;

3. job tasks can be broken down into smaller units so that two women could share what was previously one job;

4. the organization should offer more professional jobs that do not entail long overtime hours for women who need to spend time with their families;

5. consulting jobs could be made available to women who cannot work on a continuous basis;

6. women in certain careers, such as accounting, programming, systems work, may be able to do some of their work at home. In some cases, the installation of home computer terminals will allow this.

Some progress toward this direction is indicated in the literature (Catalyst, 1981). Seventy-three percent of the U.S. corporations indicated that they favored flexible working hours for parents, but in reality, only 37 percent actually provided this futuristic practice.

If parenting women are not provided for in the corporate scheme, it is the corporation which will be the loser.

Can the modern corporation really stand to lose the contributions of the continually growing number of professional women who work in the business organization? The economic and human loss is unconscionable.

Implications for Teachers and Trainers

Teachers and trainers need to be aware of the career lifestyle goals of their students. They should assume responsibility for educating their students not only in professional and technical content areas, but in the realities of the corporate workplace. Also of great importance is assisting students to plan for anticipated career lifestyles.

Most undergraduate students do not understand the lifestyle demands of a middle or higher level management job. In order for students not to be disillusioned with their career-lifestyle, they must understand the realities of the corporate world. It should be the responsibility of educators to help make students aware of corporate lifestyle demands.

Simply being subjects in career research seems to have initiated self insight and career awareness on the part of the female students who participated in this study. When students understand their goals and the realities of the corporate world they can decide either to form a realistic career plan or to modify their goals to fit their perceived lifestyle needs.

Educators can help students become aware of their career-lifestyle goals and the realities of the corporate workplace by encouraging them to engage in some of the following activities:

1. examine research related to career lifestyles of professional women;
2. participate in appropriate career-awareness programs aimed at women;
3. participate in professional women's groups and networks;
4. participate in professional business organizations;
5. interview professional women currently in management-level positions;
6. survey local and regional corporate organizations as to their career interruption policies;
7. participate in internship programs while still in school.

Educators should communicate to those in charge of corporate policy the need for responsive corporate career-interruption policies. Some of the means used could include having the educator:

1. provide the results of research relating to career lifestyle needs of professional women to key members of the corporate organization;

2. participate in professional organizations that allow for the informal discussion of the problems professional women face;

3. prepare formal programs for professional organizations related to career lifestyle needs of women;

4. present seminars for corporations related to career-lifestyle needs of women.

When students are educated as to the realities of the corporate workplace and corporate executives are cognizant of the realities of today's career lifestyles, teachers and trainers will have gone a long way toward meeting the goals set forth in this paper.

REFERENCES

Catalyst Career and Family Center. "Corporation and Two-Career Families: Directions for the Future." *Catalyst,* 1981.

The Chronicle of Higher Education. "Proportion of Degrees Awarded to Women." Sept. 17, 1979 (19:12).

_____. "Proportion of Degrees Awarded to Women." June 15, 1981 (22:8).

Harmon, L. W. "The Life and Career Plans of Young Adult Women: A Follow-Up Study." *Journal of Counseling Psychology,* 1981, 28, pp. 416-27.

U.S. Department of Labor. *Employment in Perspective: Working Women.* No. 1, First Quarter 1980.

_____. *Employment in Perspective: Working Women.* Summary 1982.

U.S. News and World Report. "What Americans Told the Census Takers." May 3, 1982, p. 12.

Women and Organizations:
A Study of Mentorship[1]

Carol M. Michael, Miami University
David M. Hunt, Miami University

The mentoring of young professionals by older, more experienced professionals has been occurring for generations. Only recently, however, has mentoring been labeled a critical factor in the career success of young professionals and become the topic of formal research ("Everyone Who Makes It Has a Mentor," *Harvard Business Review*, 1978).

It has long been acknowledged that mentorship is important to the advancement of men to top positions in business, academia, law, and medicine. Relatively little research has been done, however, on the role mentorship has played in the advancement of women in these traditionally male-dominated fields.

Because of the ever-increasing number of women entering these fields, the importance of mentors to the future success of these women needs to be examined. The purpose of this paper is to present an initial framework for future research on mentorship and to illustrate its use in an exploratory examination of samples of professional women in business management, academic administration, and medicine and law, traditionally male-dominated careers.

Mentor-protégé relationships such as master-apprentice, physician-intern, and professor-student have long existed in the predominantly male fields of business, medicine, law and academia. Membership in high level management groups, such as boards of directors and deanships in these fields, has also been predominantly male. Recently a few women professionals in these fields have begun to achieve top management ranks.

There is evidence that having a mentor is one factor which facilitates membership in the executive suite. The important contributions of mentors to the career success of young males is addressed by several authors, including Levinson (1978), Roche (1979), and Sheehy (1976). Youthful males entering the worlds of business (Levinson, 1978; Roche, 1979), the professions (Thompson, 1976), and academia

(Cameron, 1978), seem to find mentors with predictable regularity. Levinson's (1978) study of the lives and careers of forty males emphasized the importance of the mentor to the male's personal and professional development. Hennig (1971) and Sheehy (1976) have pointed out the paucity of female role models or mentors available for young adult or early mid-life adult females. Mentors are thought to be crucial to career success for women (Adams, 1979; Hennig, 1971; Scarf, 1980; Stewart, 1977). However, little is known about the frequency with which women in traditionally male-dominated fields experience mentorship or how influential these relationships are to their career success.

Review of Literature and Framework Development

Mentorship defined

The mentoring function is just one of many dyadic relationships that exist in career settings (Kanter, 1977; Shapiro, Haseltine, and Rowe, 1978). Coaches, teachers, guides, sponsors, bosses, mentors, and even relatives are often turned to for advice or for protection, and sometimes looked at as role models of the optimal traits and behaviors needed to attain success in life or in a career. Generally, the term "mentor" is used to mean teacher, adviser, or guide.

Shapiro et al. (1978) have suggested that there are differences between mentors and other adviser/support roles based on the degree of intensity and professional paternalism, indicating that the mentor-protégé relationship is indeed unique among the dyadic relationships. On the continuum suggested by Shapiro et al. (1978), the mentor role appears to be more intense, emotionally charged, hierarchical, parental, and has more restrictions attached to it than do other adviser relationships.

Further evidence of the uniqueness of mentors versus bosses, coaches, teachers, and gurus is provided by Sheehy (1976) who stated that persons in these roles seem to take more detached positions, leaving relatives and mentors in positions of more intimate relationships with those they advise and counsel. Mentors are often described as parent-like figures (Levinson, 1978; Shapiro et al., 1978; Sheehy, 1976). A nonparental career-role model function is also detailed by Sheehy (1976) as she describes a mentor as a guide supporting a young adult's dreams and helping in their attainment.

To date, most descriptions of the mentor-protégé relationship are male-oriented. In Webster's *New Collegiate Dictionary* (1976) a different spelling of protégé is suggested when referring to a woman—protégée.[2] Levinson (1978) also defines mentorship primarily in the male gender, noting its importance in the development of young males.

A developing framework

To examine the nature of mentorship and its outcomes better, current knowledge

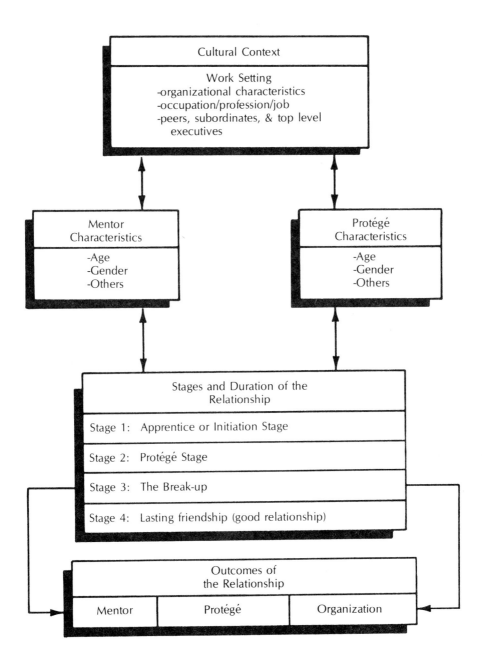

Figure 1: A suggested framework for the study of mentorship

has been used to develop a framework for its analysis. The framework consists of four major parts: (1) the context within which mentor-protégé relations emerge, (2) the characteristics of the mentor and of the protégé, (3) the functions and stages in the mentorship process, and (4) the outcomes or benefits that result from the mentor-protégé relationship (Figure 1).

The context

Several variables within the work setting serve to encourage or to constrain mentor-protégé relationships. Kanter (1977) emphasized the importance of the total context within which mentorship exists. The relationships between the mentor and top level executives in an organization, and protégés and peers are relevant to the central mentor-protégé dyad. Mentors can provide influential connections with top level executives. Peers are involved as a frame of reference for measuring the career success of the protégé and in networks providing the protégé with a source of support.

Cameron (1978) reports that some women believe that an "old girl's network" can be formed to function the same way as "old boy networks." Mentors frequently introduce their protégés to established networks of powerful individuals. Peers, on the other hand, often create their own networks for support and information. Shapiro et al. (1978) describe these women's networks, helping other women, as networks of peer pals rather than mentors.

The position of the protégé within the organizational hierarchy may also affect the availability of mentors. As a person moves up the hierarchy towards greater subjectivity, he/she can afford the favoritism of mentorship. Some would-be mentors may be more attracted to persons with proven track records. On the other hand, the number of persons available to mentor naturally diminishes as a person advances in the career hierarchy.

The type of organization that would be a willing user of mentorship is described by Kanter (1977) as follows: an organization with enhanced opportunity, with enthusiasm for innovation versus conservative resistance, and with structural supports for more equal treatment of women and minorities. According to Kanter (1977), overly bureaucratic organizations tend to produce a mentality of powerlessness, and women in particular may be overcrowded into supervisory or professional positions where their authority is restricted. These bureaucratic organizations are characterized by centralization, numerous levels in the hierarchy, and limitations on the decision-maker's domain.

In addition to these support relationships and organizational characteristics within the work setting, commonality in careers or occupations may affect mentor-protégé relations. The basis for this statement appears to be the concept of homophily, defined by Rogers and Bhowmik (1971) as the degree to which pairs of individuals who interact are similar with regard to attributes, beliefs, values, and social factors. Thus, professionals within the same career are more likely to develop mentor-protégé relationships than those in different fields due to their common interests.

Characteristics of the mentor and protégé

The characteristics of the mentor and of the protégé are critical determinants as to whether a relationship will be formed. One of the most infuential characteristics seems to be gender.

Levinson (1978) has stated that protégés need to have mentors of the same sex, based on the concept of homophily. Levinson's argument is based on a sample of men who were pursuing careers in traditionally male-dominated fields; no comparison of mixed sex relationships was provided.

A typology of mentor-protégé relations shows that three of the four possible mentor-protégé dyads involve women (Figure 2).[3]

Gender
of
Protégé

		Male	Female
Gender of Mentor	Male	Cell 1	Cell 2
	Female	Cell 3	Cell 4

Figure 2:   Gender-based typology of mentor-protégé relationships

Levinson's (1978) study focused only on forty men who had male mentors, Cell 1. Roche (1979) provided additional evidence of the importance of mentors to young adult males entering business careers.

Adams (1979) interviewed and reported on successful women who entered male-dominated fields and had male mentors, Cell 2. Stewart (1976) reported that career-oriented women in their thirties sought mentors much as young adult males have done.

Cook (1979), Shapiro et al. (1978), and Sheehy (1976) have all noted the obvious scarcity of female role models or mentors in traditionally male-dominated careers. This shortage is reflected in the literature where there is very little discussion of Cell 3 and Cell 4 cases. Information about female-mentored relationships is particularly scarce in the world of male-dominated careers. The complexities of balancing career and family/mother responsibilities may be a critical reason why mixed sex mentor-protégé relations are not as prevalent (Kanter, 1977; Sheehy, 1976). Sheehy (1976) suggests further evidence on this paucity of mixed gender cases and states that good or successful mixed dyads call for an increased level of maturity on the part of the mentor to cope with the possibility of sexual relations and keep the mentor-protégé relationships on a career basis.

A further examination of the characteristics of mentors is crucial to understanding and determining whether women can effectively act as mentors for male protégés, Cell 3. Female mentors of male protégés within male-dominated careers such as business, academia, and the professions would seem to require a high degree of position or career security. Cell 3 also presents an area for the examination of the role of female mentors in traditionally female careers. The principle of androgyny may apply to both Cell 2 and 3 relationships as noted by Shapiro et al. (1978).

Roche (1979) lists seven key characteristics that mentors have, and that protégés should look for in selecting a mentor: (1) willingness of the mentor to share his/her knowledge and understanding, (2) knowledge of the organization and its people, (3) rank of the mentor, (4) peer respect, (5) knowledge of the use of power, (6) upward mobility, and (7) organizational power.

The protégé must have certain characteristics in order to attract the attention of the potential mentor. At least a few years younger than their mentor, young, aspiring executives who are frequently described as "shining stars" are usually the ones chosen as protégés (Levinson, 1978). Kanter (1977) suggests that protégés are selected by mentors because the protégé: (1) has good performance, (2) has the right social background, (3) knows some of the officers socially, (4) looks good in a suit, (5) is socially similar, (6) has the opportunity to demonstrate the extraordinary, and (7) has high visibility.

These characteristics pose several problems for female protégés who wish to select either a male or female mentor. In the male mentor-female protégé (Cell 2) relationship the notorious Agee-Cunningham case serves to illustrate some of the problems of these characteristics when applied to females (Sheehy, 1980). In particular, a different social background and/or lack of social similarity presented problems for Mary Cunningham.

Another problem facing female protégés is that they are frequently entering second careers (after raising a family). This shift in careers means that they are at a different stage in their life cycle than are their youthful male counterparts.

Stages in the mentor-protégé relationship

Once the two role partners have identified each other, their relative positions become more apparent and their roles are more clearly defined in this first or apprentice stage of the relationship. Levinson (1978) has described this as the initiation phase of the relationship.

During the second stage of the relationship the apprentice or pupil advances skills to the point of being considered a protégé and is given opportunities to make key decisions (Roche, 1979). The mentor is proud of the pupil's progress and flattered by the attention accorded him/her in this reflective way. This is the protégé stage of the relationship: the protégé's work is not yet recognized for its own merit, but as the by-product of the mentor's instruction, encouragement, support, and advice. As the protégé develops a need for individuality and to have his/her work recognized on its own merit, the relationship enters the next stage.

The break-up stage serves to describe the termination of the mentor-protégé relationship. The relationship may be terminated for a variety of reasons. The protégé may develop a need for individuality, the mentor may not accept the protégé as a peer, the protégé may aspire to the job held by the mentor, or the protégé may need to relocate due to a spouse's career.

Sometimes this break-up is very stormy as Sheehy (1976) has suggested. Emotional ties are not always easily broken. The mixed sex mentor-protégé cases may present a more complex relationship to break off than same sex relationships (Stewart, 1977).

The break-up is necessary, but it is not necessarily the end of a full-term mentor-protégé relationship. Lasting friendships have frequently been reported in these relationships (Adams, 1979; Cook, 1979; Levinson, 1978; Sheehy, 1976; Stewart, 1977). In fact, it would seem that the complete mentor-protégé relationship is characterized by this lasting friendship stage. The protégé has progressed to peer or higher status and becomes a mentor him or herself, but has not severed ties with the mentor, who still provides counsel and support. Now a more equal status exists between mentor and protégé and a lasting friendship often develops.

Outcomes/benefits of mentorship

Benefits of the mentor-protégé relationship accrue to the two role partners and to the organization or career field in which they work. Mentorship provides several advantages to the protégé. In Roche's (1979) survey of executives, former protégés (versus nonmentored executives) were found to be better educated, less mobile, to plan their career more, have higher salaries, be more highly satisfied with their career progress, and to derive greater satisfaction from their work.

Cameron (1978) points out that benefits of mentorship in graduate level education are evident in financial aid, job placement, research project training, collaboration on publications, and personal or emotional support. Benefits to the profession may also result in that mentoring helps produce active members in a professional society who are self-confident and knowledgeable enough to become successful scholars.

According to Jennings (1967) there is now a developmental ethic in business which was not present 20 years ago. This ethic holds the manager responsible for developing talent. The manager's own promotions are thus facilitated by her/his adequate training of a replacement.

Not all the outcomes of mentorship are positive. Stewart (1977) and Sheehy (1976) suggest that some mentor-protégé relationships which break up involve emotional and psychological complications. Women protégés are particularly likely to develop emotional ties with their male mentors according to Stewart (1977). When the mentor refuses to accept the protégé as a peer, or is emotionally not mature enough to cope with protégé independence, break-ups can be very dysfunctional.

Use of framework in research

Examination of the framework can result in the generation of many important questions on the topic of mentorship. A sample of these research questions is provided in Exhibit 1.

Research questions:

1. How frequently do women in various professions have mentors?
2. What position does the mentor hold in the organization?
3. Are mentors of women professionals in male-dominated fields male or female?
4. Is gender an important factor in the success of the relationship?
5. What characteristics are most important in a mentor?
6. When do women in these professions find mentors?
7. At what ages do women find mentors?
8. How are mentor-protégé relationships initiated?
9. Are the protégés and mentors good friends at the end of the relationship?
10. How have these relationships aided the protégé?
11. What influence has the relationship had on the career success of the protégé?

Exhibit 1:   A sampling of research questions on mentorship

Design of the Study

Purpose

The literature reviewed and the framework that has been suggested served as a basis for an exploratory study to examine mentorship as it relates to women in traditionally male-dominated fields. Specifically, the purposes of the study were:

(1)   To determine how frequently these women had been protégés of mentors

(2)   To determine the nature of these protégé-mentor relationships and

(3)   To determine the impact of the protégé-mentor relationships on the career success of the women.

Sample

Thirty women in the fields of business, academia, medicine, and law were selected for the sample. These fields were chosen as representations of fields which have traditionally been male-dominated and fields into which increasing numbers of women are seeking entry. It was decided to examine these three fields concurrently to represent a variety of traditionally male-dominated fields and to permit exploratory comparisons between the three groups of career women.

Twelve women in academic administration at a major university, twelve business women at the management level, and seven professional women in medicine or law were selected by position (as a measure of career success) and availability for inclusion in the study. A variety of positions at several levels of academic and business management were represented.

Data collection

Data were collected in a semi-structured interview conducted by the first author. The interview procedures used were consistent with those used by Stewart (1977) and others. The questions which were asked included the eleven questions generated in the examination of the research framework. In twenty-eight cases, the interviews were conducted in person; in two cases extensive interviews were conducted by telephone.

Results and discussion

Over 70 percent of the women interviewed had previously had a mentor.[4] Over 80 percent of the academic women, two-thirds of the business women, and 57 percent of the professional women had a mentor during their careers.

The number of women with mentors in this sample indicates that women do have mentors more frequently than Levinson (1978) had indicated. Seven of the twenty-two women who had mentors had more than one. One woman who was a vice president of a business had a total of twelve mentors in various companies during her career progression. Business women more frequently had multiple mentors than either academic administrative or professional women. This might have been predicted since business women are more likely to change companies and progress through more positions in a formal hierarchy during their career advancement than are either academic or professional women. The latter groups of women had a higher percentage of their mentor relationships while they were pursuing graduate education in preparation for their careers than did business women.

In some cases multiple mentors were identified by the participants. In these cases, a representative sample of the relationships was chosen for further description and analysis.

Most of the mentors described were older people in the same career as the younger person, supporting Levinson's statements (1978). In a majority of the cases, the mentor was either the woman's department or division head or her immediate supervisor. This finding supports Roche's survey report findings (1979).

In slightly more than half of the cases of mentorship (12), the first (or only) mentor the woman had was a woman (Cell 4). Both business and professional women had male mentors more frequently than female mentors (Cell 2).

The academic women, on the other hand, were more likely to have had female mentors than were males (Cell 4). This could be predicted since there are relatively few professional women in dentistry, law, and medicine or in the middle or upper management levels of business, whereas there are more women in university professorships, especially within the educational fields in which women have traditionally pursued careers.

Seven of the women reported having had more than one mentor. In four of these cases there were mentors of each gender.

It seems that the gender of the mentor is not only heavily dependent upon the nature of the field, but also upon the level of management involved. In cases where there were sequential mentors, it was found that the first mentor is more likely to be female (Cell 4). Subsequent mentors are more likely to be male (Cell 2). This is not only true in some businesses, but in academic circles as well. Early in a woman's career she is likely to encounter other women in lower level management positions. As her career progresses and she is promoted she is more likely to encounter men, who have traditionally held middle or high level management positions. This finding supports the statement by Levinson (1978) and others that there is a general scarcity of women to mentor other women. This is true especially at high levels within an organization.

In eight cases (36%), the women said that the gender of their mentor was an important factor in the success of the relationship. In two of these cases a male mentor was thought to have had more power and influence than a female since the fields were male-dominated. In other instances women thought having a woman as a mentor was particularly helpful since the mentor could serve as both a role model and as a personal friend who understood her (as a person and as a woman).

The characteristics which the women identified most frequently as most important for a mentor were commitment and expertise in the profession. A sensitive and supportive nature, objectivity, a willingness to share expertise and time, possession of admirable personal qualities, openness, interest in the individual and her potential and willingness to allow freedom and personal challenge were also frequently cited. Willingness of the mentors to share their knowledge and understanding was also cited by Roche (1979) as a key characteristic to look for in mentors.

For seven of the twenty-two women with mentorships (32%), the mentor relationship began during college; for thirteen (59%) it began on their jobs. Of the thirteen relationships which began during the women's jobs, nine relationships began within the first year of employment. Three other relationships began within five years; one relationship began later.

In sixteen cases of mentorship (73%) the women protégés were under the age of thirty-three. In the remaining 27% of the cases, however, the women ranged from age thirty-three to forty-four. In four of the work-related relationships, the women who obtained mentors were forty years of age or older. Though these cases are in the minority, it seems that some women acquire mentors at an older age than the men described by Levinson (1978).

Nine of the respondents did not know how the relationship was actually initiated or thought it was mutually initiated. In ten cases, the mentor was thought to have initiated the relationships. In four cases involving the business and professional women, the protégé initiated the relationship.

Nearly three-fourths of the women who had mentors later became colleagues with them. Eighty-six percent of the women said they were friends with their mentors during the relationship. Nearly 90 percent of these women reported that they remained friends after the relationship had ended. This finding supports the research results of Adams (1979), Cook (1979), Levinson (1978), Sheehy (1976), and Stewart (1977).

When asked to describe how their mentors had aided them in their professions, the most frequently cited benefit was encouragement. The relationship was also credited with instilling self-confidence, developing special skills needed in the present or future job, helping in the evaluation of the protégé's strengths and weaknesses, and aiding in the analysis of professional issues and setting of professional goals. Many of these functions are similar to those cited by Levinson (1978).

At least fifteen of the women interviewed said that their mentors had a great deal of influence on their career success and personal development. Four women said that their mentor relationship was directly responsible for their career choice. Thus, the reported importance of the mentor to their career success clearly supports the survey findings reported by Roche (1979).

Implications for Teachers and Trainers

The literature reviewed and the research reported in this paper suggest that the career training and development of women should include coverage of the role of mentors and the other types of support relationships that are important to professional development. To use this topic effectively to aid professional women in their career development, the objectives of the teacher/trainer should be:

(a) to introduce women to the informal side of organizational life as well as the formal side,

(b) to acquaint women with the roles mentors and other support relationships can play in their professional development, and

(c) to suggest ways in which professional women can acquire and maintain the support of more experienced professionals.

Selected suggestions on how to accomplish these objectives are as follows:

1. Since the mentor type of support relationship is frequently part of the "informal organization," professional women need to gain an understanding of the informal side of organizational life and how it can affect their career development. Suggested reading for background and discussion includes:

Harragan, B. L. *Games Mother Never Taught You: Corporate Gamesmanship for Women.* New York: Warner Books, 1977.

Kanter, R. M. and Stein, B. A. *A Tale of "O": On Being Different in an Organization.* New York: Harper and Row, 1980.

2. Teachers and trainers can help acquaint professional women with the roles mentors and other support figures have in their professional development in a variety of ways. An understanding of the basic research in the area is important. Suggested materials for reading and discussion include the following:

   Everyone Who Makes It Has a Mentor. *Harvard Business Review,* July-August 1978, *56*(4), 89-101.

   Hennig, M., and Jardin, A. *The Managerial Woman.* Garden City, New York: Anchor Press/ Doubleday, 1977.

   Kanter, R. M. *Men and Women of the Corporation.* New York: Basic Books, Inc., 1977.

   Levinson, D. J., Darrow, C. M., Klein, E. B., Levinson, M. H., and McKee, B. *The Seasons of a Man's Life.* New York: Ballantine Books, 1978.

   Missirian, A. K. The Process of Mentoring in the Career Development of Female Managers. Unpublished doctoral dissertation, University of Massachusetts, 1980.

   Roche, G. R. Much Ado about Mentors. *Harvard Business Review,* January-February 1979, *57*(1), 17-28.

   Shapiro, E., Haseltine, F. P., and Rowe, M. P. Moving Up: Role Models, Mentors, and the Patron System. *Sloan Management Review,* Spring 1978, *19*(3), 51-58.

3. Speakers from a variety of organizations who have been mentors and/or protégés can facilitate understanding and spark interest. Having several mentor/protégé pairs as a panel to describe their relationships from the viewpoint of each participant and to answer questions would be especially beneficial. As a guide for presentation and questions the Hunt and Michael framework is suggested.

   Hunt, D., and Michael, C. Mentorship: A Career Training and Development Tool. *Academy of Management Review,* July 1983, *8*(3), 475-585.

4. Some research findings suggest that it is usually the mentor who initiates a support relationship and that it is the career performance and attitude of the prospective protégé which attracts the mentor's attention. Ways in which prospective protégés can attract the attention of desirable mentors and acquaint them with their work should be discussed.

5. Teachers and trainers may themselves need to consider serving as a mentor to a less experienced professional woman in their field. Not only will they be helping another professional develop, but they will be advancing the organization and their field of specialization.

6. Further research is needed on the topic of mentorship. Teachers and trainers should consider doing their own research on mentorship and should encourage capable students to do major research projects on the topic. Comparative studies that cut across occupations and organizations can provide additional

information about occupational, organizational, and cultural differences with regard to mentorship in the work environment.

7. To place mentorship in its proper perspective, it should be pointed out that it is only one of a variety of helpful support relationships in the professional development of women. Teachers and trainers should discuss the formation of peer support groups both in and outside the organization. Women should be encouraged to investigate the professional women's networks which are open by field of specialization or geographical area. Members from professional women's networks should be invited to speak to the group and directories and membership information should be shared.

NOTES

1. Earlier versions of papers on this topic were presented at the Midwest Conference on Women and Organizations, Kalamazoo, 1982, and at the Midwest Academy of Management Meeting, Columbus, 1982.
2. In this paper, the term "protégé" is spelled the same whether it refers to males or females.
3. Three of the four possible relationships also involve men.
4. In this research a mentor was defined as a person who took a personal interest in the protégé's career and guided and sponsored the protégé.

REFERENCES

Adams, J. *Women on Top.* New York: Hawthorn Press, 1979.

Cameron, S. W. "Women Faculty in Academia: Sponsorship, Informal Networks, and Scholarly Success." Unpublished Doctoral Dissertation, University of Michigan, 1978.

Cook, M. F. "Is the Mentor Relationship Primarily a Male Experience?" *Personnel Administrator,* November 1979, 24 (11), 82-86.

"Everyone Who Makes It Has a Mentor." *Harvard Business Review,* July-August 1978, 56 (2), 89-101.

Hennig, M. M., and Jardin, A. *The Managerial Woman.* New York: Doubleday, 1977.

Hennig, M. "Career Development for Women Executives." Unpublished Doctoral Dissertation, Harvard University, 1971.

Hunt, D. M., and Michael, C. M. "Mentorship: A Career Training and Development Tool." *The Academy of Management Review,* July 1983, 8 (3), 475-85.

Jennings, E. E. "The Mobile Manager: A Study of the New Generation of Top Executives." Unpublished Doctoral Dissertation, University of Michigan, 1967.

Kanter, R. M. *Men and Women of the Corporation.* New York: Basic Books, 1977.

Levinson, D. J. *The Seasons of a Man's Life.* New York: A. A. Knopf, 1978.

Roche, G. R. "Much Ado about Mentors." *Harvard Business Review,* January-February 1979, 57 (1), 14-28.

Rogers, E. M., and Bhowmik, D. K. "Homophily-Heterophily: Relational Concepts for Communication Research." *Public Opinion Quarterly,* 1971, 34, 523-38.

Scarf, M. *Unfinished Business: Pressure Points in the Lives of Women.* New York: Doubleday & Co., Inc., 1980.

Shapiro, E. C., Haseltine, F. P., and Rowe, M. P. "Moving Up: Role Models, Mentors, and the Patron System." *Sloan Management Review,* Spring 1978, 19 (3), 51-58.

Sheehy, G. *Passages: Predictable Crises of Adult Life.* New York: E. P. Dutton and Co., 1976.

_____. "Ambition and the Angel: The Mary Cunningham Saga." *The Washington Post,* October 12-16, 1980.

Stewart, W. A. "A Psychosocial Study of the Formation of the Early Adult Life Structure in Women." Unpublished Doctoral Dissertation, Columbia University, 1977.

Thompson, P. H. "Tear Down the Pyramids." *Exchange: A Journal of Teaching Theory and Techniques,* Fall/Winter 1976, 21 (4), 19-25.

Webster's New Collegiate Dictionary. Massachusetts: G. & C. Merriman Co., 1976.

Attitudes Toward Equal Employment Opportunity[1]

Lizabeth A. Barclay, Oakland University
Mitchell W. Fields, Texas A&M University

Equal Employment Opportunity (EEO) compliance was designed to protect subgroups from discriminatory practices. While various test fairness models have been examined for their effects on fair selection standards, and numerous guides have been written for management practitioners (Arvey, 1979; Hayes, 1980; Kandel, 1977), little formal research has been done on employee attitudes toward EEO until recently.

Chacko (1982) has conducted one of the few studies on attitudes toward EEO. His study involved data collection on 55 female managers. The study examined whether these female managers perceived gender to be an important factor in their selection. Those who did think gender was important, displayed less satisfaction and commitment than did those who did not perceive gender as involved in their selection. Chacko (1982) believes that "these results suggest certain inherent difficulties with affirmative action and equal employment opportunity programs (p. 122.)."

A recent study by Fernandez (1981) also examines equal employment opportunity. Fernandez conducted surveys at a number of large corporations to determine whether females and minorities needed special training in order to enter and advance in the corporate world. The results of his study provide insight for Chacko's (1982) work. He found that "54 percent of all managers agree that most male managers make female managers feel they got their jobs because of EEO targets and not because of ability (p. 88)." This certainly could help account for Chacko's finding concerning the relationship of perceived selection criteria and satisfaction. If one were repeatedly told that one did not have the requisite abilities for one's job, evaluation of outcomes associated with the job could suffer. In a related finding, Fernandez also found that white males were anti-EEO and females and minorities were generally pro-EEO.

While Chacko (1982) provides very useful exploratory information, additional research needs to be conducted. Chacko did not examine women in different (i.e., traditional versus nontraditional) jobs. He also did not assess their orientation toward appropriate roles for women. Both situation (job) and person (orientation) variables need to be examined in order to address issues recently raised by Riger and Galligan (1980). Riger and Galligan (1980) state that there are different implications associated with person versus situation paradigms. Fernandez (1981), while conducting a more comprehensive study, did not examine situation and person variables either. In addition, recent work on person perception by Bankart and Wittenbraker (1980), indicates that the orientation of the perceiver is an important variable to consider when examining attitudes.

In an attempt to extend the research of Chacko and Fernandez, this study tests the following hypotheses:

Nontraditionally oriented females in traditional jobs will have significantly more positive attitudes toward Equal Employment Opportunity than will traditionally oriented females in nontraditional jobs.

and

There will be no significant difference in attitudes toward Equal Employment Opportunity for traditionally oriented females in traditional jobs as compared to nontraditionally oriented females in nontraditional jobs.

Method

Subjects

The subjects of this investigation were 336 females drawn from a larger group of respondents who had completed a more comprehensive survey at a major corporation. The females in this study were those who were employed in traditionally female jobs (80 percent or more of the incumbents were female) and those who were employed in nontraditionally female jobs (20 percent or fewer of the incumbents were female).[2]

In addition to determining job type, respondents were asked to complete a number of scales. A brief description of these scales follows.

Scales

Attitudes toward Equal Employment Opportunity

Respondents were presented with ten statements concerning Equal Employment Opportunity. The scale is presented in Exhibit 1. These statements were both positive and negative. Respondents were asked to check the items with which they agreed. In order to compute a score for a respondent's attitude toward EEO, scale scores for each of the items were computed via Thurstone scaling (Torgerson, 1967). Item scale scores were computed on the basis of item rank ordering done by ten judges (graduate students). Matrix transformation was employed in order to compute scale values. An individual respondent's score was based on the sum of the scale values for the items checked divided by the number of items the respondent had checked. A positive score indicates a relatively positive attitude toward EEO, while a negative score indicates a relatively negative attitude toward EEO. The median score of this scale for the larger survey effort was .059.

The following statements are about Equal Employment Opportunity Programs. Please check the statements which most accurately reflect your feelings. You may check as many or as few as you wish, however, we want your *candid and accurate personal opinion* even if it contradicts widely held opinions.

Equal Employment Opportunity programs . . .

_____ provide the same opportunity for everyone to get a job.

_____ are hard on the employer, because of the costs of administering the programs.

_____ are not well-administered, too much red tape.

_____ help stop discrimination.

_____ are unnecessary, because people with ability can progress regardless of race or sex.

_____ quotas force organizations to hire people for jobs for which they are not qualified.

_____ sometimes end in costly court cases when there has been no discrimination.

_____ have caused "reverse discrimination."

_____ provide equal pay for work of equal value.

_____ provide advancement and versatility in organizations for minorities and women.

Exhibit 1. EEO attitudes

Sex stereotype scale

This instrument consists of ten items selected from a larger scale (Kirkpatrick, 1963). The items provide an assessment of attitudes toward current sex roles. Coefficient alpha for the scale was computed at .74 for the entire set of subjects. The scale included items such as: "Women are generally too nervous and highstrung to make good professionals;" "Men are more aggressive and achievement-oriented than women;" and "Women should freely compete with men in every sphere of economic activity." A median split based on the entire group of respondents, not just the subgroup considered in this study, classified subjects as holding traditional versus nontraditional beliefs in roles for women.

Data analysis

One-way analyses of variance were used to test the stated hypotheses.

Results

Table 1 presents the means and standard deviations for the four groups on the EEO scale.

TABLE 1

EEO Scale Means and Standard Deviations

Job Type	Orientation	Mean	Standard Deviation
Nontraditional	Nontraditional	.18	.93
Nontraditional	Traditional	−.02	.77
Traditional	Nontraditional	.44	.90
Traditional	Traditional	.29	1.25

Table 2 presents the one-way analysis of variance which was used to evaluate the first hypothesis. The hypothesis was confirmed. Women who were nontraditionally oriented and in traditional jobs held significantly more positive views toward EEO than did traditionally oriented women in nontraditional jobs.

TABLE 2

Analysis of Variance for EEO Attitudes by
Incongruent (Job-Role) Females

Source	df	SS	MS	F

Between
  Nontraditional Job—
    Traditional Orientation
    vs. Traditional Job—
    Nontraditional Orientation
	1	4.55	4.55	6.96*

Within	105	68.74	.07	
Total	106	73.29		

*$p < .01$

Note: Some missing data with regard to classification into jobs exists so there is a slight difference
between the number of subjects reported earlier and those accounted for in Tables 2 and 3.

The second hypothesis was also confirmed. Table 3 presents the results of the analysis of variance. The two groups were not significantly different.

TABLE 3

Analysis of Variance for EEO Attitudes by
Congruent (Job-Role) Females

Source	df	SS	MS	F
Between Nontraditional Congruents vs. Traditional Congruents	1	.32	.32	.34
Within	234	224.29	.96	
Total	235	224.61		

Discussion

Women who are in jobs with limited opportunity for advancement and have nontraditional orientations hold positive attitudes toward EEO while traditionally oriented women in nontraditional jobs hold anti-EEO attitudes. O'Leary (1977) has detailed the historical existence of "privileged" minority group members who are resistant to social change. The women in this group may see their positions as unique and are unwilling to change the status quo (i.e., open these nontraditional jobs to *more* women). EEO would be viewed as a mechanism of unwanted change. While the anti-EEO attitudes of this group can be explained, it would be useful to examine *why* traditionally oriented women would take such jobs. As several explanations can be offered (e.g., more financial reward, unique status), the area should be given more study.

Women in congruent positions (traditional job—traditional orientation, nontraditional job—nontraditional orientation) held attitudes toward EEO which were intermediate to the groups (the incongruents) in the first hypothesis. It would appear that if one chooses a job which is consistent (i.e., congruent) with one's orientation there is less reactivity (whether positive or negative) toward change mechanisms.

Kreps and Clark (1975) and Riger and Galligan (1980) report that female workers are concentrated in lower status job categories. Researchers should be very careful not to ignore the women in these lower level jobs. While the problems of women entering nontraditional jobs warrant investigation, the problems of women in traditional jobs (and their attitudes) are no less important. Additionally, these two groups cannot be treated as homogeneous within themselves. This study had indicated that women's orientations have an effect on how they view mechanisms which supposedly assist them. Future research should consider the points raised here in order to develop research frameworks which include all women at work.

Implications for Teachers and Trainers

In a recent article, Milkovich and Krzystofiak (1979) state that: "Equal opportunity, a noble policy, must be translated into specific programs and behaviors; intentions must be translated into actions to achieve desired results (p. 359)." What kinds of programs are needed; what kinds of behaviors are appropriate? The research in this paper suggests that training programs designed to deal with Equal Employment Opportunity should take women's varying attitudes and job levels into consideration.

According to Wexley and Latham (1981), a successful training and development program initially needs a "systematic determination of training needs (p. 234)." The primary objective of the trainer should be to communicate the law and its intents. If this is successfully accomplished, misconceptions about EEO policy can be dealt with and discriminatory behaviors hopefully eliminated.

This study, taken with Chacko's (1982) and Fernandez's (1981) findings, recommends several approaches for organizations and their training departments.

1. Women with nontraditional orientations and traditional jobs may have established their employment in the organization as a means of gaining access to the organization. Once employed, these women may have aspirations of entering managerial or professional jobs. One set of development programs could address themselves to women in traditional positions (or for that matter, males in nonexempt positions) who want to become upwardly mobile. This could be accomplished through tuition reimbursement plans or internal programs aimed at developing professional and/or managerial skills. While this sounds good, anecdotal evidence suggests that in some organizations, the acquisition of a degree does not enhance intra-organizational mobility. The training department may wish to set up workshops on career development within the organization. These workshops would have to deal with diagnosing personal strengths, detail coping strategies to use when experiencing a career plateau, and so forth. At the same time, information about EEO should be provided so that these individuals can more realistically assess reasons for slow career movement.

2. Another important consideration which derives from this study deals with the lack of homogeneity in female attitudes. Traditionally oriented women in nontraditional jobs may have to be trained about EEO in a manner similar to majority males. Fernandez (1981) found that participants suggested special training for minorities and females "be enlarged to include white men and be primarily for them (p. 268)" as these males were the individuals experiencing difficulty with the changing corporation. It would appear that anti-EEO females function from

a similar perspective. Training programs for these individuals, especially since these are managerial types, must focus on the facts and reality of EEO law. The utility of EEO for the organization must be detailed. In addition, role playing and awareness training may be incorporated into the fact sessions so that the participants can gain a wider perspective.

The organization should also realize that transfer of training may not always occur. Organizational policy should be modified to include EEO behaviors in performance evaluations as this may provide an incentive to practice the material presented in training.

3. Training programs should be expanded to include all members of the corporation. Just because some groups are pro- or anti-EEO does not mean that they have correct information about the laws and regulations. A side issue in this study, although not reported here, dealt with EEO knowledge. Nonmanagerial employees possessed less information about the laws than did managers. This misinformation may by dysfunctional for organizations as unnecessary litigation could occur. Although it might be too costly to send all organizational participants to formal training, a resource center could be set up to include EEO information. In fact, this could occur in conjunction with a career center. Having information available and accessible can help to dispel the misconception that companies "keep" this information from employees.

NOTES

1. The authors would like to thank Michael Pendergrass for his assistance in the development of the EEO scale and Andres Inn for his help in the Thurstone scaling of it.
2. The 20% cutoff allows identification of gender dominated positions in a manner similar to Moore and Rickel (1980).

REFERENCES

Arvey, R. D. *Fairness in Selecting Employees.* Reading, MA: Addison-Wesley, 1979.

Bankart, C. P. and Wittenbraker, J. B. "Sex-Role Orientation of Perceivers and Targets as Variables in the Person Perception Process." *The Psychological Record,* 1980, 30, 143-53.

Chacko, T. I. "Women and Equal Employment Opportunity: Some Unintended Effects." *Journal of Applied Psychology,* 1982, 67, 119-23.

Fernandez, J. P. *Racism and Sexism in Corporate Life.* Lexington: D. C. Heath & Co., 1981.

Hayes, H. P. *Realism in EEO.* New York: John Wiley & Sons, 1980.

Kandel, W. L. "Introduction to EEO Laws and Regulations." In R. Freiberg (Ed.), *The Manager's Guide to Equal Employment Opportunity.* New York: Executive Enterprises Co., Inc., 1977.

Kirkpatrick, C. "The Construction of a Belief Scale for Measuring Attitudes toward Feminism." *Journal of Social Psychology,* 1963, 7, 421-37.

Kreps, J. and Clark, R. *Sex, Age and Work: The Changing Composition of the Labor Force.* Baltimore: Johns Hopkins University Press, 1975.

Milkovich, G. T. and Krzystofiak, F. "On the Road to Equal Employment Opportunity." In W. F. Glueck (Ed.), *Personnel, a Book of Readings.* Dallas: Business Publications, 1979.

Moore, L. M. and Rickel, A. U. "Characteristics of Women in Traditional and Nontraditional Managerial Roles." *Personnel Psychology,* 1980, 33, 317-33.

O'Leary, V. E. *Toward Understanding Women.* Monterey, Ca.: Brooks/Cole Publishing Co., 1977.

Riger, S. and Galligan, P. " Women in Management, an Exploration of Competing Paradigms." *American Psychologist,* 1980, 35, 902-10.

Torgerson, W. S. *Theory and Methods of Scaling.* New York: John Wiley & Sons, Inc., 1967.

Wexley, K. N. and Latham, G. P. *Developing and Training Human Resources in Organizations.* Glenview: Scott, Foresman and Co., 1981.

The Costs of Seeking Redress from Discrimination[1]

Sandra E. Gleason, Michigan State University

An important development in response to the growth of the women's movement during the 1970s was increased attention devoted to educating women about their legal rights in the workplace. These educational activities took a variety of forms, but their focus was typically on the statutes providing legal protection, such as the Civil Rights Act and the Equal Pay Act, the institutional mechanisms available for the expression of a complaint, such as filing with the Equal Employment Opportunity Commission (EEOC), and the potential benefits to the woman who decides to file a sex discrimination complaint using these formal complaint channels. In contrast, little attention has been given to the monetary and nonmonetary costs of filing complaints from the perspective of the complainant. The purpose of this paper, therefore, is to describe the experiences reported by women who filed sex discrimination complaints in the federal government and the implications of these experiences for the trainers of professional women. The survey respondents were professionals employed in middle and upper level civil service jobs who had participated in and/or belonged to CHANGE (Check Harassment and Negligence in Government Employment).

Methodology

The basic problem confronted in the study of professional women who file sex discrimination complaints is that they are a rare population, and the true incidence of their complaints is unknown. Based on data for the period from 1972-74 for the federal civil service, a rough estimate of all persons filing written complaints is less than 1% of white collar civil servants (Rosenbloom, 1977). Consequently, the case study of CHANGE was employed to identify women who had filed, or had considered filing, a sex discrimination complaint against the federal government (filers). Women seeking a support group to help them make the decision

199

to file and/or provide support and information during the processing of a complaint have participated in CHANGE since its creation in 1974. It operates in the Washington, D.C. metropolitan area and serves only federally employed women.

The questionnaire focused primarily on two major issues relating to the costs imposed on the women by the complaint process, in addition to determining the outcome of the complaint and collecting a variety of demographic information: what costs were expected prior to filing a complaint, and what costs were actually experienced. Costs were defined broadly to include both monetary expenditures as well as nonmonetary costs, including the loss of leisure time, additional stress at home and on the job, and health problems. The attention given to the costs of filing was based on the hypothesis that a woman will decide to file a sex discrimination charge only if she believes that the expected costs of this activity will be less than the expected benefits received. Since she is protecting the value of economic opportunities to which a job provides access (her job property rights), the costs and benefits should be viewed in both monetary and nonmonetary terms in order to make an informed decision about filing (Gleason, 1981).

The questionnaire was mailed in 1982 to 60 current addresses provided by CHANGE. Three follow-up letters were sent to nonrespondents. Eighteen completed questionnaires were returned (a response rate of 30%), as well as five letters explaining why the questionnaire was not completed. The letters provided such miscellaneous explanations for the failure to complete the questionnaire as complaint records being in storage or that a woman had attended some CHANGE meetings and decided not to file. However, a recurrent comment in all of the correspondence as well as in notes written on the questionnaires indicated how upsetting it was to the respondent to think about her case. One letter stated: "Each time I thought about the cost of the suit I became so upset I could not sit still long enough to answer the questions." In addition, members of CHANGE have noted in personal discussions with the author that women whose cases are still in progress are very concerned about protecting their privacy, even when the responses to the survey are anonymous. Furthermore, those with cases in progress are so busy with their jobs and their cases that they have little time to complete a detailed questionnaire. This suggests that a sex discrimination complaint is an extremely sensitive and painful subject for the respondents. Thus, being reminded of such a painful experience by the completion of a questionnaire will be an experience some respondents resist, especially if they were unsuccessful in achieving their desired remedy.

Due to the study design employed and the response rate achieved, it is important to keep several considerations in mind while reviewing the findings presented below. First, the extent to which CHANGE members and participants as a group, and the respondents in particular, are representative of all women who file discrimination charges in either the public or private sector is unknown. Second, we know nothing about those women who have experienced sex discrimination but have chosen not to file a charge (nonfilers), so we cannot compare the

CHANGE filers to nonfilers. As a consequence, we cannot infer anything from this sample about actual incidence of sex discrimination or the forms in which it occurs in the workplace. Third, the survey deals with the subjective perceptions of discrimination which may or may not reflect the true events which occurred. However, the respondents were asked if they had statistical data to use as evidence for the discrimination charged, and about 80% stated they had such evidence, usually systematic patterns of discrimination within an agency. This suggests that the respondents had relatively strong cases.

Finally, the experiences of federally employed professional women may differ from those of privately employed professional women in unknown ways, due to differences in employer characteristics, although any employer may choose to resist a discrimination charge. All employers are undoubtedly aware that "repeat-players" have a variety of strategic advantages over the "one-shotters" who file against them, so an employer can be expected to lose less often and win more often than individuals in litigation (Galanter, 1975; Wanner, 1975). However, a federal agency as an employer is encouraged to extend the legal proceedings as long as possible since the Department of Justice and its staff resources are used to defend the agency if the case goes to court.

Characteristics of Filers and Their Complaints

The characteristics of the respondents shown in Table 1 indicate that these women are very different from the average female employee in either the private or public sector. All were white, most were not married and had no dependents at the time they filed. Their own earnings and family income were well above the national averages. Most were college graduates or had professional training, and about 60% held degrees in nontraditional fields for women such as business, law, and the sciences. Further, 75% had spent all or most of their working lives employed by the federal government in the Washington, D.C. area.

At the time they filed all of the respondents were in middle- or upper-level civil service positions (levels GS-9 to GS-15). This is in marked contrast with the employment distribution of women in the federal civil service. In November, 1980, women constituted 45% of the full-time workers in the federal government, but held only 22% of the positions from GS-9 to GS-15. In contrast, men constituted 55% of the full-time labor force, but held 78% of the GS-9 to GS-15 positions (U.S.O.P.M., 1980).

This respondent profile is consistent with that of the sample of professional women studied by Yohalem (1979). She found that the "respondents who claim to have been treated unequally . . . (were) principally composed of workers in male-dominated fields and neither their education, occupational choice, weekly hours of work, nor total work experience conformed to traditional sex-linked conduct" (p. 148). Yohalem also found that successful workers, the high achievers, were more likely to report discriminatory treatment, and nearly twice as many in male fields reported discrimination relative to women in female fields.

In the study reported here, the average length of employment was about 15 years at the time of the first filing of a complaint; only three respondents were eligible for early or regular retirement. The length of the employment experience in combination with an average age of 40 suggests that most of the women had been full-time employees since completing their education. A slight bimodality in the age of the filers should also be noted (Table 1) since this suggests that there may be two different groups of filers (Yohalem, 1979). One group is those relatively young women under 30 years of age who were raised in the era of the women's movement and expect equal opportunity on the job. They have had relatively little experience with discrimination, and act quickly to seek redress when it occurs. The second group is those women over forty who have lived with discrimination of various types throughout their employment experience. For them, some critical factor triggered a reaction after tolerating unfair treatment for some time, such as the desire to protect their retirement income or simply to see that justice was done. Unlike the younger women, this group is more likely to have reached the point in their careers at which they no longer have the option of moving to another job or agency to seek more equitable treatment.

The 18 women reported filing a total of 22 charges, with one respondent responsible for four cases. Fourteen cases were filed charging only sex discrimination, while 8 cases charged sex discrimination in combination with race, age, and/or religion. The usual pattern was allegations of multiple discriminatory practices, with an average of 3 acts of discrimination alleged. The most common was failure to promote (24%), followed by discriminatory treatment in giving work assignments (23%), unfair performance evaluations (14%), failure to receive important training (9%), and unequal pay (7%). It is notable that the perceived discrimination typically reflected treatment which hindered progress on the job rather than not being hired for a job.

The analysis of the processing of the complaints reported by the respondents is complicated by the substantial modifications of the prescribed federal complaint handling procedures and the resulting confusion which occurred in the decade of the 1970s, since the earliest reported case was filed in 1971 and other cases were still in progress at the time this study was conducted. However, for most respondents, up to four basic procedural stages could have been used. The first stage is informal discussions of the problem conducted within the agency with the assistance of the Equal Employment Opportunity (EEO) counselor. If these discussions are unsuccessful in resolving the complaint, then a written complaint can be filed with the agency in the second or administrative stage. Rosenbloom (1977) reports that the success rate at the first stage during 1972-74 was about 37%. Only 11% of those using first stage subsequently filed in the second stage; about one-fifth of these written complaints alleged sex discrimination in FY75.

TABLE 1

Characteristics of Women Who Filed Complaints (n = 18)

Characteristics	Number	Percentage*
Education		
Some college	3	17
College degree	4	22
Some graduate work	5	28
MA, MS, Ph.D., JD	6	33
Number of Years of Full-Time Employment when Complaint Filed**		
6-10	6	33
11-20	5	28
21-30	6	33
Civil Service Level when Filed		
GS9-11	8	44
GS12-13	8	44
GS14-15	2	11
Age When Filed Complaint		
27-30	6	33
31-40	3	17
41-50	6	33
51-55	3	17
Marital Status When Complaint Filed		
Single, never married	8	44
Married	6	33
Divorced, Widowed	4	22
Number of Dependents When Filed		
None	11	61
One	2	11
Two or Three	5	28
Own Earnings Today		
$29,999 or less	8	44
$30,000-39,999	3	17
$40,000-44,999	4	22
$45,000 +	3	17
Family Total Income Today		
$30,000-39,999	11	61
$40,000-44,999	1	6
$45,000 +	6	33

*Percentages may not equal 100% due to rounding.

**Information missing for one person.

Furthermore, in FY74 examiners found discrimination in 17% of the cases, agency heads found discrimination in 7% of the cases, and reversed the findings of examiners in 27% of the cases. About 30% of all the FY74 agency final decisions were appealed that year.

The third stage is filing a charge with the Equal Employment Opportunity Commission if a satisfactory resolution is not reached within the agency, and the final stage is filing a legal suit in court. The success rate in litigation is also low. For example, from 1973-75 in individual claims of discrimination involving hiring, promotion, and discharge, the plaintiffs prevailed in only about one-third of the cases (Abramson, 1979).

Due to the federal complaint procedures prescribed, all of the respondents employed informal discussions to try to resolve their complaints, and many talked with a wide variety of people within the agency in addition to those specified by the official procedures. However, when these discussions failed, they had to file a written charge to pursue their complaints, but only about 20% of the respondents believed that the agency made a good faith effort to resolve the problems.

At the time of the survey, ten cases were still in progress, including three cases for which remedies had been recommended but were being appealed by the agency. Approximately 32% of the charges filed had reached stage two; 27% stage three; and 41%, the court. Approximately three-fourths of the completed cases had been settled in favor of the respondents, which is a much higher success rate than would be predicted based on the information above.

The Costs of Filing

The results of this case study suggest that both the nonmonetary and monetary costs of filing are positively correlated with the number of stages through which a complaint is processed. This reflects the structure of the federal dispute resolution system which is generally more complex than systems used in the private sector or in state and local governments (Moore, 1982) and thus entails longer periods of time to progress through the prescribed stages. Furthermore, discussions with CHANGE members suggest that without resolution of the complaint, a hardening of attitudes occurs: the agency resists the complaint and the filer begins to feel that she has nothing to lose by waiting and pursuing her complaint as far as her financial and psychological resources will permit. The longer the time involved, the more legal costs will develop, and the nonmonetary costs of retaliation, stress, and health problems are spread over more extended periods of time.

The commitment to file a sex discrimination complaint was substantial for most respondents since the average time involved in a case was 3.5 years, including those cases still in progress. The administrative stage alone required two years for many respondents, while a case which ended up in court could require ten years. One respondent was still involved in her case even though she had retired from the federal civil service. Respondents commented on their perception that the agencies and government lawyers used a wide variety of delaying tactics in processing their complaints to force them to give up. Even after a remedy was specified, the agencies employed delaying tactics to avoid paying it.

In light of the time commitment required, it is not surprising that respondents commented that they became preoccupied with their cases. Not only did they have to deal with the emotional and financial costs entailed, but their personal lives were also dominated by it as the filer spent evenings, weekends, holidays, and annual vacations working on, or worrying about, the progress of the case. However, although 80% reported a loss of leisure time, none had kept records of the amount of lost leisure time.

The activities related to the case pursued in nonwork hours were quite varied. These included talking with attorneys and others, completing work assignments with unreasonably short deadlines to ensure they could not be charged with incompetence for failing to complete an assignment, writing memos defending themselves from retaliatory activities conducted by the agency such as false claims about work attendance or performance, and collecting and preparing statistical evidence to support their case.

In addition to a loss of leisure time, respondents also experienced a wide range of other nonmonetary costs including retaliation, stress, and health problems. In only three of the cases filed in which the respondent remained employed in the agency after filing (20 cases) did the women report no experience with retaliation. Retaliation from supervisors and/or co-workers was the common experience of most respondents, and many women also reported this resulted in increased stress on the job and at home as well. The types of perceived retaliation experienced included such treatment as isolating the individual from staff support services, supervisors instructing co-workers not to talk to the individual and instructing co-workers to follow the individual into the bathroom on all occasions, failing to inform employees of important meetings which should be attended and other forms of ostracism, the removal of a typewriter and telephone from the office, having one's office moved into the file room, reduced performance evaluations, the assignment of no work or overburdening with work with unreasonably short deadlines, and denial of promotions or salary increases. These tactics are consistent with those used throughout the federal government (Ewing, 1979).

The treatment experienced was summarized by one respondent who stated that her supervisor had retaliated against her in "every way possible—I was told that I had faulty judgment to have filed." It is important to keep in mind that this retaliation was experienced during stage one (before filing a written complaint), as well as after the filing of the complaint. Furthermore, all of this retaliatory activity is illegal (Durling, 1981). Rosenbloom (1977, p. 134) suggests a possible explanation of why these actions occur despite their illegality:

. . . it is a consequence of the fact that to claim that there is discrimination in the upper reaches of the federal service is to violate a cardinal rule of bureaucratic culture
against exposing the deficiencies of the agency's leadership. Such a complaint would
inevitably militate against future promotion or acceptance . . . into the top ranks of
management, if only because it would be interpreted as displaying "poor judgment."

In addition to reduced leisure time and increased stress on the job, about 45%
of the respondents also reported increased stress in their homelife as the emotional stress of work and the financial stresses influenced their relationships with
others. One respondent stated:

(I was) unable to concentrate on my personal life, unable to concentrate on finance,
lost money in investments, devoted evenings and weekends to this case instead of
socializing and/or advancing and training for other work positions.

Another respondent commented: "What it cost the people who represented me,
my family, myself, in anger and frustration there is no way to estimate." A third
noted that there is "increased stress in general—no one understands what one
goes through when this situation exists."

Two other aspects of the nonmonetary costs of filing were also mentioned. Fif-
ty percent of the respondents noted they had developed new medical problems
and/or aggravated existing health problems which required them to take sick leave
and had led to some medical bills which were not covered by insurance. Furthermore, two noted that their careers had been ruined as the result of blacklisting
and being labeled as "troublemakers."[2]

The monetary costs to the respondents varied considerably depending on the
arrangements for paying the legal costs, including attorney's fees and other costs,
such as xeroxing and travel, the extent to which the respondents could perform
the statistical and legal work for their own cases, and the stage to which the complaint was pursued. About 50% of the women had a "pay as you go" arrangement with their attorneys, and 80% of these respondents used only their personal
and family financial resources. In general, the further the case was pursued, the
more expensive it became, with the greatest expenses occurring due to litigation
in the court stage.

The reported expenses actually paid by the respondents with completed cases
ranged from $1100 spent in 1980 pursuing a case through the administrative stage[3]
to a maximum of $20,000 paid over a seven-year period from 1973-79. In this
latter situation the respondent was later reimbursed for her legal fees when she
won her case. However, she noted that her attorney had not charged her for the
full costs of the suit, and was awarded $56,000 in legal fees. Respondents noted
that today the costs of an individual case litigated in court can be expected to
range from $20,000 to $30,000.

A conservative estimate of the average expenditures for those on the "pay as
you go" plan was about $2100 a year during the time spent pursuing their cases,[4]
but higher annual costs could occur if the case was litigated. One woman noted

she had decided not to litigate simply because she could not afford the monetary expense. However, these costs refer to individual cases only. Class action suits cost considerably more in total even though the costs can be shared among the members of the class. A Title VII class action suit could cost (in 1981 dollars) as much as $350,000, including $15,000 to $25,000 for statistical work and $10,000 for an expert witness (Norton, 1981).

The personal monetary costs are reduced by contingency fee or *pro bono publico* arrangements (the government pays the fees if the case is won), but only about 40% of the respondents had the latter arrangement. Some nonmonetary assistance in the form of free attorney services was received by about 45% of the respondents, but very few received financial assistance from public interest groups. The latter assistance appeared to be tied to the filing of court suits. Thus, the typical pattern which emerges from the experiences of the respondents is paying for all of the legal fees and other costs, such as depositions, xeroxing, travel, and meals away from home, out of their own pocket with reimbursement only after a case is won.

This review of the experiences of the respondents raises the question of how well prepared they were for what happened to them. Generally, the actual costs experienced were greater than the costs expected, and approximately 80% of the respondents indicated they were not adequately prepared for the events which occurred either before they filed a written complaint or afterwards. Prior to attempting to resolve their concerns with informal discussions in stage one, about 37% did not anticipate any costs of any type, while the rest expected some but not all of the costs actually experienced. Even after their experiences during the informal process, about one-quarter did not consider any costs before filing their written charge. One respondent stated in explanation: "I didn't estimate costs ahead of time because I expected the complaint to be settled when it was filed because it is so compelling."

This underestimation of the actual costs experienced occurred despite information-seeking activities by all of the respondents who tried to inform themselves about what to expect. The most underestimated nonmonetary costs were the extent of retaliation at work, the various types of stress, and the time required for processing the complaint. Furthermore, about 50% indicated they had not estimated the expected monetary costs. However, a variety of sources of information were cited as being helpful. References used most frequently for general information were the agency EEO counselors, followed by attorneys, CHANGE members, other women in the agency, and Federally Employed Women (FEW). Attorneys and CHANGE members were the most used source of information to determine the expected monetary costs.

The experiences of the CHANGE respondents as they pursued sex discrimination complaints in the federal government suggest that their expectations of fair treatment on the job and just treatment in the correction of perceived sex discrimination were not matched by the reality of the complaint handling system. These filers experienced substantial monetary and nonmonetary costs while employing procedures designed to keep the costs to all parties low and settle workplace problems within the agency. It is clear from their experiences that filing a discrimination complaint in the federal government is not an exercise for the faint-hearted, those with low incomes, and those without a solid social and/or family support system to help deal with the nonmonetary costs. Furthermore, by-products of this complaint process appear to include several social costs. When retaliation takes the form of withholding work assignments and reduces employee morale, the productivity of the employee filer will be reduced. Stress-induced illnesses increase medical costs paid by taxpayers. The legal costs incurred by the government to fight valid discrimination complaints represent a misallocation of taxpayer financed resources, including those of the women seeking redress. One respondent summed up the situation:

> I did all my own work until one night I realized that the agency had a team of lawyers working on their payroll who were going to appear against me at a hearing. . . . This is when I finally realized it was me against the resources of the U.S. Government.

The nonmonetary and monetary costs experienced by the respondents forces one to ask the question: "Were the benefits received by the filer worth these costs?" Unfortunately, at this time, the answer is unclear for these respondents. Three different outcomes for completed cases were identified, but there is no way to determine which pattern is most prevalent. First, some women received no monetary payments for themselves, but their cases established precedents for improved procedures within agencies and legal precedents in court decisions which will benefit other women and encourage more equal treatment of women in federal agencies. Their reward was, therefore, the psychological reward of helping others. In contrast, other respondents lost their cases with no gain to anyone, and have been left with a great deal of anger and frustration at a system which they perceive to be unfair and unreasonable and which permits discrimination to survive and even thrive. A third group of women indicated they won their cases and received personal monetary rewards including promotions, back pay, training opportunities and reimbursement for legal fees, and may have received some psychological benefits as well. However, most respondents were unable or unwilling to specify the dollar value of these remedies. One respondent did specify that she received a two-year back pay settlement of $54,000, but one has to question whether this is adequate compensation for the opportunity costs of spending virtually all of one's free time on a case for extended periods of time. Although evidence on the average monetary benefits of filing is sketchy, the average benefits for individual complaints handled by the EEOC in FY77 were about $1651 (Abramson, 1979); this amount rose to $3200 in FY82 (Norton, 1981).

Implications for Teachers and Trainers

The research reported in this paper suggests that training designed to prepare professional women to deal with discriminatory treatment in the workplace should be refocused from a narrow emphasis on the identification of legally protected rights to a broader focus on training women to make well-informed decisions about how to assert their rights with the lowest personal and professional costs. In particular, more emphasis on strategies and skills which can be used to resolve a sex discrimination complaint without filing a written complaint is needed since the monetary and nonmonetary costs of filing are so high. However, when informal measures fail, a woman also should be well prepared for the experience she is undertaking. The two sets of recommendations discussed below, therefore, focus on training women to handle workplace problems informally and to make informed decisions prior to using formal institutional mechanisms such as filing a grievance or filing with the EEOC.

The primary objective of the trainer should be to train women to handle their workplace problems themselves so that filing a written complaint is unnecessary. There are five recommendations for accomplishing this objective.

1. It is important that trainers realize that women dealing with perceived discriminatory treatment in the workplace are coping with anger at the unfairness of that treatment. Women are prone to deny this anger, and may blame themselves for what has happened to them rather than realizing that other women also have been systematically treated in a similar manner. Stress also is generated both in the workplace and at home as a result of coping with discrimination and the anger it generates. Trainers therefore should address the issues of anger awareness and stress management or provide referrals to courses on these topics.

2. As a consequence of this anger and stress, women may find it difficult to evaluate their situation objectively. The role of the trainer therefore is to help women clarify the nature of the problem being confronted and the desired outcome.

3. Trainers should encourage the use of creative problem-solving techniques to explore a wide variety of potential solutions available to accomplish the desired outcome, with particular attention to defining those acceptable solutions with the lowest cost to the individual and the highest probability of success. Among the options to be considered should be the development of skills to help women handle workplace problems more effectively, including negotiation, dispute resolution, assertiveness, and male/female communications skills.

4. In addition to skills development, women should be taught how to document the sex discrimination they experience so that they have strong evidence to use in informal negotiations. Specific actions women can take to accumulate evidence should be discussed in training programs. These include keeping a book of anecdotal information on events which occur, talking to other women in the office to find out if they have had similar experiences and how they handled their experiences, keeping notes on meetings held about the problem, talking to supervisors, and collecting information on promotion and training opportunities to see if others also have been treated in a discriminatory manner.

5. Finally, it is important to remind women that family, friends, involvement

in civic and professional organizations, and networks of professional friends are crucial in providing support and helping a woman maintain a positive self image while coping with workplace problems. Trainers can teach networking skills and facilitate the creation of support groups such as CHANGE to deal specifically with EEO problems.

The experiences of the CHANGE respondents indicate that some attempts to settle sex discrimination complaints informally do not succeed. Trainers can assist women who have reached this point by implementing the following three recommendations.

1. Trainers who focus on the legal statutes and institutional complaint mechanisms which require filing a written complaint are focusing their training too narrowly. Women need to be prepared for the full consequences of filing a complaint, including the expected monetary and nonmonetary costs and benefits. This can be accomplished by inviting a woman who has been through the experience of filing a written complaint to speak about her experiences and how and why she ultimately decided to file.

2. Trainers should also encourage a healthy skepticism about the probability of receiving redress for the perceived discrimination. One way to accomplish this is to invite an attorney specializing in EEO cases to discuss the importance of employing an attorney who specializes in EEO law, how to select an attorney, the experiences of their clients, how the monetary costs are determined and the various financial arrangements which can be negotiated with attorneys, the factors which determine the probability of success, the types of evidence needed, and the legal standards of proof which must be satisfied.

3. Women should be encouraged to seek advice from a wide variety of sources prior to filing to ensure they are well informed before making a decision. These sources should include women's rights organizations such as the Women's Equity Action League (WEAL), support groups such as CHANGE, attorneys specializing in EEO cases, and other women who have had to handle the same or similar problems. One important contribution of the trainer is to compile a list of these resources available to her classes and to discuss the types of information each resource can provide.

NOTES

1. The author gratefully acknowledges the research assistance of Marcia Mendicino and helpful comments by Renee Lipson, management consultant.
2. One respondent noted that the man against whom she filed and won her case continued in a normal career progression. In contrast, she estimated that the discriminatory treatment received

from this man, combined with the subsequent retaliation and career destruction which limited her employment options and advancement potential, cost her over the rest of her life a minimum of $375,000 which she will never recover despite winning several discrimination cases.
3. This case ended at the administrative stage when the woman resigned due to harassment and requested that the case be closed.
4. These are conservative estimates due to two factors. First, these data have not been adjusted for inflation over the period from 1975 to 1982 when the costs were incurred and therefore should be considered as underestimates of costs. While such an adjustment is desirable for comparability over several years, it was not possible to make a satisfactory adjustment due to the variations in the accuracy of the reported dates. Second, the respondents usually did not keep detailed records of their expenditures.

REFERENCES

Abramson, J. *Old Boys New Women: The Politics of Sex Discrimination.* New York: Praeger Publishers, 1979.

Bodily, S. "When Should You Go to Court?" *Harvard Business Review,* 1981, 59, 103-13.

Durling, B. "Retaliation: A Misunderstood Form of Employment Discrimination." *Personnel Journal,* 1981, 60, 555-58.

Ewing, D. "Canning Directions: How the Government Rids Itself of Troublemakers." *Harpers,* 1979, 259, 16-22.

Galanter, M. "Afterward: Explaining Litigation." *Law and Society Review,* 1975, 9, 347-68.

Gleason, S. "The Probability of Redress: Seeking External Support." In B. L. Forisha and B. H. Goldman (Eds.), *Outsiders on the Inside: Women in Organizations.* Englewood Cliffs, N.J.: Prentice-Hall, 1981, pp. 171-87.

Lester, R. *Reasoning about Discrimination.* Princeton, N.J.: Princeton University Press, 1980.

Moore, C. "Awarding Attorney's Fees in Federal Sector Arbitration." *The Arbitration Journal,* 1982, 37, 38-47.

Norton, E. "An Assessment From an Enforcement Perspective." In U.S. Commission on Civil Rights, *Consultations on the Affirmative Action Statement of the U.S. Commission on Civil Rights, Vol. I: Papers Presented.* Washington, D.C., Feb. 10 and March 10-11, 1981, pp. 75-81.

Rosenbloom, D. *Federal Equal Employment Opportunity: Politics and Public Personnel Administration.* New York: Praeger Publishers, 1977.

U.S. Office of Personnel Management. *Equal Employment Opportunity Statistics—Federal Civilian Work Force Statistics.* Washington, D.C.: U.S. Government Printing Office, 1980.

Wanner, C. "Public Ordering of Private Relations." *Law and Society Review,* 1975, 9, 293-306.

Yohalem, A. *The Careers of Professional Women.* Montclair, N.J.: Allanheld Osmun and Company, 1979.

The Role of Sports
in Developing Female Managers

Kathleen C. Brannen, Creighton University
Randolph M. Feezel, Creighton University

On the same day that an article headlined, "Team Sports Players Have Business Edge" appeared, another article in the same newspaper carried the caption: "Feminists Call Title IX Move Major Attack." The first article reported on a seminar for upwardly mobile working women which teaches that "a woman should know her chances of getting ahead at any level probably are better if she's played a team sport or had military training" (McCormack, 1981, p. 17). The second article noted that the Reagan administration has decided to take another look at the rule barring sex discrimination in school sports. "For one thing, the department appears to be leaning toward an interpretation that would limit the scope of Title IX to schools whose athletic programs receive federal funds instead of any school which receives any federal funds" ("Feminists Call Title IX Move Major Attack," 1981, p. 37). So it seems that before we have discovered for sure what sports participation can do for women, there are forces at work to limit that opportunity. The purpose of this paper is twofold: (1) To arouse interest in research to determine the type or the kind of sports participation that would be most beneficial to women, and (2) To then become active supporters of sports programs that would best suit the needs of women. This paper begins with a philosophical look at women and sports participation. Student responses to questions about sports programs and sports participation follow. The conclusion briefly relates these ideas to our knowledge about organizational behavior.

Women and Sports Participation

There is a familiar justification or vindication of sports that is offered at times by its defenders. We have all heard it—"Sports build character." The philosopher

Paul Weiss (1969) puts it in the following way, although he does not endorse the argument:

> It is sometimes contended that athletics not only builds bodies but character. Character, it has long been known, is best forged by making men face crises in the little; by being pushed up against limits they define themselves. If they are made to do this again and again in the same areas, firm habits are established, enabling the men to act without much reflection and yet with surety and precision. Properly trained, the men gradually learn how to act quickly and yet successfully; properly aimed, their action will be productive of what enriches while it satisfies. As a result of their athletic activity the men will become more alert to the insistence and rights of others, both those with whom they play and those against whom they play (pp. 28-29).

Anyone who defends or promotes sports because of the possible production of some valuable human qualities must be endorsing, at least in some general sense, the character-building argument for sports. The response to this particular argument, when it is offered in a loose and unqualified way and when it attempts to say something exclusive about the nature of sports and moral education, may be damaging to the defender of sports. For the moral education of the child sometimes is well-developed long before his or her first little league practice, and the effects of sports participation may lead to the growth of personal characteristics which are far from virtuous. Thus, it may be more appropriate to say that sports *reveal* character rather than build it.

All of this suggests that the development of character, virtues, personal attributes—however one might wish to describe the genesis of the personality of individuals—is a very complex process and a development about which one must be very careful when speculating. But to admit that there are clear counter examples to the character-building argument for sports is not to deny that participation in sports sometimes is extremely valuable and that it provides a relevant atmosphere in which certain valuable human qualities might be properly developed. In this more tentative way, it seems to be appropriate to speculate about the effects of sports participation on the personality of females.

One of the most valuable consequences of the women's liberation movement has been the intense and sustained effort to understand the way in which sexual stereotyping has permeated the institutions of society. Certainly women have been excluded in a variety of ways from sports, and the exclusion may well have reinforced the stereotyping of women as passive, vulnerable, timid, physically awkward, weak, and unable to cope with failure. In fact, it has been argued that the very concept of sport contains a male bias, because of the conceptual identification of sports with supposedly more masculine qualities like aggressiveness, strength, assertiveness, size, speed, and power (Young, 1979; English, 1978). The more difficult questions revolve around whether some aspects of such an identification are historical accidents (insofar as grace and coordination might just as well have been emphasized) and whether some aspects of such a "male" conceptual bias have little or nothing to do with an essentially male personality. It is the latter which is of special interest, because the stereotypical passivity and nonassertiveness of the female naturally has wider cultural effects, revealed not only by exclusion from sports, but also by exclusion from the central professions and institutions of leadership and authority in our society. Without committing oneself to anything like a strong causal connection, one might think about the possibility that participation in sports is a possible occasion for the development of qualities which are valuable and human, neither exclusively masculine nor feminine, and which are effective in other areas of life.

Michael Novak, in his wonderful meditation, *The Joy of Sports,* and in his usual suggestive and provocative way, takes up these issues in the chapter "Of Women and Sports." While recognizing that a strong case can be made for the "feminizing" of males, he thinks about this in a different and more personal way. Speaking of his two daughters he says:

> Nonetheless, I wish my two daughters had greater opportunities to play baseball, basketball, and football than they do at present. While the boys on our block are playing their rather vicious games of stickball, football, and basketball, most of the girls at present go for long chatty walks. Perhaps they should. Yet I see my son developing qualities that most of the girls do not seem to acquire. I wish my daughters had equivalent institutional support. Institutions are critical for individual growth (Novak, 1976).

Novak's sense of tentativeness and honesty should be appreciated here. He's not sure; he wonders; he speculates. Later, he again recognizes the tenuousness of his claims: "Perhaps it is chauvinistic and deeply erroneous to wish that the training of women were more like the training of men—that competitive team sports should come to play as large a role in the childhood and growth of women as they do in those of men" (Novak, 1976, p. 203). Yet we think his intuitions are sound, because the qualities we are referring to are important for the growth of a human being. Novak describes a situation with which nearly any parent whose child has participated in a sport can identify. Early in the little league season his son makes an error and is disconsolate; he wants to quit, yet remains on the team. Late in the season, the boy contributes significantly to a victory in the finals. "From bum to hero in a single season. The range of his emotions, his self-confidence, his capacity to accept failure, and his easy familiarity with the desire to quit increased dramatically" (Novak, 1976, p. 196). These are the powerful human and moral ambiguities which sport dramatizes over and over again, which girls should have the opportunity to experience.

Novak offers one other suggestive personal account. His eight-year-old daughter, after considerable agonizing, decides not to become a cheerleader, no doubt a delightful and beautiful little apparition, with pompoms and uniform. Shortly after the difficult decision, father and daughter stand her brother and a friend in a game of touch football. After fumbling on the first play, she falls down, gets up crying, and wants to join her mother and the baby on the sidelines. The next play is immediately called and she outruns her brother on "a brilliant long touchdown run." Perhaps these examples are overly idealized; perhaps not. Undoubtedly, a child might learn in other areas of life what it means to submit to discipline, pursue excellence, experience pain, failure and risk (as well as consummate joy), relate to others, learn one's role in a social organism, and start to realize what it means to understand one's limitations. But if these themes are as important as they seem to be, at least for some who participate in sports, they are no less important for girls than for boys, and perhaps even more so.

Do Students Care About Sports Programs for Women?

To set the stage for a discussion about organizational change and innovation, students in a Fall term Principles of Management class were asked to complete a brief questionnaire on several innovations. Two questions are pertinent to this paper: (1) Federal government deregulation is an important goal for this country, and (2) Title IX support for sports programs for women in our schools should be maintained. The response choices were: 5 =strongly agree, 4 =agree, 3 =neither agree nor disagree, 2 =disagree and 1 =strongly disagree. There was no significant difference between the responses of males and females for either question. The mean response for Question 1 was 3.2 with a standard deviation of .816. The mean response for Question 2 was 3.6 with a standard deviation of 1.11. Although it may be encouraging to know that males and females respond similarly, their response is somewhat apathetic toward both deregulation and sports programs for women. If sports participation for women provides a significant advantage in career development, then awareness of its value must be communicated to students as well as to others. The following section asks a group of business students how they feel sports participation can contribute to career preparation.

How Sports Participation Can Help You Prepare for a Career

A discussion was held in a Spring term Principles of Management class about rumored plans to revise the rules prohibiting sex discrimination by schools that receive federal funds under Title IX. As a follow-up to that discussion, students were given the following optional, extra credit assignment: Give one concrete example of how sports participation can help you prepare for a career. A response was worth 4 percentage points on the final exam, and could be completed as a take-home assignment. The students participated as follows:

Class	Total	Respondents	% Responding
Male	60	38	63%
Female	54	40	74%
TOTAL	114	78	68%

An item analysis of the response is presented in Table 1.

TABLE 1

How Sports Participation Can Help You Prepare for a Career

Comment	Male	Female	Total
Teamwork	21	18	39
Develop Interpersonal Relationships	8	27	35
Competition	13	12	25
Discipline/Responsibility	9	12	21
Work With/Support Others	5	16	21
Goal Accomplishment	14	6	20
Goal Setting	1	11	12
Stress/Work Under Pressure	4	7	11
Learn Specific Function/Relationship of Parts to the Whole	11	0	11
Cooperation	4	5	9
Learn Success/Failure	3	6	9
Communication Skills	2	6	8
Leadership/Decision Making	6	1	7
Individual/Team Goal Overlap	7	1	8
Motivation	3	3	6
Develop Self Worth	0	6	6
Loyalty/Spirit of Unity	2	3	5
Become a Well-Rounded Person	2	0	2
Managers Are Like Coaches	2	0	2
Learn Respect for Opponents	1	0	1
A Place To Make Mistakes	1	0	1
TOTAL	119	140	259

The student population provided a convenience sample, and the responses are neither generalizable nor necessarily representative of a larger or different population. The responses are presented primarily for the purpose of providing some information as an aid to future questionnaire development.

The respondents are business students who have been taught to think in terms of market competition and management teams. We would hypothesize that this student sample can relate the advantages of sports participation to a career more readily than nonbusiness students or other young people. The female students who chose to respond used examples of personal sports experience rather than hypothetical examples or abstract concepts.

What can we glean from these responses? Sports participation provides a variety of experiences. Several responses are presented below as examples to ponder over. Teamwork is seen as the most beneficial outcome of sports participation by both males and females. Further study is needed to determine if the concept "teamwork" means the same thing in our culture to females as it does to males. Only

23% of the respondents who mentioned the development of interpersonal relationships were male. The connection between interpersonal relationships and teamwork as perceived by males and by females needs to be studied. Why is goal accomplishment mentioned most frequently by males, while goal setting is most frequently mentioned by females? Can a case be made for the notion that at the present time females see sports as a place to make better friends while males view sports as training for a tougher environment in the work world? (For example, a) Develop Interpersonal Relationships—response 77% female, b) Work With/Support Others—response 76% female, c) Communication Skills—response 75% female, d) Learn Specific Function/Relationship of Parts to the Whole—response 100% male, e) Leadership/Decision Making—response 86% male, and e) Individual/Team Goal Overlap—response 88% male.)

A sample of responses

A sample of responses are presented below:

(1) Teamwork, a complex way of understanding and interacting with your group, is the primary asset learned through sports participation. Whether your skills are needed as a leader or as "the worker" who carries out necessary actions, playing on an athletic team hones your abilities and reactions that are used everyday in the business world. You can learn about people and yourself while getting a good workout (male).

(2) To be successful in sports competition, teamwork is essential. The success of the team depends on the interdependence of all players. Learning that one must rely on others to do their part, and that others are relying on you to accomplish a specific goal can help one prepare for a career in management. Ridding oneself of the notion that "if I want a job done, I'll do it myself" will help when working in groups. Learning to delegate duties and being responsible for one's own duties is an important function, and can be gained from sports competition—teamwork (female).

(3) I played football for 4 years during high school as linebacker. Football did many things for me which have helped me in later life, such as giving me a competitive spirit, teaching me how to work effectively in a group, and showing me how to be aggressive; however, the one quality that has helped me most in later life which I acquired from playing sports is self-determination. That inner willpower I got from playing football has been indispensible to me in later life. Indirectly, sports has taught me how to stay up that extra hour for an exam, how to force myself to stay home from the bar and catch up on my assignments, and how to control my emotions when the social situation does not fit my feelings (male).

(4) If it is true that people don't need to be taught group behavior, why then do many organizations find it necessary to send employees to sensitivity training groups? College classes can't always provide this experience, but team sports can. Team sports are very effective at this because they can help develop a better understanding of others and oneself (male).

(5) My one example of how participation in sports can help you prepare for a career can be summed up in one word—TEAMWORK. Through sports participation you learn how to combine your individual skills, not only to accomplish your task

but also to enhance your teammates' capabilities. That is the essence of teamwork—bringing out the best traits of those with whom you work (male).

(6) I have been involved in volleyball for many years. I feel it has greatly helped prepare me for a career because through it I have learned how to compete and how to handle pressure situations. But one of the most important things I have learned is how to work together with others as a team to achieve a common goal. I have found that the key to winning is to support and encourage each other, and to have trust and confidence in the others to get the balls that come to them and to be able to cover for others when they don't get it or mishandle the ball (female).

(7) One crucial point should be made about the importance of team sports and its aiding in career preparation—it allows one to experience the forementioned experiences in a detached atmosphere in which mistakes are not costly as they would be in real life situations. Therefore, it allows a person the chance to make mistakes and learn from them without much harm or injury occurring (male).

(8) The one thing that everyone learns in sports of all kinds is patience. For an example, in high school I played basketball. I worked as hard at basketball as anything I've ever done. I sweated and strained and tried so hard. But I never started, I never played that much, I was always a bench rider. The one thing I learned was a vast amount of patience. Sports is not always full of success, and you must be patient to wait for the successes. This is a good trait to have in any career. There will be losses in life as well as in sports, and you better have patience to wait for your victories (male).

All of the students who responded were positive in their attitudes toward sports participation. They find no difficulty in seeing a positive relationship between sports participation and career development.

Why Should We Care About Sports Programs for Women?

Those of us who teach personnel have been far more concerned about the aftermath of Title VII dealing with sex discrimination in employment than with Title IX of the Education Amendments of the Civil Rights Act. We have assumed that those who qualify themselves through education can make their way up the organization within an EEO environment. The ideas presented in this paper show that it is most probable that participation in sports should be a part of that education. In addition to the preparation of mind, body, and spirit which many women have missed; it seems there is also a carryover of sport experience to the work world itself. What have women missed?

(a) There is a literature with which most of us are unfamiliar. *Sport in the Sociocultural Process* by Marie Hart is a good place to begin an introduction to the sport literature.

(b) There is a jargon which most women do not understand. Harragan says that, "Male business terminology is almost foreign speech to women, replete as it is with secret codes, double meanings, and colloquial slang. Translation is essentially a matter of making the nonspecific specific because identical words or phrases can have a vague, abstract, philosophical meaning in the female culture but a concrete, explicit, practical meaning in the male culture" (1977, pp. 69-70). Sports lingo is a part of this vocabulary along with military derivations and sexual allusions, according to Harragan.

(c) Because sport has affected our culture and the organizations which exist within it, ignorance of sport has a detrimental effect on the ability of many women (and men) to correctly interpret what is observed in the business world. The social structure of organizations includes "a system of social roles and behavior norms; of understandings about "proper" behavior, and about "proper" attitudes, values, and motives" (Klein and Ritti, 1980, p. 10). Organizational behavior is affected by mutually shared understandings among members as to what is right and proper behavior. "These shared understandings are not set down as written rules and contracts of the organization, but exist as common expectations concerning behavior" (Klein and Ritti, 1980, pp. 59-60). What is the source of these common expectations?

(d) A part of the organizational socialization process takes place at presocializing institutions. Sports participation can be a part of this experience. "The presocializing experience takes place in a formal setting and is aimed at inculcating proper values, attitudes, and motives, often in the context of skills training. . . . The university and the training academy are generally seen as institutions whose function is to convey skills necessary to future occupations. But we feel that the functions of selection and indoctrination are even more important" (Klein and Ritti, 1980, pp. 125, 143).

The authors feel that the role of sports in developing female managers is a research area which needs exploration. We hope the readers will share an interest in this topic and become participants in sports and in sports research for managers.

Implications for Teachers and Trainers

The research reported in this paper lists a number of characteristics of sports participation which the student respondents feel will be an asset to them on the job. None of the respondents thought that sports participation would be a hindrance to career success. While teachers and trainers can spend some time evaluating how the various characteristics make a valuable contribution to career preparation, in many cases the more important activity is to help women without sports training learn to play "catch up." There are three areas of "catch up" for women:

1. Learn the use of sport analogies to understand behavior at work (Keidel, 1984). Both work organizations and various sports are microcosms of our culture and of the larger society in which we live. Those who learned to interpret the larger culture through an understanding of sports activity will use this understanding to interpret the meaning of organizational behavior or activity whenever possible. Whether the particular analogy is accurate or inaccurate is not as important as the fact that people are behaving in response to *their*

perception of reality. To understand the behavior of others, you must understand their perspective. If their perspective is a sports analogy, then you must know the analogy to make sense of the behavior of others. Learn to listen for sports terminology in everyday discussions, especially at work. Make a list of the use of sports terms in work settings. One of the first things a female engineer did after starting her job was to subscribe to *Sports Illustrated*. If you have not been involved in sports during your youth, subscribe to *Women's Sports* to see how female athletes perceive the world.

2. Learn how to be perceived as a team player. Women as members or potential members of the management team need to manage their impression so that it is both positive and predictable to others.

   Teamwork was the most frequently mentioned aid to career preparation mentioned by the student respondents. One of the most fundamental concepts that carries over from the sports arena to the world of work is that of "team player." Whether or not one is judged to be a "team player" at work is a basic classification used by most men. If you fail to be perceived as a team player, other positive traits that you possess will count for little when it comes to support from those you assume to be your colleagues. You are not on their team! The team is comprised of those capable of winning, and only team players really get the idea. You have probably seen and heard many references to the "old boys network." People are classified by sex, by job title, by level in the organization, and by whether or not they are "into physical fitness." One way into the network of decision makers is to become involved in fitness activities with others at work, because you will find an overlap between the two groups. It is never too late to become involved in sports. Schools in most areas are looking for soccer coaches. Start with a group of first graders and learn with them!

3. Explain what behavior you expect from others by using sports terminology. Women managers tend to get a different response from co-workers than their male counterparts. This differential response may have nothing to do with the capability of female managers. We refer to the movement of women into nontraditional positions such as management. If management is a nontraditional occupation for females, then males have not been socialized to respond to females as managers. We hear complaints that people do not take women seriously, or that we tend to be viewed as another mom. One way to communicate to others how you perceive your role, so that they in turn can respond to that role, is to communicate in sports terminology. Are you the coach? Who's on the first string? Is this just practice, or is it a conference game? One of the reasons that sports terminology is used so frequently is that it is good shorthand. A capable young M.B.A. with good job skills was dismayed to encounter a male colleague who took over a task that really fell under her job description. Later she told him that his behavior reminded her of a center fielder who ran to catch a fly ball in right field territory. He paused in amaze-

ment and said, "You really do understand that!" Now he is aware that she knows the rules used by team players.

Suggested activities for trainers:

1. Have the participants compile a list of different types of coaches. In addition to coaches for different sports you will get a list of leadership types. Males or females who play a number of sports soon learn that there are different types of coaches just as there are different types of managers. The way a coach treats a team member is more directly related to the style of the coach than to the individual being coached.

2. Assign participants to write an incident about a problem at work that involves personal relationships. Have the class translate the incident into a team sport situation.

3. Compile a list of sports terminology that is used to explain human behavior at work. For example, a faculty member was discussing the probable outcome of a decision before the Rank and Tenure Committee compared to the decisions of the past few years, noting that decisions from past years were not necessarily relevant (because members change and no minutes are kept). "Yes," another faculty member replied, "It's a whole new ball game." The conversation ended, because complete communication had taken place. Other examples are: team player, playing your own position, good sport, second string player, tough competitor, ball hog, plays to the stands, a good play.

4. The following is a list of the distinguishing characteristics of modern sports (Guttmann, 1978): secularism, equality of opportunity to compete and in the conditions of competition, specialization of roles, rationalization, bureaucratic organization, quantification, and the quest for records. Discuss how these characteristics are used in sports and whether or not they also serve to illustrate the modern corporation.

5. The average teen-age male who has participated in the usual collection of sports has learned some of the following items. Use them for discussion to evaluate how knowledge of sports translates into job knowledge.
   a) There are many kinds of coaches (managers). Some know what they are doing; others do not. If you are going to play on the team, then you will follow the advice of the coach even if you do not agree with it.
   b) Some referees know the rules and how to apply them, others are not as good (performance evaluators).
   c) Some players are picked for the all stars (promotion) because of game performance, others are son of the coach (and thus received early and extensive coaching and training and practice).
   d) A game schedule is designed so that each team plays every other team in the league during the season. A little inclement weather does not justify upsetting the schedule.

e) The rules of the game were around before you started playing. It's not your job to change (or complain about) the rules. Just learn to play by the rules.

f) Trickery, deception, harassment, and foul play are some of the things which teachers won't teach children, but they are used in sports and in other human interrelationships.

6. Schedule a soccer game for the class members to provide an opportunity for males and females to compete against each other. For help with this assignment see "Soccer: Simulation of Organizational Issues For Women and Men" (Bowen and Bowen, 1982).

REFERENCES

Bowen, D. D., and Bowen, P. "Soccer: Simulation of Organizational Issues for Women and Men." *Exchange: The Organizational Behavior Teaching Journal,* 1982, 7, (1), 32-37.

English, J. "Sex Equality in Sports." *Philosophy and Public Affairs,* 1978, 7, (3), 269-77.

"Feminists Call Title IX Move Major Attack." *Omaha World Herald,* November 13, 1981, p. 37.

Guttmann, A. *From Ritual to Record: The Nature of Modern Sports.* New York: Columbia University Press, 1978.

Harragan, B. L. *Games Mother Never Taught You: Corporate Gamesmanship for Women.* New York: Rawson Associates Publishers, Inc., 1977.

Hart, M. *Sport in the Sociocultural Process.* Dubuque, Iowa: Wm. C. Brown Company Publishers, 1972.

Keidel, R. W. "Baseball, Football, and Basketball: Models for Business." *Organizational Dynamics,* 1984, 12, (3), 4-18.

Klein, S. M., and Ritti, R. R. *Understanding Organizational Behavior.* Boston: Kent Publishing Company, 1980.

McCormack, P. "Team Sports Players have Business Edge." *Omaha World Herald,* November 13, 1981, p. 17.

Novak, M. *The Joy of Sports.* New York: Basic Books, Inc., 1976.

Weiss, P. *Sport: A Philosophic Inquiry.* Carbondale: Southern Illinois University Press, 1969.

Young, I. M. "The Exclusion of Women from Sport: Conceptual and Existential Dimensions." *Philosophy in Context,* 1979, (9), 44-53.

About the Authors

LIZABETH A. BARCLAY has been in the School of Economics and Management at Oakland University since 1980. She earned her Ph.D. in Industrial/Organizational Psychology from Wayne State University in 1981. Her most recent research focuses on equal employment opportunity, personnel issues, and social learning theory.

BRENDA MARSHALL BECKMAN is currently Dean of Academic Affairs for General Education at Delta College. In 1982, Ms. Beckman was the recipient of an American Association of University Professor Award for Governance and in 1983 was selected as a National Forum participant through the American Council of Education's Identification Program for the Advancement of Women in Higher Education Administration. She has also been actively involved in the highly successful "Leaders for the 80s Program" for the advancement of women in community college administration. She earned her B.A. in Political Science from Oakland University, her M.A. in Political Science from Central Michigan University, and has done further graduate work in Political Science and Public Administration at Michigan State University.

KATHLEEN C. BRANNEN has been an Assistant Professor of Management at Creighton University since 1979. She earned her bachelor's degree from Xavier University, Cincinnati, Ohio, her M.B.A. degree from Creighton University, and her Ph.D. from the University of Nebraska. Her doctoral dissertation studied the movement of women into management as the diffusion of an innovation. Dr. Brannen is the Small Business Institute Director at Creighton. Her research interests include career success for women in both large organizations and owner/managed small businesses.

THERESA L. CLOW has been in the Business Administration Department at Stephens College, Columbia, MO since 1980. She earned her bachelor's degree from Stephens College in 1973, her MA from the University of Northern Colorado in 1980, and is currently completing her PhD in Higher and Adult Education at the University of Missouri at Columbia. She teaches business and management courses to residential students and to adults in an external degree program. She is associated with a consulting and training firm, Success Research, which conducts seminars on success. The seminars include topics such as decision-making and negotiation. Her background includes negotiation and contract administration experience with both the federal government and industry.

RANDOLPH M. FEEZEL is Associate Professor of Philosophy at Creighton University. He received his B.S. and M.A. from the University of Oklahoma, and his Ph.D. from State University of New York at Buffalo in 1977. His current research interests include topics in ethics, aesthetics, contemporary philosophy, and philosophy of sport. Other essays on the philosophy of sport include "Sport: Pursuit of Bodily Excellence or Play? An Examination of Paul Weiss's Account of Sport," "Play, Freedom, and Sport," and "Play and the Absurd."

MARGARET FENN, Professor Emerita of the University of Washington, has just returned from New Zealand where she was a Fulbright Lecturer at Victoria University in Wellington and invited lecturer on every campus in New Zealand. She was the founder of the extremely successful Women Plus Business Conference in Seattle which is in its seventh year. Many have benefited from the knowledge and experience shared in her books for women, *Making It in Management* (recently translated into the Dutch language) and *In the Spotlight.*

MITCHELL W. FIELDS has been in the Department of Psychology at Texas A & M University since 1982. He earned his Ph.D. in Industrial/Organizational Psychology from Wayne State University in 1982. His research interests include: equal employment opportunity, psychometrics, leadership, and quality of working life.

SANDRA GLEASON has been an assistant professor in the School of Labor and Industrial Relations of Michigan State University since 1981. She earned a B.A. from Smith College, a M.A. from Northwestern University, and a Ph.D. in economics from Michigan State University in 1978. Prior to joining the faculty of Michigan State University she taught in several colleges, and worked at the Federal Trade Commission while a Brookings Institution Economic Policy Fellow. Her research interests include comparable worth in pay, the measurement of the quality of legal services, and the effectiveness of prison vocational training.

MARIE R. HODGE has been in the Department of Management at Bowling Green State University full-time since 1981. Prior to that, she served as Assistant Dean in the College of Business Administration for fourteen years. She earned her Bachelor's and Master's in Business Administration at Northwestern University in 1938 and 1939, respectively. Because of the large increase in the number of women entering the College during the decade of the '70s, much of her programming and research concerns have centered around women's needs and concerns.

DAVID M. HUNT is a professor of organizational behavior and management at Miami University, Oxford, Ohio. His background and research interest areas include international management with an emphasis on Asia and career development programs with a focus on women and minority interests.

DIANE MCKINNEY KELLOGG is an Assistant Professor of Management at Bentley College in Waltham, Massachusetts. In addition to teaching Organizational Behavior, Interpersonal Relations, Career Development, and Women and Men as Colleagues in Organizations, she is an Organization Development consultant and trainer to clients in both the public and private sectors. She has been a featured speaker nationally on issues related to women's professional development. Her current research with female executives explores their career paths and the balance between their private and personal lives. Her doctoral work was completed at Harvard University.

CAROL M. MICHAEL is a professor of home economics and consumer sciences at Miami University, Oxford, Ohio. As an adviser of students preparing for professional positions as home economists in business, her research interests include the career development of women in business with an emphasis on the role of support relationships.

CLAIRE A. SCOTT MILLER, President of C. Scott Miller Associates, has been a human resource specialist for over ten years. Her experience includes work in industry and higher education, where she developed and taught a graduate-level course in career development. She has conducted workshops in decision making, leadership, time management, dual career, and managing career and family. Her education includes a B.A. from Denison, an M.S. from Bowling Green University, and continuing education from Harvard-Radcliffe.

While directing the Dual Career Project for RESOURCE: Careers, she was on leave of absence from the General Electric Company where she was in professional relations, and taught courses in Career Development for Women; Career Management, and Conducting Performance Appraisals.

RESOURCE: Careers, a nonprofit career development and referral service for professionals, has served clients since 1974. Funded originally by The Cleveland Foundation and now financed mainly by client and corporate membership fees, it is a unique organization dealing with the realities of the current employment market, the changing status of professional women, and the economics of our time.

Ms. Miller can be reached at 1329 Melrose Drive, Cleveland, Ohio 44145, 216-327-2200.

JANINE A. MOON has held various positions in the Training Department of United Telephone Company of Ohio since 1979, and has been an independent training and development consultant since 1976. She earned her bachelor's degree from

Bowling Green State University, and her master's degree from Ohio State University. She is currently completing work in organization development through National Training Laboratories (NTL) Institute. Active in her professional association, the American Society for Training and Development, Ms. Moon is a member of the ASTD Women's Network Executive Committee and functions as the national coordinator of nine Network regional coordinators. She is a frequent workshop leader at professional conferences, and conducts seminars for businesses and organizations in communication, conflict, power, positioning, and networking.

LYNDA L. MOORE is an Assistant Professor of Management at Simmons College in Boston, Massachusetts where she teaches courses in Management, Organizational Behavior, and Behavioral Implications of Women in Management. She is active in a number of national organizations dealing with women in management and has made numerous presentations at professional meetings. Dr. Moore was the Conference Coordinator and Program Chair of the Third Annual Conference on Women and Organizations which was held at Simmons College in August 1984. In addition to consulting to organizations on human resource management and development issues, Dr. Moore is currently conducting research on the career concepts of women managers and the "competencies" needed by undergraduate women majoring in management. Her doctorate is from the University of Massachusetts.

SANDRA MORGAN is Assistant Professor of Human Resource Management in the Stuart School of Business Administration, Illinois Institute of Technology. Dr. Morgan's consulting is in organization change, career management, and management development. Her research interests range from the work/family balance and stress in employed couples to the introduction of technological change in office and factory environments. She received her S.M. and Ph.D. from MIT's Sloan School of Management, an Ed.M. (elementary) from the Harvard Graduate School of Education, and a B.A. in social psychology from Smith College.

DOROTHEA NUECHTERLEIN is the Executive Director of the Valparaiso University Guild, a nationwide women's support organization that recruits students, raises funds, and serves as a public relations arm of the University. Formerly an instructor in sociology, she received a B.A. from Valparaiso in 1960 and an M.A. from Queen's University of Ontario in 1978. She is a Ph.D. student at the University of Chicago, heads a social service project for Valparaiso University, and writes extensively on women's roles and other social issues. Married and the mother of three, she has experienced family/career conflict.

KRYSTAL G. PAULSEN is Manager, Training and Development for Upjohn HealthCare Services, Inc., in Kalamazoo, Michigan. Formerly, she was both administrator of management and executive development programs and faculty member in the College of Business at Western Michigan University. With master's degrees in both business administration and liberal arts, she retains a strong interest in the concerns and development of professional women.

LINDA SUGARMAN has been in the Accounting Department of the College of Business Administration at The University of Akron since 1970 and prior to that, taught accounting at Mercer County Community College in New Jersey. She holds the CPA certificate in both Ohio and New York. Her BBA (1962) and MS (1968) were earned at Hofstra University, Hempstead, New York. In addition to her academic career, she has had experience in business and in public accounting. She has presented papers related to professional women and career lifestyles for the American Vocational Association, the Midwest Accounting Association, and the Midwest Conference on Women and Organizations. Her publications have been in the areas of business and education.

SHIRLEY A. VAN HOEVEN has been in the Department of Communication Arts and Sciences at Western Michigan University since 1970. She graduated from Hope College in 1965 with a bachelor's degree in Speech and English. Her M.A. (1970) and Ed.D. (1976) degrees were earned at Western Michigan University in Communication Arts and Sciences and Educational Leadership, respectively. Dr. Van Hoeven's teaching and research interests are concerned with the impact of communication upon power, leadership, and conflict. She continues to conduct workshops for men and women in organizational settings. Currently an Associate Professor, Van Hoeven is Director of the Graduate Program in the Department of Communication.

Annotated Bibliography of Books
Women in Management

In the spirit of sharing, so essential to the Women and Organizations Conference, an annotated bibliography of some of the books available on some of the issues of interest to teachers and trainers of professional women was prepared and distributed at the 1983 Conference. While far from complete, readers may find it useful in their initial explorations of new areas. My students find it helpful as a "starting point" in their research for required papers.

The bibliography is, in fact, a result of student efforts! Students in my Women in Management class are required to submit an annotated list of references with each of their papers. Collecting these over the last 2-3 years and classifying them by topic made pulling together such a bibliography relatively painless. I am pleased to share it with you and hope that you and your students find it useful.

Assertiveness

Adams, L. *Effectiveness Training for Women.* New York: Wynden Books, 1979. The book gives a step by step method of how women can overcome traditional female passivity and dependence. It suggests ways to master fears of self disclosure, confrontation and conflict, allowing you to protect your rights without feeling unfeminine.

Baer, J. *How to be an Assertive (not Aggressive) Woman.* Brattleboro, Vermont: The Book Press, 1976. Baer offers easy to follow plans that allow the reader to identify their own assertiveness problems, how to respond to others, how to say no, and how to express anger. She indicates how to overcome society's stereotypes of being female.

Bower, S. A. and Bower, G. H. *Asserting Yourself: A Practical Guide for Positive Change.* Mass: Addison-Wesley Publishing Company, 1976. This is a self-program that helps the reader analyze present assertiveness skills and then provides a guide on how to improve areas of weakness. It includes such topics as improving self-esteem, coping with stress and assertiveness techniques.

Phelps, S. and Austin, N. *The Assertive Woman.* San Luis Obispo, California: Impact Publishers, 1975. An excellent analysis of what assertive behavior represents, this book presents information on all areas of one's life. Situation analysis is employed very well to demonstrate different types of behavior. It is also a self-help guide intended to assist women as they grow into assertive individuals.

Smith, M. J. *When I Say No I Feel Guilty.* New York: The Dial Press, 1975. This is a book that uses novel dialogue to explain how to deal with other people in the commercial world, authority relationships, and close relationships of equality.

Beginning a Business

Griffin, B. C. *A Successful Business of Your Own*. Los Angeles: Sherborne Press, 1974. An excellent book on starting and maintaining a business of your own. Includes extra tips for women.

Jessup, C., and Chipps, G. *The Woman's Guide to Starting a Business*, New York: Holt, Rinehart, and Winston, 1979. A thorough guide for women considering a business of their own. Covers many areas of concern.

Kuriloff, A. H. and Hemphill, J. M., Jr. *How to Start Your Own Business and Succeed*. New York: McGraw-Hill, 1981. A handbook with worksheets designed to solidify your ideas. A very direct and to-the-point book on starting a business.

Leslie, M. and Selton, D. *New Businesses Women Can Start and Successfully Operate*. Rockville Centre, New York: Farnsworth Publishing Company, Inc., 1977. A brief review on how to start your own business. Realistic examples of women and their businesses throughout the book.

McCaslin, B. and McNamara, P. *Be Your Own Boss*. Englewood Cliffs, NJ: Prentice-Hall, Inc., 1980. A modern woman's guide to planning and running her business. Covers many areas of business relations.

Office of Management Assistance, U. S. Small Business Administration. *Women's Handbook*. Washington, D. C., 1980. A handbook filled with the many kinds of assistance the U. S. Small Business Administration has for women entering the ranks of small business ownership.

Szykitka, W. *How to Be Your Own Boss*. New York: New American Library, 1978. A guide on how to be your own boss. A complete handbook for starting and running a small business.

Taylor, C. *Women and The Business Game: Strategies for Successful Ownership*. New York: Cornerstone Library, 1980. Although targeted to women, this is a good book for anyone interested in starting or owning a business. It is written so that the first time business reader can understand—it even includes a section on business jargon.

Winston, S. *The Entrepreneurial Woman*. New York: Newsweek Books, 1979. Based on a series of case studies, the author addresses the characteristics, issues, and concerns of women entrepreneurs. From her limited analysis, offers practical advice for a woman entertaining the notion of going into business for herself.

Career Planning

Angel, J. L. *Why and How to Prepare an Effective Job Résumé*. (5th edition) New York: Uniworld Business Publication, 1972. A very extensive study of résumé writing. Actual résumés are used to illustrate a technical approach to writing a résumé.

Arbarbanel, K. and Siegel, C. *Women's Work Book*. New York: Pracje Publishers, 1975. Offers practical advice for women just entering the job market, going back to work after an absence, or thinking about changing jobs. Tells how to find a job, how to acquire a job, and how to deal with sex discrimination on the job.

Bolles, R. N. *What Color Is Your Parachute?*. Berkeley, CA: Ten Speed Press, 1978. A valuable guide developed to help define career goals and provide step-by-step instruction on how to get a job. Gives background on how to prepare for a job interview, how to write a résumé, what to do or say during an interview, and even what to do after you have found a job.

_____. *The Three Boxes of Life*. Berkeley, CA: Ten Speed Press, 1978. A comprehensive work book for Life/Work planning. Everyone should have a copy. It covers so much territory that it should be used as a reference book by anyone who cares about her/his life.

Biegeleisen, J. I. *Job Résumés.* New York: Grosset and Dunlap Publishers, 1982. This reference book provides guidelines and samples for preparing a résumé and cover letter. Contains excellent guidelines and sample questions for interviewing.

Bostwick, B. E. *Résumé Writing.* New York: John Wiley and Sons, 1980. A comprehensive and in-depth review of different styles of résumés. Discusses what, why, who, where, and how concerning résumé writing. Gives examples of completed résumés.

Burack, E. H.; Albrecht, M.; and Seitler, H. *Growing: A Woman's Guide to Career Satisfaction.* Belmont, CA: Lifetime Learning Publications, 1980. A self-help guide intended for the working woman who wants to plan and direct her own more fully rewarding career. The book is laden with inventories, profiles, models, and exercises so that the reader can assess her own skills and goals. The self-help materials represent tools from which a woman can choose to manage her own development more effectively.

Dickhut, H. W. and Davis, M. J. *Professional Résumé/Job Search Guide.* Chicago: Management Counselors, Inc., 1975. Written in an easy-to-read and understand style, designed for the first-time résumé writer. Includes many helpful hints for cover letters, résumés, and follow-up letters.

Fader, S. S. *From Kitchen to Career.* New York: Stein and Day Publishers, 1977. The variety of situations that are covered in this book make it relevant to almost any woman whether or not she wants or needs to work for money. It is the kind of book that will help a woman who is scared to develop courage. It gives valid reasons for investing time and money into the volunteer work, which may be necessary to convince the woman who is full of doubt.

_____. *Successfully Ever After.* New York: McGraw-Hill Book Company, 1982. A young woman's guide to career happiness. The focus is on how to succeed during the months and years after you land a job. Deals with job and career questions, and problems and anxieties women struggle with.

German, R., and Arnold, P. *Bernard Haldane Associates' Job and Career Building.* New York: Harper and Row, 1980. This book offers a complete range of tools for building a career step-by-step, job by job, from one's present position to the ultimate career goal. The book is directed towards men and women who are out of work, ready to work for the first time, rejoining the work world, eager to move upward, or anxious to change careers.

Ginn, R. J. *The College Graduate's Career Guide.* New York: Charles Scribner's Sons, 1981. This manual takes the prospective employee step by step through the career planning process. It is particularly directed towards the college graduate making his/her first entrance into the job market.

Hall, D. T. *Careers in Organizations.* Santa Monica, CA: Goodyear Publishing Company, Inc., 1976. An excellent source that discusses the stages of careers and why careers are important.

Higginson, M. V., and Quick, T. L. *The Ambitious Woman's Guide to Successful Careers.* New York: AMACOM, 1975. Analysis of past socialization of women and how it affects their career planning and success. Solutions are available for ambitious women.

Jackson, T. *The Perfect Résumé.* Garden City, New York: Anchor Books, 1981. This is the book that gives you the definition for the perfect résumé and the ten most common résumé writing mistakes.

McDaniels, C. *Developing a Professional Vita or Résumé.* Garrett Park, Maryland: Garrett Park Press, 1978. This is a volume that defines credentials, papers, professional summary, résumé and vita for you. It gives you the option of what type of front you want to present.

Mitchell, J. S. *I Can Be Anything.* College Entrance Examination Board, 1975. Describes careers for young women. Stresses that you can choose what direction your life is to take.

Occupational Outlook Handbook. Published by the U. S. government, this source reviews all types of occupations in all industries in the U. S. Information includes future employment projections, working conditions, earnings, and general requirements for each position.

Osipow, S. H. *Emerging Woman: Career Analysis and Outlook.* Columbus, Ohio: Charles E. Merrill Publishing Company, 1975. This book describes the major theories of career development and conceptual approaches to understanding vocational choice or development.

Pogrebin, L. C. *Getting Your's.* New York: David McKay Company, 1975. A down-to-earth, informative guide to the female working world. Details how to spot dead-end jobs, gives career advice on finding a good job, gives advice on how to handle occupational hazards (e.g., getting fired, sexuality traps, and male chauvinist bosses) and what to do about sex discrimination.

Recruiting Trends. Chicago: Enterprise Publications. This publication provides interviewers with up-to-date information on interviewing questions and techniques.

Reed, J. (Ed.) *Résumés That Get Jobs: How to Write Your Best Résumé.* New York: Arco Publishing Co., Inc., 1976. An amplified résumé is the term that is used in this volume to describe a résumé that is more than 1 page long but not yet a vita.

Wright, J. W. *The American Almanac of Jobs and Salaries.* New York: Avon Books, 1981. Offers brief descriptions of the professions listed and the range of salaries.

Communication

Barbara, D. A. *Your Speech Reveals Your Personality.* Springfield IL: Charles C. Thomas Publisher, 1958. Analysis of speech and personality. Focus is on the behavioral aspects of speakers and suggests that speech problems are psychological.

Burgoon, J. K. and Saine, T. *The Unspoken Dialogue: An Introduction to Nonverbal Communication.* Boston: Houghton Mifflin Co., 1978. Covers all aspects of nonverbal communication. It has a few paragraphs pertaining to women but mostly defines nonverbal communication and what different gestures mean.

Giblin, L. *How You Can Have Confidence and Power.* Englewood Cliffs, NJ: Prentice Hall, Inc., 1956. Giblin tells the reader the key to success is knowing how to deal with people. You are given practical instructions on how to walk, how to shake hands, and how to control the tone of your voice to produce the right response in the other person.

Hinde, R. A. *Nonverbal Communication.* Cambridge, Mass: Cambridge University Press, 1975. This book analyzes nonverbal communication by the use of experiments. An information theorist, a biologist, and a linguist give input on species differences in communication, and the relation of nonverbal communication to verbal language. It is mostly a scientific approach to nonverbal communication and does not differentiate between male and female.

Siegman, A. W. and Feldstein, S. *Nonverbal Behavior and Communication.* Hillsdale, NJ: Lawrence Erlbaum Associates, 1978. This book covers animal as well as human communication. It analyzes nonverbal communication through experiments and contains many statistics. It gives some good clues on how control is gained with nonverbal communication.

Spiegel, J. and Pavel, M. *Message of the Body.* New York: The Free Press, 1974. This book uses art drawings and manikins for analysis of how body-stance affects how we are perceived. Groups of people are surveyed as to what messages they receive from the art forms. The book is overrun with statistics.

Warschaur, L. A. *Winning by Negotiation.* New York: Berkley Books, 1980. A "how to" book on communicating and negotiating with others so that everyone wins.

Discrimination

Astin, H. S. and Harway, M. *Sex Discrimination in Career Counseling and Education.* New York:

Praeger Publishers, 1977. An exploration of many studies done on sex discrimination in counseling and education. Gives both sides of controversies.

Blau, F. D. *Equal Pay in the Office.* Lexington, Mass.: Lexington Books, D. C. Heath, 1980. A study of the causes and consequences of sex segregation in the labor market. Examines the relationship of differences in employment distribution of male and female workers among firms to the male-female pay differential within selected white-collar occupations.

Madden, J. J. *The Economics of Sex Discrimination.* Lexington, Mass: Lexington Books, D. C. Heath, 1973. Statistical evaluation of sex discrimination and how it affects the economy of the United States.

Peres, R. *Dealing With Employment Discrimination.* New York: McGraw-Hill Book Co., 1978. A practical and realistic work in the field of unlawful employment discrimination, written primarily for employees. Provides a concise and useful understanding of the legal subject of discrimination, sets forth workable guidelines for the prevention of discrimination in complaints and gives resolution of existing complaints.

Dress

Cho, E., and Grower, L. *Looking Terrific.* New York: G. P. Putnam's Sons, 1978. Focuses on the language of clothing and how it affects your life. Helps you consider the special needs of your lifestyle and how to accommodate them through clothing.

Hemingway, P. D. *The Well-Dressed Woman.* New York: David McKay Co., Inc., 1977. Emphasizes how to create that well-dressed look necessary for business women. Tells you how to recognize correctly fitting garments, good fabrics, and how to put together a basic business wardrobe.

Malloy, J. T. *Women's Dress for Success Book.* New York: Wainer Books, Inc., 1977. Explains how women can use their appearance as an effective tool for becoming a more successful manager. The advice is succinctly given and remains practical throughout.

Dual Career Couples

Bird, C. *The Two-Paycheck Marriage.* New York: Simon and Schuster, 1979. Based on research this book discusses eight types of dual-career marriages. It tells about the options two paychecks offer a couple and the price they will have to pay for these options.

Hall, F. S., and Hall, D. T. *The Two-Career Couple.* Reading, Mass: Addison-Wesley Publishing Company, 1979. An excellent analysis of the issues and problems confronting couples who attempt to integrate two careers in one household. Practical and varied insights and techniques are developed for teaching couples how they can convert "stresses into greater self-direction and mutual fulfillment."

Holmstrom, L. L. *The Two-Career Family.* Cambridge, Mass: Schenkman, 1972. Although findings presented in this book were based on a small, nonrandomized sample, one can gain meaningful insights into the dual-career family. Family life cycle, divisions of labor, and competitiveness are among the topics discussed.

Rice, D. G. *Dual-Career Marriage.* New York: The Free Press, A Division of Macmillan Publishing Company, Inc., 1979. This book discusses the strains and structural problems that can be encountered by dual-career couples. It also provides helpful insight on techniques and methods for solving these problems.

Rapport, R. and Rapport, R. N. *Dual Career Families.* New York: Pelican, 1971. This work is one of the earliest dual-career studies. Five British families were carefully studied and results of the study are reported.

_____. *Dual Career Families Re-Examined.* New York: Harper and Row, Publishers, 1977. This is a continuation of their first book in which the authors attempt to discuss issues raised in the first edition. They also examine these same families in light of the social changes in the intervening decade.

Health

Freudenberger, H. *Burn Out: The High Cost of High Achievement.* New York: Doubleday and Co., Inc., 1980. The author describes burn-out and its symptoms, workable cures, and preventative advice to help potential victims recognize the problems and correct them.

Friedman, J. and Roseman, S. *Type A Behavior and Your Heart.* New York: Alfred A. Knopf, 1974. A thorough book that discusses various personality types and their relationship to coronary diseases. The importance of stress and its effects on the heart are emphasized.

Goldberg, P. *Executive Health.* New York: McGraw-Hill, 1978. This book covers basically 3 areas of health and its correlation to stress. First, the ailments to which business people are particularly vulnerable; second, what is being done to correct health complaints; and third, a how-to section for improving health.

Grissum, M. and Spingler, C. *Women and Health Care.* Boston: Little, Brown and Company, 1976. A historical look at the origins and types of power in relation to women and the health care system.

Krause, E. A. *Power and Illness: The Political Sociology of Health and Medical Care.* New York: Elsevier, 1977. This work of general political sociology shows how health care problems are intimately involved with the political, social, and economic struggles of the day.

History of Women

Altbach, E. H. *From Feminism to Liberation.* Cambridge, Mass: Schenkman Publishing Co., Inc., 1971. This collection of works aims to further the critical analysis of the Women's Liberation movement and its revolutionary potential.

Blaxcell, M. and Reagan, B. (Eds.). *Women and the Workplace.* Chicago: The University of Chicago Press, 1976. An excellent collection of readings about the implications of occupational segregation. This book covers such subjects as familial constraints, policy issues, social institutions, economic dimensions, and the historical roots of occupational segregations.

Cott, N. F. and Pleck, E. H. *A Heritage of Her Own.* New York: Simon and Schuster, 1979. The book goes beyond the stereotypical roles assigned to women in conventional histories written by males. It examines the vital themes that transcend history, the intimate relationships between women and men, women and women, women and the workplace, and women and the home.

Fremon, S. *Women and Men: Traditions and Trends.* New York: H. W. Wilson Company, 1977. The book discusses the changing situation of women in recent decades. It analyzes the problems faced by both women and men in the stages of their lives focusing on early conditioning to sex roles and later reinforcement.

Gornick, V. *Essays in Feminism.* New York: Harper and Row, 1978. Essays on feminist issues, published over a nine-year period in the *Village Voice.*

Hymorwitz, C. and Weissman, M. *A History of Women in America.* New York: Bantam Books, Inc., 1978. Traces the history of women in America, their trials and tribulations, the progress that has been made and that which still needs to be made.

Kessler-Harris, A. *Women Have Always Worked: A Historical Overview.* Old Westbury, New York: The Feminist Press, 1981. This book explores the history of the working lives of women in the U. S. from the colonial period to the present. The author discusses the meaning of work in women's lives, household labor, paid employment, social reform work, and the changing nature of the contemporary work force.

Kreps, J. M. *Women and the American Economy: A Look to the 1980's.* Englewood Cliffs, NJ: Prentice-Hall, Inc., 1976. Examines the effect the changes in the number of women in the labor force are having and will continue to have on the economic potential of our nation. Paints a fascinating picture of women—how they are reshaping our economy and society—and offers an interesting preview of how women will influence this nation in the next decade.

Kuhn, A. and Wolpe, A. M. *Feminism and Materialism: Women and Modes of Production.* Boston: Routtedge and Kegan Paul, 1978. The papers presented in this volume focus on the two main themes of family and the labor process, since precise analysis of women's position in these two areas is necessary to understand the past as well as the present. Several of the works are actual case studies and present an international viewpoint rather than just an American view on the status of women in the world.

Lerner, G. *The Female Experience: An American Documentary.* Indianapolis: The Bobbs-Merrill Company, 1977. The focus of the book is what it has meant to be a woman in America, how women have passed through the life cycle from youth to death, how women have moved out into male-dominated society and how they have defined themselves, while developing various forms of feminist consciousness.

Robertson, P. *An Experience of Women: Pattern and Change in 19th Century Europe.* Philadelphia: Temple University Press, 1982. This is an excellent book on the women's movement in 19th century Europe. It is extremely worthwhile reading because I could see some of the roots of the feminist movement in America. Also this book has a brilliant bibliography to use for future research.

Sanguiliano, I. *In Her Time.* New York: Marrow Quill Paperbacks, 1980. A really excellent book dealing with women's lives and various crises and transitions one can expect to pass through. She deals with and interviews primarily middleclass women. The book stresses growth—it's beautiful.

Smith, R. E. *The Subtle Revolution: Women at Work.* Washington, D. C.: The Urban Institute, 1979. An analysis of working women from many different perspectives. The book presents research tracing the growth and increasing diversity of the female labor force. Since the turn of the century, it examines the prospects for women in the labor market and highlights their problems and needs.

Sweet, J. A. *Women in the Labor Force.* New York: Seminar Press, 1973. This book investigates employment status in relation to the family, education, family economic pressure, and age. In addition, the effects of various aspects of marital and fertility history such as age at marriage, number of times married, and the length of the first birth interval on current employment.

Laws

Berger, M. *Litigation on Behalf of Women: A Review for the Ford Foundation.* New York: Ford Foundation, 1980. This is a very compact study about the importance of litigation in the women's rights movement. Also it gives a very good explanation of Title VII and IX and other legislation concerning women.

DeCrow, K. *Sexist Justice.* New York: Random House, Inc., 1974. Gives an analysis of the laws, legislators, judges, lawyers, and law professors that make up our legal system and how they are prejudicial against women.

Eisler, D. *The Equal Rights Handbook.* New York: Avon Books, 1979. A well-organized and researched look at the implications of an Equal Rights Amendment with tactics to employ in the fight for this end.

Farley, J. *Affirmative Action and the Woman Worker.* New York: AMACOM, 1979. This book is concerned with the many ramifications of affirmative action along with implementation of this program. It reviews the situation that prompted enactment of affirmative action legislation and shows why legislators have seen fit to intervene in areas that were traditionally done by management.

U. S. Equal Employment Opportunity Commission. *Affirmative Action and Equal Employment.* Vol. 1. Washington, D. C.: U. S. Government Printing Office, 1974. A detailed outline of the legal basis of affirmative action and the basic steps to developing an effective affirmative action program.

Leadership and Power

Brady, M.; Dyer, L.; and Parriott, S. *Woman Power!* Los Angeles: J. P. Taicher, Inc., 1981. This is a humorous book written in a satirical style, about women making it to the top and what awaits them there.

Chesler, P. and Goodman, E. J. *Women, Money, and Power.* New York: William Morrow and Co., 1976. This book presents 16 chapters on the socio-economic condition of women in the context of social trends, male-female relationships, the education of women, future employment, and leadership needs. This book is an excellent exploration into the importance of power, myth, and reality.

Hart, L. B. *Moving Up! Women and Leadership.* New York: AMACOM, 1980. This book is addressed to women exploring new roles in the changing job environment. This practical book not only speaks from the woman's point-of-view, but also covers the essential aspects of leadership.

Hochschild, A. R. *Women and the Power to Change.* New York: McGraw-Hill, 1975. The author suggests that whole economic and social patterns must be rearranged if women are to gain equity in the workplace. The egalitarian marriage, with a radically different definition of career, must become normative.

Killian, R. A. *The Working Woman: A Male Manager's View.* American Management Association, 1971. Provides specific, practical guides to male and female leaders for achieving maximum harmony and performance results with women.

Korda, M. *Power! How to Get It, How to Use It.* New York: Random House, 1975. A very convincing, readable explanation of "how to use, recognize, and live with power." The author discusses power people, power games, and power symbols. A chapter on Women and Power describes what some women have done to increase their power status.

Mitton, D. G. and Liligren-Mitton, B. *Managerial Clout.* Englewood Cliffs, NJ: Prentice-Hall, Inc., 1980. Although not limited to a woman's perspective, these authors explain the value of a tool women are often perceived as lacking—clout. This self-help guide specifically explains techniques and methods whereby the reader can change her attitudes and actions so that she can be perceived as a person with clout. Emphasis remains throughout on developing a style of mutual respect in transactions so ultimately the reader can manage with the willing cooperation of others—whether bosses, peers, or subordinates.

Miscellaneous

Becker, B. *Decisions, Getting What You Want.* New York: Grosset and Dunlap, 1978. The author gives a step-by-step program that helps you make better decisions and increases skill in the decision-making process.

Bulmer, C. and Carmichael, L. J. *Employment and Labor-Relations Policy.* Lexington, Mass: Lexington Books, D. C. Heath, 1980. Examines many issues of labor-management policy affecting employment and labor. Judges the presidential leadership and government reorganization and how they affect equal employment opportunities.

Dobson, T. and Miller, V. *Giving in to Get Your Way.* New York: Delacatc Press, 1978. A unique method, based on a Japanese style of self defense, of handling conflict, social problems, and psychological attack.

Forisha, B. L. and Goldman, B. *Outsiders on the Inside: Women and Organizations.* Englewood Cliffs, NJ: Prentice-Hall, Inc., 1981. Based on a seminar given at the University of Michigan in

1979. Brings together the work of recognized experts on working women. An excellent book covering all aspects of what the working woman needs to know and what qualities she needs to have to get ahead.

Frost, J. and Wilmont, W. *Interpersonal Conflict.* Dubuque, Iowa: Brown Co., 1978. This book examines the various views of conflict, the role of power in conflict, and offers strategies of intervention for managing conflict.

Ginzberg, E. and Yohalem, A. *Educated American Women: Self Portraits.* New York: Columbia University Press, 1966. This book analyzes a specific group of educated women. The authors have woven together and discussed similarities and dissimilarities, then painted a portrait of the educated American woman.

Kaufman, G. and Blakeley, M. K. *Pulling Our Own Strings: Feminist Humor and Satire.* Bloomington, Ind: Indiana University Press, 1980. This volume of satire and humor is one of the best to come out in a long time. It pokes fun at many things women take for granted and lets us laugh at ourselves.

Neal, P. E. and Tutko, T. A. *Coaching Girls and Women: Psychological Perspectives.* Boston: Allyn and Bacon, 1976. Gives psychological aspects of women in sports. Supports evidence that women can handle more pressure and stress than men.

Neubeck, K. J. *Social Problems: A Critical Approach.* Glenview, IL: Scott, Foresman and Company, 1979. This is a text for the study of social problems in the U. S. It deals with inequality in schools and the environment. It does not deal specifically with business but it gives some understanding in the socialization process.

Stearns, P. N. *Be A Man! Males in Modern Society.* New York: Holmes and Meier Publishers, Inc., 1979. Describes the evolution of Western man, his roles and how they have changed, and how men had to struggle with them.

Networking

Kleiman, C. *Woman's Networks.* New York: Lippincott and Crowell, Publishers, 1980. Concisely introduces the importance of networking for women in business, the professions, health and sports fields, politics and labor, and the arts. Advice is offered on how to establish a network, and the book concludes with a list of national, state, and local U. S. women's networks.

Stern, B. B. *Is Networking for You?* Englewood Cliffs, NJ: Prentice-Hall, Inc., 1981. Traces the history of networking from its beginnings as the "Old Boy Network." Gives many reasons why it is important to understand how networks operate and how to organize your own network, including the pitfalls and the glories.

Welch, M. S. *Networking: The Great New Way for Women to Get Ahead.* Harcourt Brace Jovanovich, Inc., New York, New York, 1980. This book shows women how to be part of networking. Success stories are depicted in this book about women whose networks have helped them to better jobs and higher salaries. Also described in this book is how to form your own network.

Organizational Politics

Culbert, S. A. and McDonough, J. J. *The Invisible War.* New York: John Wiley and Sons, Inc., 1980. An extremely stimulating and readable book on the political struggles in organizations. It offers unique perspectives on self-motivation and resulting deception in communication, on leadership, and on power. Concepts are explained through their application to real-life examples.

Dubrin, A. J. *Winning at Office Politics.* New York: Van Roshand Rienhold Company, 1978. It is a unisex guide to practicing sensible office politics at every job level no matter what organization. It includes such topics as understanding office politics, strategies for gaining favor.

Harragan, B. L. *Games Mother Never Taught You.* New York: Warner Books, 1977. An excellent analysis of why women don't share the male executive's perspective of corporate gamesmanship. The book is dedicated to introducing women to the unwritten rules, male jargon, and feminine attitudes that handicap women. The author's emphasis remains on how a woman knowledgeable about these things can successfully use her own perspective within the corporate framework.

Kennedy, M. M. *Office Politics.* Chicago: Follett Publishing Co., 1980. A practical guide to dealing with politics at work. The author first examines popular beliefs about politics and work, then leads the reader through a process coping with the reality of work. Her presentation includes tips on political analysis, career and strategy planning, mentoring, extraordinary politics, and managing politics in the organization.

Self-Help

Berne, P. E.; Dublin, J., and Muchnick, S. *You've Got a Great Past Ahead of You.* Indianapolis: The Bobbs-Merrill Co., 1980. This book is designed to get women to do the thinking which is preliminary to actual planning. It will not help you plan, but it will help you get started with the thinking that is absolutely essential.

Billings, V. *The Woman's Book.* Los Angeles: Wollstonecraft, Inc., 1974. The author explains the ways of dependent and independent behavior, what is meant by equality, and what feminine means. Also, what types of behavior to practice in order to improve your life in various areas.

Carnegie, D. *How to Win Friends and Influence People.* New York: Pocket Books, 1944. The original self-help in which all that you need to be an instant success is set forth in an easy style.

Carriere, R. and Hart, J. *Psychological Fitness, 21 Days to Feeling Good.* New York: Harcourt Brace Jovanovich, 1979. A self-help book that contains exercises and programs of change concerning many aspects of life such as worries, depression, frustration, loneliness, and other emotional problems.

Fast, J. *Creative Coping: A Guide to Positive Living.* New York: William Morrow and Company, Inc., 1976. This book includes many stress factors that challenge our coping ability. These aspects are reviewed and then techniques are suggested on how to master these anxiety-producing situations.

Snelling, R. *The Opportunity Explosion.* New York: The MacMillan Co., 1969. Some of the information is out of date but the general message is still appropriate. Specifically "you can overcome any problem with enough of the right kinds of positive effort."

Sexual Harassment

Backhouse, C. and Cohen, L. *Sexual Harassment on the Job.* Englewood Cliffs, NJ: Prentice-Hall, Inc., 1981. Using statistical studies, interviews with executives and personnel managers, case studies, historical records, and court cases the authors show how pervasive sexual harassment is in the workplace.

MacKinnon, C. A. *Sexual Harassment of Working Women.* Salt Lake City: The Murry Printing Company, 1979. Covers all facts of sexual harassment of working women and how laws and society have dealt with it.

Socialization and Stereotypes

Carmichael, C. *Nonsexist Childraising.* Boston: Beacon Press, 1977. The author presents a view of child raising from the feminist viewpoint. She is practical, however, in her recommendations because she sees reality clearly. She provides key guidelines in evaluating books for sexism.

Epstein, C. F. *Woman's Place.* Los Angeles: University of California, 1970. Myths and stereotypes are discussed, as well as data on the fears of succeeding for women. Hardships and barriers of the external environment are also dealt with.

Fasteau, M. F. *The Male Machine.* New York: McGraw-Hill Book Publishing Company, 1974. Discusses the "male mystique" and how destructive male stereotypes are to men. Also examines interactions with women, how men conduct themselves in work, social life, and so forth.

Fisher, E. *Women's Creation.* New York: Doubleday, 1980. A very interesting and well-written work touching on many thought-provoking subjects. Demonstrates that links between aggression and maleness are without scientific substance. Suggests that current evolution theories, positing hunting as a more advanced and creative human activity than gathering, have devalued and falsified women's true contributions.

Muff, J. (Ed.). *Socialization, Sexism, and Stereotyping: Women's Issues for Nursing.* St. Louis: Mosby, 1982. The book discusses developmental and discrimination issues for women in general and nurses in particular. Strategies for dealing with sexism and improving self-esteem are offered.

O'Kelly, C. G. *Women and Men in Society.* New York: D. Van Nostrand Company, 1980. The central theme of this book is that although the roles of men and women vary widely from society to society, gender roles can be explained by social variables. This book is an excellent reference for women's studies courses dealing with gender roles and sexual stratification.

Orasanu, J., Slater, M. K., and Adler, L. L. (Eds.). *Language, Sex and Gender: Does a Difference Make A Difference.* New York: The New York Academy of Sciences, 1979. This book is a collection of papers that throw a light on a series of questions raised concerning gender-marked features of speech and implications of those differences for social realities.

Reeves, N. *Womankind, Beyond the Stereotypes.* Chicago: Aldine Publishing Company, 1973. A very large and complete volume dealing in detail with every imaginable subject pertaining to women. Divided into two major sections, the first written by the author, and the second submitted by a variety of contributors.

Richardson, L. W. *The Dynamics of Sex and Gender.* Boston: Houghton Mifflin Company, 1981. The chapter on mass media (chapter 5) provided me with insights I haven't encountered in such detail elsewhere. This book says it all regarding women's plight from a sociological perspective.

Rivers, C.; Barnett, R., and Baruch, G. *Beyond Sugar and Spice: How Women Grow, Learn and Thrive.* New York: Ballantine Books, 1979. Explores reasons why women feel that they should be taken care of in adulthood. Suggests ways of helping young girls to grow up to be able to take care of themselves.

Robinson, L. S. *Sex, Class and Culture.* Bloomington, Ind: Indiana University Press, 1978. A book of 12 essays written between 1968 and 1977 on the work that women do and its relation to cultural expression. They are the author's attempt to figure out what she thinks and why she thinks that way.

Teitelbaum, M. S., Lancaster, J., Barfield, A., Brown, J., Stewart, V., and Fee, E. *Sex Differences.* Garden City, NY: Anchor Books, 1976. Explains how and sometimes why males and females act or react differently in different situations.

Williams, J. H. *Psychology of Women.* Toronto: George J. McLeod Limited, 1977. Examines why myths come about, how they are continued, and how they become stereotypes.

Success

Adams, J. *Women on Top.* New York: Berkley Books, 1979. Looks at successful women, how they got there, how they stay there. Also examines their personal lives, their rewards and problems.

Cannie, J. K. *The Woman's Guide to Management Success: How to Win Power in the Real Organizational World.* Englewood Cliffs, NJ: Prentice-Hall, Inc., 1979. Deals with developing and delivering behavioral skills for professional and personal development. Chapters deal with such topics as: what makes people tick, getting comfortable managing others, negotiating and persuading, conflicts, and decision making.

Knudson, R. B. (Ed.). *Women and Success: The Anatomy of Achievement.* New York: William Morrow and Company, 1973. The editor of this collection of works by women on the success of their lives is concerned by the lack of professional women in our society and is attempting to present viewpoints from women who have achieved success in their fields.

Korda, M. *Success!* New York: Ballantine Books, 1978. This book gives you the inside track on how to set goals and achieve them, that is, set up "game plans of success." While more for men than women, it does include a section on women and success.

Kennedy, M. M. *Career Knockouts—How to Battle Back.* New York: Warner Books, 1980. Describes in detail factors that can knock you out of your career. A career guidebook for the 80s that can help you re-evaluate your job attitudes and your organization's problems. Includes probing questions and self tests and gives winning strategies for success.

Malloy, J. T. *Malloy's Live for Success.* New York: William Morrow and Company, Inc., 1981. Provides information and guidelines on how to be successful in the business world. Covers such topics as body language, verbal patterns, interviews, sales, communications, and office politics.

Seaman, F. and Latimer, A. *Winning at Work.* Philadephia: Running Press, 1979. Although not a thorough analysis, the book presents many practical suggestions for solving the basic problems of women who want to achieve satisfaction and gain recognition for a job well done in the office or home. Issues regarding rejection, decision-making, power, criticism, and success are addressed, and the authors conclude the book with a useful annotated bibliography on the issues addressed in the text.

Swell, L. *Success: You Can Make It Happen.* New York: Simon and Schuster, 1976. A step-by-step course to learn to mobilize personal strengths, identify a system of values and write a personal "success chart." Through a program of building on the positive areas of our lives, this guide helps the individual to set short- and long-term goals. Shows readers how to be the best they can be, living in harmony with themselves and increasing their successes each day.

Stress

Albrecht, K. *Stress and the Manager.* Englewood Cliffs, NJ: Prentice-Hall, Inc., 1979. An explanation of stress and how it affects a person in a management position. Teaches managers how to live and work with stress.

Cooper, C. L. and Marshall, J. *Understanding Executive Stress.* New York: P. B. I. Books, 1977. Provides the reader with a better understanding of the sources of stress acting upon the manager.

Forbes, R. *Corporate Stress.* New York: Doubleday and Company Inc., 1979. The purpose of this book is intended not to teach you how to eliminate stress, but how to learn with it. It helps the reader identify an optimal level of stress to enhance productivity and job satisfaction.

Frew, D. R. *Management of Stress.* Chicago: Nelson-Hall Co., 1977. Deals with stress in work and nonwork situations, and how to improve both.

Gherman, E. M. *Stress and the Bottom Line.* New York: AMACOM, 1981. This book is an excellent working manual for handling stress. It will help the individual deal with personal and corporate stress, both positive and negative. It is designed to help people cope effectively with stress-creating situations in our society.

Kiev, A. *A Strategy for Handling Executive Stress.* Chicago: Nelson-Hall Company, 1974. Gives the reader ideas of how to handle stress better and examines behavioral factors which contribute to stress in management.

Kinzer, N. *Stress and the American Woman.* New York: Anchor Press, 1979. A book that studies 119 women from West Point to determine the effects of professional advancement and its relationships to stress-related illness. She advises how to work in a competitive world by keeping one's femininity which may serve as a "natural" protection against stress-induced diseases.

McQuade, W. and Aikman, A. *Stress.* New York: E. P. Dutton and Company, Inc., 1974. A complete book that discusses the results of stress especially the physical effects. It explains how both the mind and body handle stress and how to cope with it.

Norfolk, D. *The Stress Factor.* New York: Simon and Schuster, 1977. Norfolk describes the biology of stress, the origin of stress, the control of stress, and how to turn problems and frustrations of life into purposeful, problem-solving action.

Parrino, J. J. *From Panic to Power, the Positive Use of Stress.* New York: John Wiley and Sons, 1979. This book follows three case studies of individuals in different stress situations. It traces their progress from recognition of the problem through successful coping behavior.

Parker, R. S. *Emotional Common Sense.* New York: Harper and Row, 1973. This book concerns itself with a self-understanding of behavior, recognizing stress and methods of coping with stress.

Selye, H. *Stress without Distress.* Philadelphia: J. B. Lippincott Company, 1974. Selye explains the physiological mechanisms of stress and offers advice on avoiding stress that is harmful.

Time Management

Barret, R. *Executive Time-Control Program.* Englewood Cliffs, NJ: Prentice-Hall, Inc., 1964. This manual is designed as a programmed scheduling system. It shows that organizational planning and realistic forecasting are the only means by which executive output can be increased.

Fanning, R. and Fanning, T. *Get It All Done and Still Be Human.* New York: Ballantine Books, 1980. A time-management workshop designed to help you make better use of your time. Provides many useful tools and ideas.

Goldfein, D. *Every Woman's Guide to Time Management.* Millbrac, California: Les Femmes Publishing, 1977. Donna Goldfein analyzes the time traps as well as the proven techniques of organization that will help one free precious hours to pursue personal interests.

Lakein, A. *How to Get Control of Your Time and Your Life.* New York: The New American Library, 1973. A practical, no-nonsense guide to managing your personal and business time. Shows you how to set short-term and long-term goals, establish priorities, organize a daily schedule, and achieve better self-understanding. Provides tips for building will power, creating quiet time, defeating unpleasant tasks, and keeping yourself on target.

Love, S. F. *Mastery and Management of Time.* Englewood Cliffs, NJ: Prentice-Hall, Inc., 1978. How to make more effective and efficient use of your time, i.e., accomplish more with the time you have.

Mackenzie, R. A. *The Time Trap.* New York: AMACOM, 1972. This book is packed with practical, easy to apply tips that you can use to make yourself more productive than you ever thought possible. You can learn to lower the pressure on yourself more and get much more accomplished by using sensible time management techniques, such as discovering your top-ten time-wasters, setting goals and priorities, and planning your time effectively. An excellent book, makes you enthusiastic about changing your habits.

McCay, J. T. *The Management of Time.* Englewood Cliffs, N.J: Prentice-Hall, Inc., 1959. This book sets forth a practical method for overcoming time pressures today, and preparing for the much greater time demands of the coming decade. Going beyond superficial time-saving techniques, the author underscores the intimate relationship between time pressures and rate of personal growth.

Tennor, D., *Super Self: A Woman's Guide to Self-Management.* New York: Funk and Wagnalls, 1977. You start with a daily schedule and work your way into finding out your hidden low points of the day and how best to work around them. You can learn to become assertive and competent all by reading this one book and following the instructions in it.

Webber, R. A. *Time and Management.* New York: Van Nostrand Reinhold Company, 1972. A book to help you gain insight into yourself, give you a perspective of your time, on insight into your behavior at work, and to help you understand how time affects managerial behavior and decision making.

Webber, R. *Time is Money.* New York: The Free Press, 1980. Shows you how to gain control of time that means money with tested tactics that work. Begins by taking a look at shorter-term time management, discussing the reasons for managing time through lists and diaries.

Women in Management

Bird, C. *Everything a Woman Needs to Know to Get Paid What She's Worth in the 1980's.* New York: Bantam Books, 1980. Contains all the latest information on salaries, statistics, legal rights, and job tactics. Has very useful information on what are the best jobs for women, how to acquire these jobs, how to move ahead once you're in, how to start your own business, and how to use the law to get what you deserve.

Colwill, N. *The New Partnership: Women and Men in Organizations.* Palo Alto: Mayfield Publishing Company, 1982. The male/female coalition in organizations is addressed from the perspective of role theory, trait measurement attributions of success, power, communication and leadership. Chapter 2, specifically, covers sex-role stereotyping.

Douglass, L. S. *Women In Business.* Englewood Cliffs, NJ: Prentice-Hall Inc., 1980. This book shows women in business how they can make themselves marketable, and the importance of understanding and liking who we really are. It features self-exploration, assessment, guidance, and building your own support system.

Fenn, M. *Making It In Management.* Englewood Cliffs, NJ: Prentice-Hall Inc., 1978. Sufficiently introduces women to the management process, explains why women haven't easily fit into that process, and suggests techniques women have available to break down the barriers to becoming successful managers. Its brevity makes the book a good introduction for women discovering some of the issues they need to explore as they enter management ranks.

———. *In the Spotlight—Women Executives in a Changing Environment.* Englewood Cliffs, NJ: Prentice-Hall, 1980. Covers subjects such as organizational conflict, conflict management, management of change, and the art of negotiation from a woman's perspective.

Fidell, L. S. and DeLamater, J. *Women In the Professions: What's All the Fuss About.* California: Sage Publications, 1971. The editors of this book collected essays on women in the business world. They also gave helpful hints on interviewing, meetings. They are a success in the business world.

Gordon, F. E. and Strober, M. H. *Bringing Women into Management.* New York: McGraw-Hill Book Company, 1975. A compilation of articles written by noted experts on women's issues as they relate to women in management. The last third of the book contains vignettes showing institutional and subtle barriers women have encountered. This book is particularly "tuned in" to the business-oriented female.

Hennig, M. and Jardim, A. *The Managerial Woman.* New York: Pocket Books, 1976. These authors analyze what events, attitudes, skills, and techniques were responsible for the success of twenty-five successful women managers and address the implications for aspiring women managers. Their excellent analysis is insightful and important for both men and women struggling to integrate a "mixed corporation" intelligently and successfully.

Josefowitz, N. *Paths to Power.* Reading, Mass: Addison-Wesley Publishing Co., 1980. This useful and encouraging book shows women how to get ahead in the business world without compromising their values or ideals. Lending personal insights and sympathetic counsel, Dr. Josefowitz offers supportive advice to any woman at any stage in her career—from first job to top executive. Offers invaluable information on what skills you'll need to get a job, get promoted, motivate subordinates, manage time, handle stress, and become a more forceful leader. Offers specific tips on writing a résumé, understanding the power structure, being in the right place at the right time, finding a sponsor, and more.

Kanter, R. M. *Men and Women of the Corporation.* New York: Basic Books, Inc., Publishers, 1971. Another excellent book based on an actual field study. Examines the relationship of men and women within a corporation and offers unique and convincing reasons why women have been excluded from power positons—reasons which go beyond sex-role stereotyping. Her suggestions for change are concrete, practical, and inviting.

Lee, N. *Targeting the Top.* New York: Doubleday and Company, Inc., 1980. A complete, comprehensive resource book exploring basic management know-how for women. The author discusses ways for prospective women managers to plan an effective career strategy to get to the top.

Pinkstaff, M. A. and Wilkinson, A. B. *Women at Work: Overcoming the Obstacles.* Reading, Mass: Addison-Wesley Publishing Co., 1979. This book addresses problems unique to women in business and industry and offers techniques for overcoming them. Topics discussed include self-image, family relationship, mentors, ambition, anger, stress.

Place, I. and Plummer, S. *Women in Management.* Illinois: VGM Career Horizons, 1982. Presents information middle managers and supervisors should be familiar with. Brings practical insight into the management arena and helps the reader walk through a business career from setting goals and objectives to a management Self-Rating Checklist.

Thompson, A. M. and Wood, M. D. *Management Strategies for Women or, Now That I'm Boss How Do I Run This Place?* New York: Simon and Schuster, 1980. The book covers such matters as power, planning, financing, appraising, and decision making for women in management positions. It is designed with self-tests, checklists, and games and exercises.

Williams, M. G. *The New Executive Woman.* Radnor, PA: Chilton Books Company, 1972. A practical guide book for striving executive women which is founded on the personal experiences of women who succeeded as executives. The text addresses a variety of situations and problems about which the fledgling executive woman needs forewarning; these include traveling, managing office space, and office sex relationships. Sound strategies are offered for the secretary aspiring for promotion to management and for any woman wanting to assume responsibility for increasing her chances of executive success.

Women, Work, and Family

Bernard, J. *Women, Wives, Mothers.* Chicago: Aldine Publishing Co., 1975. This book pulls together research, theory, and polemics about the status and problems of women as they relate to public policy. Includes discussion of "manpower" development, concepts of self-fulfillment and sex roles, and the present women's liberation movement.

Callahan, S. C. *The Working Mother.* New York: The MacMillan Co., 1971. This book is based on interviews with working mothers, their decisions to work full- or part-time, arrangements for child care, household management, and work routines.

Duvall, E. M. *Marriage and Family Development.* Philadelphia: J. B. Lippincott Company, 1977. The text's basic thesis is that developmental stages are predictable and identifiable as the family moves through its life cycle. Contemporary isues such as flexible gender roles, the equal rights movement and marital options are reflected in this fifth edition of the text.

Feinstein, K. *Working Women and Families.* Beverly Hills, California: Sage Publishing Co., 1979.

The focus of this book is on working women and families. Outlined are the problems and pressures created by the movement of women into the labor force, plus concrete proposals for alleviating these difficulties.

Greenleaf, B. K. *Help: A Handbook for Working Mothers*. New York: Thomas Y. Crowell, 1978. The handbook is loaded with ideas for scheduling and organizing home and work. Preparations and planning is stressed by the author. Practical tips are offered for mothers.

Grieff, B. and Munter, P. *Tradeoffs: Executive, Family, and Organizational Life*. New York: The New American Library, 1980. Deals with the tradeoffs involved with pursuing a career, a family, or both. The decisions one makes are hard, but some suggestions are presented to help deal with those you choose. Femininity on the job, dual careers, open communication, and time planning are a few areas covered.

Jaggar, A. M. and Strudl, P. R. *Feminist Frameworks: Alternative Theoretical Accounts of the Relationships Between Women and Men*. New York: McGraw-Hill Book Company, 1978. A volume of theoretical and practical applications of women in society. From conservative to liberal viewpoints.

Mott, F. L. *Women, Work and Family*. Lexington, Mass: Lexington Books, D. C. Heath and Company, 1978. A collection of very analytical articles supplying hard facts and numbers in various issues affecting women, their lives, and their families.

Norris, G. and Miller, J. A. *The Working Mother's Complete Handbook*. St. Louis: E. P. Dutton, 1979. This handbook presents a variety of information for the mom reentering the work force. Although it is quite complete and interesting, the authors spend more than their share of time speaking to conflict, quiet, and the reasons mothers go to work.

Nye, F. I. *Family Relationships, Rewards, and Costs*. Beverly Hills: Sage Publications, Inc., 1982. This book represents very general, very versatile theories. Basic concepts of rewards, costs, and propositions which underly these theories are cited.

Ogden, R. W. *How to Succeed in Business and Marriage*. New York: AMACOM, 1978. Although this book is written from the male perspective, it offers good information on the basic problems encountered when committed to both a career in business and a family life.

Russell, A. and Fitzgibbons, P. *Career and Conflict*. Englewood Cliffs, NJ: Prentice-Hall, Inc., 1982. Uses real-life case studies and personal experiences to suggest ways for women to begin making choices about the direction of their personal and professional lives. It covers the conflicts you face when you must choose between marriage and a single life, having children or remaining child-free, giving up a career and staying home, when to have children, when to go back to work, and how to combine both worlds. The insight of the authors on how to combine both worlds is excellent.

Skolnick, A. and Skolnick, J. (Eds.). *Family in Transition*. Boston: Little, Brown and Co., 1980. Contains an excellent selection of articles on the evolving family, sexuality and sex roles, couples, parents and children, variations in household and life style, and other related subjects.

Annotated Bibliography of Films and Videotapes

Again, a "sampling" only of the films and videotapes available for teaching and training professional women. Special thanks go to Betty Fouch and Anita Pinder, of the Media Services Department at Western Michigan University, for compiling this list for the 1983 Conference on Women and Organizations.

Videotapes:

What You Are is What You Were When. 88:00 videotape, 3/4" cassette format, color, $750.00 sale price, 1977. The culmination of hundreds of workshops, lectures, and programs by Dr. Morris Massey to help people understand and deal with their value judgments.

Dr. Massey's presentation is in the "no holds barred, tell it like it is" mode—in the language and terms of today.

Twentieth Century-Fox, Video, Inc.
23705 Industrial Park Dr.
Farmington Hills, MI 48024
ph. 313-477-7800

What You Are Isn't Necessarily What You Will Be. 61:00, videotape, 3/4" cassette format, color, $500.00 sale price 1980. Dr. Morris Massey presents an in-depth analysis of basic value systems of people in the 40-to-60 year age range, comparing these systems with the values of people who are 20-to-30 years old.

Dr. Massey then discusses how conflicting behaviors result from the differences between these value systems.

Twentieth Century-Fox Video, Inc.
(see above address)

Women in Management: Critical Incidents. 13:39, 1/2" VHS or 3/4" U-matic cassette format, b&w, $70.00 sale price, 1979. A series of 11 vignettes produced in cooperation with the Policy, Planning, and Administration Concentration in the School of Social Work designed to promote discussion of reaction to conflicts which may affect the role of women in management positions.

Among the titles contained are "We Already Have One Woman" and "But Does Your Husband Mind?"

Western Michigan University
Media Services
Kalamazoo, MI 49008
ph. 616-383-4927

Women's Work: Management. 28:00, 3/4" cassette format, color, 1978, free. Developed to meet the need for information about management careers for women. Designed for use by teachers in career education and social studies classes and by guidance counselors, this videotape provides in-depth portraits of women students and professionals giving their personal views about the opportunities, problems, and rewards of a management career.

Aetna Life and Casualty
Film Librarian
Public Relations & Advertising Dept.
Hartford, CT 06156

Women (Worlds of Abraham Kaplan Series). 29:10, 3/4" cassette format, b&w, 1972. Provides a candid view of some of women's biological, cultural, emotional, and psychological differences from men. Discusses the identity problems women have and points out that the crisis of female identity has a lot to do with the crisis of male identity.

The University of Michigan
Media Resource Center
416 Fourth St.
Ann Arbor, MI 48109
ph. 313-764-5360

The Joy of Being Fully Human (a lecture of Leo Buscaglia). 60:00, 3/4" cassette, b&w, $78.00 sale price. Contains thought-provoking experiences and ideas about love and life in the special Buscaglia style. Dr. Buscaglia is professor of Love at the University of Southern California.

PBS Video
475 L'Enfant Plaza, S.W.
Washington D.C. 20024
202-488-5220

Sneak Preview: Women in Danger. 29:00, 3/4" cassette, color, $175.00 sale price. Are women exploited in today's cinema? Are movies the cause of this exploitation or just reflecting trends in our society? Acclaimed film critics Roger Ebert and Gene Siskel analyze this disturbing new trend in movies.

PBS Video
475 L'Enfant Plaza West, S.W.
Washington, D.C. 20024
toll-free ph. 800-424-7963

Identifying Sexist Behaviors at Work. 10:00, 3/4" cassette, videotape, $250.00 for 5-year lease or $125 for 6-month lease. A dramatic demonstration of sexist behavior in a typical office environment.

Discrimination in the Employment Interview. 10:00, 3/4" cassette, videotape, $250.00 for 5-year lease or $125 for 6-month lease. An interview in which a manager asks a number of questions that were acceptable in the past—but now are recognized as discriminatory.

Control Data Corporation
Education Distribution Center
3111 Sibley Memorial Drive
Eagan, Minnesota 55121

The Productivity/Quality of Work Life. A series of seven videotapes (about 13 minutes each) with the following titles: 1. Human Resources in the 1980s; 2. The "Moving" and "Stuck"; 3. Getting Them Moving; 4. Powerlessness Corrupts; 5. Turning on the Power; 6. Twelve Minutes a Day; 7. Organizing for Productivity.
  Sale price of each module: $500.00 Complete series: $3,485.00

A Tale of "0": On Being Different, videotape, 1979, 3/4 " cassette, 20:00 Illustrates the predictable group dynamics which occur when people interact under conditions of unequal representation.

Goodmeasure, Inc.
Media Department
Box 3004
Cambridge, MA 02139
ph. 617-492-2714

Looking at Leadership: A 5-Part Video Series, purchase: $950 (full series), $350 (first tape), $250 (subsequent tapes), $25 (preview). NABW's *Looking at Leadership* is a video-workshop series that enables potential leaders to become productive leaders. You'll hear thirty successful women talk about important management and leadership skills. Their experience in business, government, education, and volunteer organizations will help you recognize your own leadership aptitude. Listen to the leaders answer these and other important management questions: Do you plan as well as you might? Can you run effective meetings? Do you take conflict personnally? How do you sort out priorities? What's the key to motivating people? How can you make the most of the resources around you? What makes an effective public speaker?

The series has been developed by the National Association of Bank Women (NABW) under a grant from the Lilly Endowment with matching monies supplied by other foundations (Ford, International Paper, Coors), over 150 banks, and individual groups and members of the NABW. The Association undertook the project in 1980 because of a recognized need for leadership training among its own 30,000 members. After researching the consistency of this need with representatives of other organizations, the NABW saw that, as a volunteer association, it was not alone.

Therefore, the premise of *Looking at Leadership* is that any volunteer association—community or civic group, board of trustees, network or professional society—can be a vehicle through which people, and women particularly , can practice leadership skills. These increased capabilities will automatically enhance that organization and will transfer to all other roles which a leader may have in addition to a volunteer job.

The five programs in the series include: 1. New Perspectives: The Changing Styles of Leadership; 2. Getting Started: Prelude to Planning; 3. Making Things Happen: Leadership in Action; 4. Dealing with Differences: Managing Conflict, 5. Making Presentations: Speaking in Public.

Each tape comes with complete workshop materials, including leader guide and 20 participant workshops.

NABW Educational Foundation
500 N. Michigan Avenue, Suite 1400
Chicago, IL 60611
ph. 312-661-1700

Films

Men Under Siege: Life With the Modern Women, 33:00, color, 1979, 16mm: $515, video: $300. A searching film account of how men are reacting to the changing sexual and social revolution created by American women, as they seek equality and additional power. Men and women from all walks of life express a wide range of feelings about their work . . . their sexual relations . . . their families and marriages.

ABC Wide World of Learning
1330 Avenue of the Americas
New York, NY 10019

The Workplace Hustle, 30:00, color, 1980, 16mm: $520, video: $520. Sexual harassment in the workplace is an agonizing, continuing problem still plaguing men and women alike. This film, narrated by Ed Asner and featuring author Lin Farley, focuses attention on the damaging effects of unchecked harassment on both employers and employees. It encourages men and women to talk candidly about their attitudes toward sexuality—and each other—and suggests specific steps women should take, if they become victims of harassment. Comprehensive print materials, plus training seminars and workshops are available.

ABC Wide World of Learning
1330 Avenue of the Americas
New York, NY 10019

Bottom Line Communicating: Get to the Point, 18:30, color, purchase: $450 film or video, preview: $50. A film about strategy in communication—different kinds of communication require different kinds of strategy.

Barr Films
3490 E. Foothill Blvd.
P.O. Box 5667
Pasadena, CA 91107

A Case of Working Smarter, not Harder, 16:00, color, purchase: $425 16mm film or video. MacGregor's out of the office playing golf again! A few months ago, he was the guy whose over-filled ashtray looked neater than his desk! So what's he doing these days—stuffing work into his credenza? And why do his people and peers like him so much? This true-life case study makes clear the difference between delegating and dumping. Comprehensive leaders guide available.

CRM/McGraw-Hill
P.O. Box 641
Del Mar, CA 92014
714-453-5000

Managing Stress, 33:00, color, 16mm: $545, video: $520, rental: $55. Explores the types of stress generated from within an individual, from interpersonal relationships, and from within organizations. The wider variety of stress reactions are examined, including those that manifest themselves in physical illness. Then, the range of techniques for alleviating stress are shown, the object being to bring stress energy under control so that its beneficial aspects are maximized and the harmful aspects can be minimized.

CRM/McGraw-Hill
110 Fifteenth Street
Del Mar, CA 92014

Creative Problem Solving: How to Get Better Ideas, 28:00, color, 16mm: $525, video: $495, rental: $55. Creative solutions are stifled when people fear they will look ridiculous. How can managers help unblock inhibitions and encourage inventiveness? Shows the critical importance of separating production of ideas from evaluation of ideas.

CRM/McGraw-Hill
P.O. Box 641
Del Mar, CA 92014
714-453-5000

One in Five, 17:00, color, 16mm and video, purchase: $525, rental: $55. One in five will have a heart attack before retirement. Five people—different ages, different jobs, different life styles—are presented as five typical examples. Statistics show that coronary disease is now a major cause of illness with more victims than all other known occupational diseases. Contrary to popular belief, the industrial/office worker is just as susceptible to coronary disease as the executive working long hours under stress.

International Film Bureau, Inc.
322 S. Michigan Ave.

Chicago, IL 60604
312-922-6621

Successful Delegation, 15:00, color, 16mm or video, purchase: $425, preview: $20. By following the growth of Evelyn from doer to managers, trainees learn how to: choose what tasks to delegate, match the person to the job to achieve optimum results, avoid the three major pitfalls of delegation, give subordinates the freedom to perform well by emphasizing results, not methods, establish controls and follow-up procedures that enhance rather than hinder the authority granted, and support the subordinate by communicating the authority granted to everyone involved in the project. Complete training package accompanies.

EFM Films
85 Main Street
Watertown, MA 02172

Joshua In a Box, 5:00, color, purchase: $135, rental: $40. A cartoon designed to illustrate the "boxes" that women individually and collectively may face in career and life planning.

Churchill Films
662 North Roberterson Blvd.
Los Angeles, CA 90069
213-657-5110

Communication: The Nonverbal Agenda, 30:00, color, purchase: $560, rental: $60. Do your gestures or expressions contradict your verbal message? This fascinating exposé will sharpen your viewers' skills by showing how to employ both verbal and nonverbal communication constructively when giving instructions.

CRM/McGraw-Hill
P.O. Box 641
Del Mar, CA 92014-9988

Group Dynamics: Groupthink, 22:00, color, purchase: $425, rental: $60. Using a management meeting as setting, this film shows your audience how to recognize when meaningful group decisions are being blocked by group dynamics and illustrates how to overcome that block.

CRM/McGraw-Hill
P.O. Box 641
Del Mar, CA 92014-9988

The Power of Listening, 26:00, color, purchase: $560, rental: $60. Dr. Anthony Alesandra shows how improved productivity results from learning the how-to of active listening.

CRM/McGraw-Hill
P.O. Box 641
Del Mar, CA 92014-9988

Killing Us Softly, 30:00, 1979, 16mm, rental: $13.00 (WMU). Using hundreds of ads from magazines, newspapers, album covers, and storefront windows, Jean Kilbourne analyzes a 40 billion dollar industry that preys on the fears and insecurities of every consumer in America. With an intriguing mixture of facts, insight, humor, and outrage, Ms. Kilbourne points out that although ads may seem harmless or funny by themselves, they add up to a powerful form of cultural conditioning through the use of sexual and psychological themes.

Films, Inc.
733 Greenbay Road
Wilmet, IL 60091

Note: the prices quoted were those available in 1983. They may have changed.